Night Whispers

'Blood Work'

Volume 01-Q3

July-August-September

Edition 01-Revision 03

Victor Robert Farrell

Night Whispers
All current
Contact & Sales Information
Can be found at
www.NightWhispers.com

Night Whispers
'Blood Work'
Volume 01–Q3

July-August-September

Dedication

This book is dedicated, very simply,

To the now four most important people

In the whole wide world to me.

My daughter Gemma,

My son Jonathan,

My grandaughter Ellie May,

And of course,

My wife

Bridget.

PREFACE

I am Pastor, Rev. Victor Robert Farrell, and these everyday Bible insights called 'Night-Whispers' have long since been a global endeavor to communicate the God of the WHOLE Bible in very raw terms to very real people. This is my passion and the reason why I founded The 66 Books Ministry, which through the grace of God and according to His will and favor, shall be preaching consecutively from each of the 66 Books of the Holy Bible, the Gospel of the Lord Jesus Christ in 16,500 of the most influential cities of the world on an annual and ongoing basis! We shall plant, 'City Simple' Churches (see www.CitySimple.Church). In this regard, these Night-Whispers accompany our endeavors by providing Every Day Bible Insights into the whole Bible, for all of our members and anyone who wants to know the God of the whole Bible.

These Night-Whispers are presented in such a way as to be read each day. They are produced on a regular basis, and the 366 daily readings for each year are presented with a unique volume number. That 'Volume' year is then divided into four Quarters. For example:

> **Year 01= Volume 01-Q1 | January-February-March**
> **Year 01= Volume 01-Q2 | April-May-June**
> **Year 01= Volume 01-Q3 | July-August-September**
> **Year 01= Volume 01-Q4 | October-November-December**
> **Year 02= Volume 02-Q1 | January-February-March**
> **Followed by Volume 3, 4, 5, 6 etc., and the associate four Quarters for the consecutive years. I am sure you get the picture!**

The point is, that you can start any volume of Night-Whispers IN ANY YEAR you wish, and AT ANY TIME you choose, because whilst these Everyday Bible Insights are fresh and relevant to each day, they are not interconnected in a way which means you have to read one volume before another. Indeed, Night-Whispers are produced as stand-alone products rather than connected volumes. Therefore, if you wish, you can also consecutively read any Quarter from any Volume you choose! For example, Volume 02-Q3 might easily be followed by Volume 05-Q4, because each book is a standalone product. May I say that along with the team at The 66 Books Ministry and Whispering Word, I do hope and pray that these particular *Night-Whispers,* will be an enormous blessing to you in *revealing just a little more to you of the God of the WHOLE BIBLE.*

Rev. Victor Robert Farrell, June 2019.

INTRODUCTION TO NIGHTWHISPERS

VOL 01-Q3- 'Blood Work'

This is our third standalone quarterly volume of Night-Whispers and we hope that these Every Day Bible Insights will be as red as the blood of Jesus and read more than all your other publications put together!

The foundation of Christian work, church planting, proclamation and global mission is the shed blood of Jesus Christ. The 'blood work' of Jesus is our only foundation and future. Before those five prized crowns are given out, the church at the end of the age shall wear along with Her Savior, a crown of many thorns. Each time we break bread and drink the cup, we remember then the blood work of Christ. "..This cup is the new covenant in My blood, which is shed for you. (Luke 22:20 NKJV)

As usual, all we earnestly desire is that you especially check the Scriptures to see if these things are so, and also to do your own digging both there in particular and elsewhere in general. May God the Holy Spirit truly guide you in this.

To that end, these NightWhispers will continue to present the God of the Bible in very raw and very real terms and also challenge you to think very differently about the coming years on planet earth. Therefore, as you find us pursuing and applying Biblically correct truth to our current cultural and geo-political and technocratic context, you will find that not only are we not politically correct, but some of the things I might suggest for your immediate consideration, well, you might find to be just a little 'out there.' However, your children of now, and the up and coming 'Alpha' generation (those born from AD 2010 onwards) will find them to be the norm. Remember, I am a Bible believing Christian, and thus part of the biggest and most solid 'conspiracy theory' ever revealed to man, and if you are a Christian, so are you! It is your responsibility to know the unfolding of the times and seasons according to God's Holy Word for never has morality been engulfed by the selfish application of the sciences like they are today. This, is being done with purpose by the great enemy of our souls both to destroy the image of God and set up his anti-God kingdom upon this earth. 'Contextual Tilting' will attempt to address just a few of those 'inroads of our enemy.' That we might be prepared to protect the image of God and rightly proclaim the Name and claims of His so Great Son, Jesus Christ our Lord.

As usual, all we earnestly desire is that you especially check the Scriptures to see if these things are so, and also to do your own digging both there in particular and elsewhere in general. May God the Holy Spirit truly guide you in this.

Some global historical acknowledgements

Now then, I have been writing these Bible Insights for many years and I have gleaned in a multitude of fine meadows and otherwise. For me to give credit where credit is due then, would not only increase the size of this quarterly volume many, many times, but I would undoubtedly miss many more people out of that massive list of those which I tried to give credit to. It is Solomon who said that *"there is nothing new under the sun"* and I believe it! Therefore, please then take it for granted that when someone like myself, who almost sees 'cut and paste' as an unspoken gift of the Holy Spirit, says he might have gleaned from another person's work, in someplace, somewhere, and at some point in time without giving appropriate credit where credit is due, that I probably have! If this is the case, it was not my intention to rob you of any glory, but if I have, then please inform me of the same and the necessary changes and/or credits will be made. Remember, I have borrowed from everywhere, I have taken from everyone. 'Everywhere' and 'everyone;' there you go, that should have you covered!

US, UK or elsewhere-or, "How do you spell that?"

To be British, is to be somewhat like 'the last of the Mohicans.' The Britain, that is, the United Kingdom I grew up in is breaking apart. No, sadly, it is broken and never to be repaired. Even so, I am of Irish & Scottish great-grandparents, grandparents and parents, and I was also born in England. Therefore, I am British and a Celt at that. In addition to this, I love North America and the South in particular, so much so, that I feel like a British Red-Neck. Does this make me a Yankophile, or loving the South in particular (and its battle flag) does it make me more especially a Dixiophile? Alternatively, maybe I could be an Americophile or a Canameriphile? Who knows? Suffice to say, that as our nations were once only divided by a common 'English' language, (America still being the residence of the majority of our English readers,) I have tried to adopt the spelling and grammar of the Americas. In this, I have no doubt failed, and in the so doing, both mixed and matched the UK and US spelling and English grammatical styles. In doing this, I confess that I am a double-minded man, and unstable in all my editorial ways. The purists, either side of the pond, I am sure will never forgive me. The rest do not care. Either way, I need your help. So, if you spot any 'howlers,' do let me know. Email me your corrections on,

getyouracttogetherman@whisperingword.com

BIBLE VERSIONS

Ah, the Bible. The true meta-narrative of the real world and therefore all things meta-physical. Well, preferring the 'Textus Receptus' or the 'Majority Text,' I have tried to use the New Separatist Bible (NSB), which is a confluence Bible based on the 1560 Geneva Bible and the 1611 Authorized version, (Pure Cambridge Edition) when I have referenced the Bible, though where necessary, for mere contemporary clarity of course, when I have I have deviated from this norm, at that time I have clearly indicated which other Bible Version has been referenced.

NIGHT-WHISPERS ARE WRITTEN FOR……..

There is so much 'devotional' material available nowadays for the Christian that a great part of me says that no more should be written. Yet I do believe that we are moving speedily to the time of the end. What devotionals are written to truly address the needs of Christians living in the approach to this period, or in this period? In my opinion, there are none. Night-Whispers then, are written for those people of this darkening time in particular. Therefore, you will find that Night-Whispers are battle rations that demand your time, attention, study and consideration. If you need a little ear tickler folks, a quick little cuddle before you go to bed at night, a sleeping pill even, indeed, if you have sold out the truth, your calling and your very self for ten shekels and a shirt, then these Bible Insights are NOT for you. They demand your thoughtful consideration and further investigation and ardent application. They need your time! Night-Whispers are written for those seekers who are looking for the God of the whole Bible. They are written for those who hate the color grey but love black and white. They are written for those who want to know the truth, even if it is unpalatable to them. They are written for the awakened; that is, for those people who know that the darkness is alive and like a black incoming tide, is infiltrating every area of present life. They are written for those people who know that a Night is coming when no man can work. They are written for those people who refuse to be spoon-fed. They are written for Bible hungry people. They are written for those who are done with distractions. They are written for those people who have not sold out to cultural compromise and refuse to sell themselves to social niceness and religious self-righteousness. They are written for those who want to cease being unpaid social workers for the unthankful and want to love and arm the saints. They are therefore written for fighters, even that growing band of brothers who are no ragged or rag-tag remnant, but rather, are the released people of 'The Revolution,' that back to the Bible, boots on the ground, present movement of God, who are done with everything that has silenced the one true church and with the removal of its voice, have killed our nations. They are written for the sold out the followers of Christ who have at last found their proclamation voice. They are written for the rooted, fruited and flowering stump. Therefore, to all you great and holy people then, who, even in this darkness might just turn the world right ways up once more, I say then this to you this very night: *"Welcome to Night-Whispers, Volume 01-Q3-'Blood Work'-" "Be strong and keep looking up for your salvation draweth nigh."*

JUST A HUCKSTER

Some young preacher will study until he has to get thick glasses to take care of his failing eyesight because he has an idea he wants to become a famous preacher. HE'S JUST A HUCKSTER buying selling and getting gain. They will ordain him and he will be known as Reverend and if he writes a book, they will make him a doctor. And he will be known as Doctor; but he's still a huckster buying and selling and getting gain.

And when the Lord comes back, HE will drive him out of the temple along with the other cattle.

A.W. Tozer

(from 'Tozer on Christian Leadership,' compiled by Ron Eggert)

John 3:30 *He must increase but I must decrease.*

STILL LOOKING

Wise men speak of trees
From the Cedar to the Hyssop
Springing from the wall
From the Aspen to the Alder
Beside the water fall

Wise men speak of animals of creeping things and fish
Of birds and bees and smooth black cats
That lap the dainty dish

Wise men sing of love and capture moments in a jar
Wise men suck the juice of days
Wise men shop at Spar

Wise men count the fallen ticks
Of old clocks running down
Wise men number muscles
That help create the frown

Wise men follow after
Wise men follow far
Wise men seek the Savior still
Beneath the wandering star

1 Kings 4:33 Also he spoke of trees, from the cedar tree of Lebanon even to the hyssop that springs out of the wall; he spoke also of animals, of birds, of creeping things, and of fish. (NKJV)

The Old 100th!

All people that on earth do dwell,
Sing to the Lord with cheerful voice.
Him serve with fear, His praise forth tell;
Come ye before Him and rejoice.

The Lord, ye know, is God indeed;
Without our aid He did us make;
We are His folk, He doth us feed,
And for His sheep He doth us take.

O enter then His gates with praise;
Approach with joy His courts unto;
Praise, laud, and bless His name always,
For it is seemly so to do.

For why? the Lord our God is good;
His mercy is for ever sure;
His truth at all times firmly stood,
And shall from age to age endure.

To Father, Son and Holy Ghost,
The God whom Heaven and earth adore,
From men and from the angel host
Be praise and glory evermore.

From 'Fourscore and Seven Psalms of David'
(Geneva, Switzerland: 1561); attributed to William Kethe

CONTENTS

Dedication vii

PREFACE ix

INTRODUCTION TO NIGHTWHISPERS xi
VOL 01-Q3- 'Blood Work' xi
Some global historical acknowledgements xii
US, UK or elsewhere-or, "How do you spell that?" xiii

NIGHT-WHISPERS ARE WRITTEN FOR……... xv

JUST A HUCKSTER xvii

STILL LOOKING xix

The Old 100th! xxi

| Vol | 01 | Q3 | NW00183 | July 01st | 1
    NIGHT-WHISPER | **SACRIFICE** 1
Blood work 1
    Hebrews 4:15 .... *1*

| Vol | 01 | Q3 | NW00184 | July 02nd | 5
    NIGHT-WHISPER | **CLEAN** 5
The many-legged vampires 5
    Proverbs 15:2 .... *5*

| Vol | 01 | Q3 | NW00185 | July 03rd | 8
    NIGHT-WHISPER | **CARE** 8
Caught by God's great cat 8
    John 3:5-8 .... *8*

| Vol | 01 | Q3 | NW00186 | July 04th | 12
    NIGHT-WHISPER | **HOPE** 12
Independence day! 12
    Genesis 3:22-24 .... *12*

| Vol | 01 | Q3 | NW00187 | July 05th | 15
   NIGHT-WHISPER | **TRUTH** 15
'Cleansing the corners,' or, 'How to deal with Night Terrors' 15
   Exodus 10:21 15

| Vol | 01 | Q3 | NW00188 | July 06th | 19
   NIGHT-WHISPER | **COURAGE** 19
When 'Amzi' looked longingly over his trailing flowered wall 19
   Ezekiel 37:1-4 19

| Vol | 01 | Q3 | NW00189 | July 07th | 22
   NIGHT-WHISPER | **HOPE** 22
Prepared packages & Doorstep gifts 22
   Hosea 14:1, 2a 22

| Vol | 01 | Q3 | NW00190 | July 08th | 24
   NIGHT-WHISPER | **CONFIDENCE** 24
'Real yeast for the bread of victory,' 24
   Revelation 1:17c, 18 24

| Vol | 01 | Q3 | NW00191 | July 09th | 27
   NIGHT-WHISPER | **DANGER** 27
The devil's garden and operation light-foot 27
   Psalms 18:29 27

| Vol | 01 | Q3 | NW00192 | July 10th | 29
   NIGHT-WHISPER | **GRACE** 29
Of pleasure and pain 29
   Jeremiah 15:18 29

| Vol | 01 | Q3 | NW00193 | July 11th | 33
   NIGHT-WHISPER | **FACE** 33
The face of grace 33
   2 Corinthians 4:6 33

| Vol | 01 | Q3 | NW00194 | July 12th | 37
   NIGHT-WHISPER | **COURAGE** 37

| The glorious twelve | 37 |
| 1 Corinthians 9:26 | 37 |

| Vol | 01 | Q3 | NW00195 | July 13th | 39
Night-Whisper | **BLESSING** 39
Paraskevidekatriaphobiai 39
Isaiah 2:6 39

| Vol | 01 | Q3 | NW00196 | July 14th | 42
Night-Whisper | **PREACH** 42
Of pig sties and palaces 42
Acts 16:14,15 42

| Vol | 01 | Q3 | NW00197 | July 15th | 45
Night-Whisper | **CHOOSE** 45
Could this be your finest hour? 45
Joel 2:15-17 45

| Vol | 01 | Q3 | NW00198 | July 16th | 48
Night-Whisper | **APPREHEND** 48
The clarity and change of the ramrod of correction 48
Philippians 3:12-14 48

| Vol | 01 | Q3 | NW00199 | July 17th | 51
Night-Whisper | **ASCEND** 51
The mighty mountain of the moral majority 51
Genesis 17:1 51

| Vol | 01 | Q3 | NW00200 | July 18th | 54
Night-Whisper | **LIFE** 54
Fighting for life 54
Psalm 10:14b 54

| Vol | 01 | Q3 | NW00201 | July 19th | 57
Night-Whisper | **HOPE** 57
Owned and loved by the Lord of the sword 57

Romans 5:3-5 .... *57*

| Vol | 01 | Q3 | NW00202 | July 20th | 61
Night-Whisper | **POWER** 61
Playing cards with Dr Vomit 61
Acts 19:11-15 .... *61*

| Vol | 01 | Q3 | NW00203 | July 21st | 64
Night-Whisper | **SPRINGS** 64
Of borders, boundaries and particular blessings 64
Joshua 15:1 .... *64*

| Vol | 01 | Q3 | NW00204 | July 22nd | 67
Night-Whisper | **DESTINY** 67
The re-naming of the shrew 67
Judges 6:12 .... *67*

| Vol | 01 | Q3 | NW00205 | July 23rd | 69
Night-Whisper | **REFRESH** 69
Enjoying the best of beers with Jesus the thirst quencher! 69
Isaiah 12:3 .... *69*

| Vol | 01 | Q3 | NW00206 | July 24th | 71
Night-Whisper | **DECLARE** 71
Something salvific? 71
1 Timothy 2:4-5 .... *71*

| Vol | 01 | Q3 | NW00207 | July 25th | 73
Night-Whisper | **GOOD** 73
Praying for pagan neighbours 73
Romans 15:1-4 .... *73*

| Vol | 01 | Q3 | NW00208 | July 26th | 75
Night-Whisper | **EFFORT** 75
Snakes and ladders 75
1 Timothy 4:7 .... *75*

| Vol | 01 | Q3 | NW00209 | July 27th | 77

NIGHT-WHISPER | **COURAGE** 77
Order no 227 77
Hebrews 10:37,38 77

| Vol | 01 | Q3 | NW00210 | July 28th | 80
NIGHT-WHISPER | **SOLID** 80
'Wibbles,' rubber valves & novelty Christians 80
Romans 1:18-23 80

| Vol | 01 | Q3 | NW00211 | July 29th | 83
NIGHT-WHISPER | **FORMATION** 83
How not to become a cold turkey Christian 83
2 Corinthians 12:1-8 83

| Vol | 01 | Q3 | NW00212 | July 30th | 87
NIGHT-WHISPER | **RESPECT** 87
Forever young 87
Numbers 11:16-17 87

| Vol | 01 | Q3 | NW00213 | July 31st | 90
NIGHT-WHISPER | **WISDOM** 90
Down the transsexual toilets 90
Genesis 1:27, 28a 90

PAUSE FOR PRAYER | 66CITIES 93

| Vol | 01 | Q3 | NW00214 | August 01st | 96
NIGHT-WHISPER | **GAIN** 96
Cutting the cost and the cost of cutting 96
Isaiah 56:3-5 96

| Vol | 01 | Q3 | NW00215 | August 02nd | 99
NIGHT-WHISPER | **PREPARE** 99
Of genitalia and gender, or the lack of both! 99
Matthew 19:8-12 99

| Vol | 01 | Q3 | NW00216 | August 03rd | 104

NIGHT-WHISPER | **COURAGE** 104
Hic sunt dracones or hic sunt remuneror 104
Numbers 13:33 .... *104*

| Vol | 01 | Q3 | NW00217 | August 04th | **106**
NIGHT-WHISPER | **CLEANSE** 106
Of socks and sweat **106**
John 13:7 .... *106*

| Vol | 01 | Q3 | NW00218 | August 05th | **108**
NIGHT-WHISPER | **SOBER** 108
The most terrible loss of a load of old bulls **108**
Titus 2:2-3 .... *108*

| Vol | 01 | Q3 | NW00219 | August 06th | **111**
NIGHT-WHISPER | **CLEAR** 111
What grows now, in the furrows of your tongue? **111**
Hosea 10:4b *111*

| Vol | 01 | Q3 | NW00220 | August 07th | **113**
NIGHT-WHISPER | **SENSE** 113
Spiritual synesthesia **113**
Ezekiel 10:14-15 .... *113*

| Vol | 01 | Q3 | NW00221 | August 08th | **116**
NIGHT-WHISPER | **TRAVEL** 116
Despite disappointments, there are always new beginnings **116**
Hebrews 11:13 .... *116*

| Vol | 01 | Q3 | NW00222 | August 09th | **121**
NIGHT-WHISPER | **SURFACE** 121
Dealing with those sounds in the night **121**
Exodus 10:21 .... *121*

| Vol | 01 | Q3 | NW00223 | August 10th | **124**
DREAM WORD | **REMEMBERED** 124
Of tear drops and pillows **124**

Psalm 56:8 .... *124*

| Vol | 01 | Q3 | NW00224 | August 11th | 127

    NIGHT-WHISPER | **SAVE** 127

Surf's up! 127

    Job 9:8   127

| Vol | 01 | Q3 | NW00225 | August 12th | 130

    NIGHT-WHISPER | **REMOVE** 130

A smack on the side of the head 130

    Hebrews 12:1,2 .... *130*

| Vol | 01 | Q3 | NW00226 | August 13th | 132

    NIGHT-WHISPER | **MARKING** 132

Letting God mark your territory 132

    Song of Solomon 2:15 .... *132*

| Vol | 01 | Q3 | NW00227 | August 14th | 134

    NIGHT-WHISPER | **PROTECTED** 134

Built by God and put beside the bulldog 134

    1 Chronicles 11:22-25 .... *134*

| Vol | 01 | Q3 | NW00228 | August 15th | 136

    NIGHT-WHISPER | **FOCUS** 136

No More Macbeth Mournings 136

    Ecclesiastes 1:1-2 .... *136*

| Vol | 01 | Q3 | NW00229 | August 16th | 139

    NIGHT-WHISPER | **RECONCILE** 139

The reconciliation of Christina The Astonishing 139

    1 Corinthians 6:19,20 .... *139*

| Vol | 01 | Q3 | NW00230 | August 17th | 143

    NIGHT-WHISPER | **LONGING** 143

Rabboni 143

    John 20:15 .... *143*

| Vol | 01 | Q3 | NW00231 | August 18th | **146**
    NIGHT-WHISPER | **RECLAIM** 146
A new anthem for the redemption of your Jerusalem **146**
    Numbers 12:6 .... *146*

| Vol | 01 | Q3 | NW00232 | August 19th | **150**
    NIGHT-WHISPER | **CHANGE** 150
Turning disaster into discovery **150**
    Lamentations 3:40-47 .... *150*

| Vol | 01 | Q3 | NW00233 | August 20th | **153**
    NIGHT-WHISPER | **TRAIN** 153
Of Butchers and Bolters **153**

| Vol | 01 | Q3 | NW00234 | August 21st | **156**
    NIGHT-WHISPER | **SAVE** 156
The sweet sauce of God **156**
    1 Corinthians 10:13 .... *156*

| Vol | 01 | Q3 | NW00235 | August 22nd | **158**
    NIGHT-WHISPER | **STICK** 158
Sticky situations demand a very sticky church **158**
    Hebrews 10:23-25 .... *158*

| Vol | 01 | Q3 | NW00236 | August 23rd | **160**
    NIGHT-WHISPER | **THINK** 160
Of men and mind control – 'What me, worry?' **160**
    2 Timothy 2:14-16 .... *160*

| Vol | 01 | Q3 | NW00237| August 24th | **162**
    NIGHT-WHISPER | **OBEY** 162
The unequivocal affirmation of the heart – hooah! **162**
    Matthew 21:28-31 .... *162*

| Vol | 01 | Q3 | NW00238 | August 25th | **164**
    NIGHT-WHISPER | **PURSUE** 164
Nothing great is easy **164**

    1 Timothy 6:10 .... *164*

| Vol | 01 | Q3 | NW00239 | August 26th | 167
    NIGHT-WHISPER | **REVEAL** 167
The man whom Jesus let die 167
    Matthew 1:18-21 .... *167*

| Vol | 01 | Q3 | NW00240 | August 27th | 170
    NIGHT-WHISPER | **PERSEVERE** 170
UB40 170
    2 Thessalonians 3:6-11 .... *170*

| Vol | 01 | Q3 | NW00241 | August 28th | 174
    NIGHT-WHISPER | **COURAGE** 174
Bight me! 174
    1 Samuel 14:6 & 12-14 .... *174*

| Vol | 01 | Q3 | NW00242 | August 29th | 177
    NIGHT-WHISPER | **NEW** 177
Driven by the demonic 177
    Revelation 18:2-6 .... *177*

| Vol | 01 | Q3 | NW00243 | August 30th | 181
    NIGHT-WHISPER | **RETURN** 181
Let's face the music and dance 181
    Deuteronomy 6:5 .... *181*

| Vol | 01 | Q3 | NW00244 | August 31st | 185
    NIGHT-WHISPER | **POWER** 185
Deep speaking 185
    John 6:63,64 .... *185*

IT'S TIME TO ORDER YOUR NEXT QUARTER OF..... 189

| Vol | 01 | Q3 | NW00245 | September 01st 191
    NIGHT-WHISPER | **CONTROL** 191
Wearing the sheath 191

Ephesians 4:26-28 .... *191*

| Vol | 01 | Q3 | NW00246 | September 02ⁿᵈ | 193
Night-Whisper | CLEAN 193
Sun down 193
Ephesians 4:26-28 .... *193*

| Vol | 01 | Q3 | NW00247 | September 03ʳᵈ | 195
Night-Whisper | FOUND 195
How far will you go? 195
Psalm 119:174-176a *195*

| Vol | 01 | Q3 | NW00248 | September 04ᵗʰ | 198
Night-Whisper | POMEGRANATE 198
Of pictures in a pomegranate 198
Exodus 39:24-26 .... *198*

| Vol | 01 | Q3 | NW00249 | September 05ᵗʰ | 200
Night-Whisper | TIME 200
The real time Lord 200
Galatians 4:1-5 .... *200*

| Vol | 01 | Q3 | NW00250 | September 06ᵗʰ | 204
Night-Whisper | HONOUR 204
She devils, sponging males and the Jerry Springer Show 204
Amos 4:1,2 .... *204*

| Vol | 01 | Q3 | NW00251 | September 07ᵗʰ | 208
Night-Whisper | COST 208
Of Hell and Texas 208
2 Samuel 23:20,23 .... *208*

| Vol | 01 | Q3 | NW00252 | September 08ᵗʰ | 211
Night-Whisper | PREPARE 211
"I can hear your strong winds blowing" 211
Matthew 24:4-8 .... *211*

| Vol | 01 | Q3 | NW00253 | September 09ᵗʰ | 215

Night-Whisper	**BUZZ**	215
God! On a vespa?	215
M Joshua 24:12,13	*215*

| Vol | 01 | Q3 | NW00254 | September 10th | 219
Night-Whisper	**POWER**	219
Big bang day and the Word of the Big Book	219
Acts 17:23-29	*219*

| Vol | 01 | Q3 | NW00255 | September 11th | 222
Night-Whisper	**REMEMBER**	222
Two Twins	222
Matthew 24:37-44	*222*

| Vol | 01 | Q3 | NW00256 | September 12th | 225
Night-Whisper	**SAFE**	225
Seeking Mark Twain and more	225
Ezekiel 47:5,6	*225*

| Vol | 01 | Q3 | NW00257 | September 13th | 228
Night-Whisper	**PUKE**	228
An old Anacreontic song for some new poet prophets	228
2 Kings 3:14,15	*228*

| Vol | 01 | Q3 | NW00258 | September 14th | 232
Night-Whisper	**WARDROBE**	232
Forgotten days	232
Jeremiah 2:32	*232*

| Vol | 01 | Q3 | NW00259 | September 15th | 234
Night-Whisper	**HOPE**	234
Searching for grovel hogs	234
Mark 12:37b	*234*

| Vol | 01 | Q3 | NW00260| September 16th | 237
| Night-Whisper | **CHARACTER** | 237 |

Equations on character and capacities **237**
- *Mark 12:37b* *237*

| Vol | 01 | Q3 | NW00261 | September 17ᵗʰ | **242**
NIGHT-WHISPER | **SERVE** 242
"We the people…" **242**
- *Matthew 6:24* *242*

| Vol | 01 | Q3 | NW00262 | September 18ᵗʰ | **245**
NIGHT-WHISPER | **CONSIDER** 245
Making the moon stand still **245**
- *Zechariah 14:7c* *245*

| Vol | 01 | Q3 | NW00263 | September 19ᵗʰ | **248**
NIGHT-WHISPER | **HUMILITY** 248
How to behead yourself **248**
- *Ezekiel 30:6* *248*

| Vol | 01 | Q3 | NW00264 | September 20ᵗʰ | **250**
NIGHT-WHISPER | **REAL** 250
Atonemints **250**
- *Matthew 21:12,13* *250*

| Vol | 01 | Q3 | NW00265 | September 21ˢᵗ | **253**
NIGHT-WHISPER | **MUSIC** 253
Bring me a musician **253**
- *2 Kings 3:14* *253*

| Vol | 01 | Q3 | NW00266 | September 22ⁿᵈ | **257**
NIGHT-WHISPER | **WAIT** 257
The marriage of midnight madness and autumn mornings **257**
- *Revelation 2:28* *257*

| Vol | 01 | Q3 | NW00267 | September 23ʳᵈ | **259**
NIGHT-WHISPER | **GLORY** 259
The floodlight of the Father **259**
- *Hebrews 1:3* *259*

| Vol | 01 | Q3 | NW00268| September 24th |..261

    NIGHT-WHISPER | **DROWN** 261

The drowning of two twins and the PO 8 Black Bart 261

    2 Samuel 13:26,27..*261*

| Vol | 01 | Q3 | NW00269 | September 25th |...264

    NIGHT-WHISPER | **SHAPE** 264

Of big girls' blouses and warrior houses 264

    2 Samuel 2:18..*264*

| Vol | 01 | Q3 | NW00270 | September 26th |...266

    NIGHT-WHISPER | **ROBUST** 266

The bare facts 266

    Ezekiel 16:25..*266*

| Vol | 01 | Q3 | NW00271 | September 27th |...270

    NIGHT-WHISPER | **BELIEVE** 270

Resurrection hopes..270

    Hebrews 11:17-19b..*270*

| Vol | 01 | Q3 | NW00272 | September 28th |...273

    NIGHT-WHISPER | **GREED** 273

The trail of tears 273

    1 Timothy 6:10...*273*

| Vol | 01 | Q3 | NW00273 | September 29th |...276

    NIGHT-WHISPER | **SATISFY** 276

No more to the dance 276

    Psalm 65:4..*276*

| Vol | 01 | Q3 | NW00274 | September 30th |...279

    NIGHT-WHISPER | **DIG** 279

The Honking Questioning of Blind Birds 279

    Job 28:7..*279*

DID YOU REMEMBER? 283

DON'T FORGET TO ORDER YOUR NEXT QUARTER OF NIGHT WHISPERS..283

THE MISSION STATEMENT OF THE 66 BOOKS MINISTRY.......285

MORE ABOUT 'THE 66 BOOKS MINISTRY'......................................287

AUTHOR BIO | PURPLE ROBERT..289

JOIN THE FELLOWSHIP OF THE BOOK 290

ANOTHER BOOK BY THE AUTHOR, VR..293
Habakkuk A Prophecy For Our Time 293

ANOTHER BOOK BY THE AUTHOR, VR..295
The 66-Minute Bible 295

AN INTRODUCTION TO 'PURPLE ROBERT' 297
Some Dangerously Different Devotionals! 297

| Vol | 01 | Q3 | NW00183 | July 01ˢᵗ |

Night-Whisper | **SACRIFICE**

Blood work

Tonight I want to look at a phrase from this marvelous verse from the book of Hebrews. Here is how it is translated in numerous different versions of the Bible saying that our Jesus is not a High Priest…..

Hebrews 4:15
"For we do not have a High Priest who cannot sympathise with our weaknesses, but was in all points tempted as we are, yet without sin."
NKJV

NKJV - who cannot sympathize with our weaknesses

KJV - which cannot be touched with the feeling of our infirmities;

MESSAGE - who is out of touch with our reality.

AMP -who is unable to understand, sympathize, and have a shared feeling with our weaknesses and infirmities and liability to the assaults of temptation,

CJB - unable to empathize with our weaknesses;

BBE - who is not able to be touched by the feelings of our feeble flesh;

WEUST -For we do not have a High Priest who is not able to enter experientially into a fellow feeling with our infirmities,

Got it? Good.

Now, taking these verses and looking at how the word for infirmities is used and also translated elsewhere in the new Testament, we can say that Jesus then, has an extended sympathetic, compassionate, reaching and touching empathy for our sickness, disease, malady, and any other weakness that can be described by an impotent feebleness caused by genetic mishap, organic failure, viral infection or the demonization of evil spirits! Why does our Great High Priest have this kind of reaching empathy and understanding of our gross maladies? Because, He was, in all points, tested as we are yet without sin.

Now it seems as though I might be saying, indeed, even suggesting that the verse might be saying that there is nothing that touches us that Jesus has not been touched by and tested by. Yet how could that be? Jesus was born a sinless individual, He thought no sin, He did no sin, and in Him was *no sin*. Now I believe that means that there was in Him, no place for sickness at all. I would go further and say that if Christ had not been crucified, He would have reached male physical maturity and then lived that way forever, never aging! Christ was never sick, and Christ was never dying. Christ our King never took the journey into decrepit old age, sans teeth, sans eyes, sans taste, sans everything and frankly, never could. How then could any one of our infirmities possibly have touched Jesus? How can our Great High Priest be so 'touched' by the same even now?

> *Christ our King never took the journey into decrepit old age, sans teeth, sans eyes, sans taste, sans everything.*

Now some folks would say that this verse is actually talking about Jesus being tempted even as we are. He feels then, our temptations to sin. Yet was Christ ever tempted as we are? He had no original sin within Him, He had no fed and still hungry monster craving the fruits of unrighteous desires of every kind within Him. When temptation was placed before Him there was no black beast within Him that leapt like a ravenous animal, its spittled neck, red with sores as it strained the leash in an attempt to bite and devour the lust of darkness set before it. How could Christ be then tempted like we are?

Christ as a youngster had all the cuts and bruises of a growing child I am sure. Maybe, He even stubbed his toe now and again but even that is possibly debatable? However, I cannot see Jesus with the measles, with the chicken pox, or with mono or any other infection come to that. How then is our High Priest touched then with the feelings of our infirmities with the diseases of our both our young life and old age? Tell me, just how can Christ be tempted as we are? Well, to these serious questions, I would say but two things:

First that in the passion of Christ, begun in the garden of Gethsemane, it was great sweaty drops of blood that mirrored for us, the terrible and titanic tragedy of the ages that was shortly to be placed upon Him, that is, all of our sin. It is Luke the physician who is the only Gospel writer to take note of this sweating of blood and it is another physician, Dr. Frederick Zugibe (Chief Medical Examiner of Rockland County, New York) who talks about "hematohidrosis". Describing this, he says that, "Around the sweat glands, there are multiple blood vessels in a net-like form. Under the pressure of great stress, the vessels constrict. Then as the anxiety passes, the blood vessels dilate to the point of rupture. The blood goes into the sweat glands. As the sweat glands are producing a lot of sweat, it pushes the blood to the surface - coming out as droplets of blood *mixed with sweat."* My goodness friends, the very thought of what was about to come upon Jesus, the sound of the dragging weight of all our screaming sins coming toward Him on the cross made the sweet Jesus sweat great drops of blood! Just the thoughtful trepidation of all the felt guilt, the full experience of the consequence of crimes unimaginable, the consequence of amputative loss, of eye poked out vision, of dreams ran aground on rocks, of great sharp disappointment, of cancer robbed organs, of all the crippling incurables and of the womb formed genetic twisted, pharmaceutically induced, knitting needle poked malady and madness of every kind, yes, even of all the sins of the whole world, from Adam onwards and even to the end of time, which were shortly to be placed upon Him, made him sweat blood! Yes, somewhere in the dark mystery of the glorious cross, this my Savior, your Savior tasted all your sin. I suppose at any time on the cross, He could have climbed off it, He could have pursued not the Father's will. However, He didn't do that. Instead, He drank the cup of damnation to the very dregs. Therefore, there was nothing that Jesus did not touch and taste of the consequences of our sin. Nothing.

> *Therefore, there was nothing that Jesus did not touch and taste of the consequences of our sin. Nothing!*

Secondly, I believe that Jesus was more tempted than we ever could be. I believe that Jesus was more tested than we ever could be. Oswald Chambers in one of his thoughts for this day around this issue comes at this verse tonight from an additional angle, which is also correct. He says, *"Our Lord's temptations and ours are in different realms until we are born again and become His brothers. The temptations of Jesus are not those of a mere man, but the temptations of God as Man. Through regeneration, the Son of God is formed in us (see Galatians 4:19), and in our physical life He has the same setting that He had on earth. Satan does not tempt us just to make us do wrong things— he tempts us to make us lose what God has put into us through regeneration, namely, the possibility of being of value to God."* I like that.

In any event, may I echo this most marvelous conclusion from the holy Scriptures………….

Listen: "Let us therefore come boldly to the throne of grace, that we may obtain mercy and find grace to help in time of need." (Hebrews 4:16 NKJV)

Pray: Thank You Jesus for this so great a 'blood work.' Lord, I come boldly to Your throne of grace this night and ask You to please touch me, heal me, help me, hold me and deliver me from the great Devourer of my soul. This is my time of need; help me obtain that which is my 'right' through being your blood bought son. Amen and let it be so!

| Vol | 01 | Q3 | NW00184 | July 02nd |

Night-Whisper | **CLEAN**

The many-legged vampires

It was early in 2007 when country music star Brad Paisley brought out two very successful songs. The first was. "When I get where I'm going," a powerful and evocative country music duet with Dolly Parton. The accompanying video produced with this song will move anyone who has lost a loved one to healing tears! In Brad's second song, he moved from the sublime to the ridiculous by producing a Benny Hill style, multiple double entendre little song, the title of which was simply, "Ticks!" Of which that never to be forgotten chorus says,

Proverbs 15:2

"The tongue of the wise uses knowledge rightly, but the mouth of fools pours forth foolishness."
NKJV

Cause I'd like to see you out in the moonlight
I'd like to kiss you way back in the sticks
I'd like to walk you through a field of wildflowers
And I'd like to check you for ticks!

What can you say to that!

When living in the redneck hills of Kentucky we were fortunate to have a couple of killer cats as our feline protectors! They culled the rodent population and the slithery things that lived on Rattlesnake Ridge and kept us safe in our beds at night both from gangs of marauding mice and malicious moles who invaded our kitchen for food. For this fine work, we would allow them to join us on our bed where they purred the night away.

Unfortunately, those fine felines had the tendency to bring onto our beds and consequently into our sheets, some tiny travelers that often attached themselves to their fur. Both my wife and I have discovered these horrible little monsters with their heads buried into the most private parts of our anatomies literally sucking the life out of us. Brad Paisley's lunatic of a lyric, "I'd like to check you for ticks!" became for us, for a wee while anyway, an absolute necessity.

You see the problem with ticks and black-legged ticks especially, is that they can be infected with the bacterium, 'borrelia burgdorferi,' which in turn, can then be passed on to humans, producing what we know as Lyme's disease. This disease is particularly nasty, in that it attacks the joints, heart and nervous system. It is a deceitful little disease as well, because its symptoms initially manifest themselves as the comparatively harmless flu bug. Because of this, the serious nature of the Tick bite and its consequences can be easily be ignored leaving in your body a ticking time bomb, which will slowly explode in the years to come. Ticks are nasty little buggers.

> *What blood sucking accusation, what life draining condemnation, what disease ridden lie, what ticking time bomb, have you gotten into bed with tonight?*

What blood sucking accusation, what life draining condemnation, what disease ridden lie, what ticking time bomb, have you gotten into bed with tonight? Nasty! Why not take a few moments to have the Holy Spirit check you for ticks tonight. Then, in quiet confession, in gentle encouragement, in prayerful and driven determination, get the tweezers of the Word of God and grab those little buggers around the middle, rock their little heads back and forth out of your skin and then crack them to death between your forgiven little finger nails. If that does not work, take some 'repentive' fire to them!

Finally my brethren, no matter how useful your well-loved acquaintances, how warm their furry fellowship, how comforting their presence when they purr the night away, if they are bringing ticks into your bed, then they have to go. He who has ears to hear, let him hear!

Listen: "He who walks with wise men will be wise, but the companion of fools will be destroyed." Prov 13:20 NKJV

Pray: Lord, tonight check me for ticks. Lord, forgive me for allowing furry fools into my life and forgive me for being a willing and complicit companion to them and their blood sucking parasites. Give me peace tonight O Lord my God, even though Your cleansing stings me. Lord tomorrow; remind me when I awake, to choose to walk with the wise. Lord from now on, my inner chamber is mine and Thine, and nothing, and no one, shall be allowed between the cleanness of our sheets. I promise You this O Lord, I promise You this, that only You and me shall occupy the bed of my peace and rest. Amen and let it be so..

Night-Whisper | **CARE**

Caught by God's great cat

In the wake of the dropping of the second atomic bomb on Japan, at a Manhattan dinner given by the Nobel prize committee, it was Walter Isaacson in his autobiography on Einstein, who noted that the great, hairy man himself, spoke at that same dinner saying, *"Alfred Nobel, the inventor of dynamite had created the Nobel award to atone for having invented the most powerful explosives ever known up to his time. Today the physicists who participated on forging the most formidable and dangerous weapons of all times are harassed by equal feelings of responsibility, not to say guilt."*

John 3:5-8

"Jesus answered, 'Most assuredly, I say to you, unless one is born of water and the Spirit, he cannot enter the kingdom of God. That which is born of the flesh is flesh, and that which is born of the Spirit is spirit. Do not marvel that I said to you, 'You must be born again.' The wind blows where it wishes, and you hear the sound of it, but cannot tell where it comes from and where it goes. So is everyone who is born of the Spirit.'" NKJV

Driven by fear, guilt and responsibility, it was in May 1946 that Einstein would take up the role of chairman and founder of 'The Emergency Committee of Atomic Scientists.' Wikipedia says that the aims of this committee were to "warn the public of the dangers associated with the development of nuclear weapons, promote the peaceful use of nuclear energy and ultimately work towards world peace, which was seen as the only way that nuclear weapons would not be used again." Einstein in fact established the committee in the wake of the "Szilárd petition" of 1945, which was presented to the United States president of the time, Mr. Harry S Truman. This petition was opposing the use of the atomic bomb on moral grounds and was signed by sixty eight scientists who had worked on the Manhattan Project, for you see, a majority of those disconnected from one another scientists, apparently did not entirely know just what they were creating at the time! Einstein, speaking as Chairman of this committee is quoted again by Isaacson as saying, *"Our generation has brought into the world the most revolutionary force since prehistoric man's discovery of fire. This basic power of the universe cannot be fitted into the outmoded concept of narrow nationalism."*

Now, whatever you think of Einstein's stance and actions, of his politics and compulsions, of his courage or naivety, is irrelevant for my point tonight. Our world is a nuclear world and the nuclear bomb cannot be un-invented! However, it is the principle stated by Einstein of "not being able to fit the most powerful force in the universe into a narrow concept" that I want you to consider this evening.

You cannot put a leash around the neck of the wind dear friends and then lead it where you will! For the wind is wild, and beyond taming and vastly unpredictable. So is God the Holy Spirit.

Actually, the most powerful force ever to have been released into the mess of humanity was the Holy Spirit Himself on the day of Pentecost. Oh yes it was! The narrow concept He has ever since been tried to be forced into, is that of religion nationalism which is better known as denominationalism. We believers in the Word of God, we holders and interpreters of this truth once delivered to the saints, have nevertheless fragmented ourselves into (at the very least) a vast multitude of protestant denominations, all of which have a slightly different flavor, bent and interpretation, on the revelation of God to us. Each of these many protestant denominations, even each of these major protestant ecclesiastical traditions, have tried to take the Holy Spirit and like some narrow nation state, have attempted to dress Him in their flag, to brand Him with their name, to dress Him up in their uniform and drop Him on their enemies in contemptible judgment and haughty exclusiveness. Tish!

You cannot capture the wind in a jar and release it where you will. For the wind is wild, it is beyond taming and it is vastly unpredictable. All you can do with the wind when it blows, is either welcome it, harness it, or shelter from it until it passes. You cannot put a leash around the neck of the wind dear friends and then lead it where you will! For the wind is wild, and beyond taming and vastly unpredictable. So is God the Holy Spirit.

God the Holy Spirit, this Divine wind if you will, is not on a suicide mission, wildly diving at the decks of our lives to simply crash burn and dissipate. No mate, this Holy God, the most magnificent Holy Spirit is on a life giving mission!

Because we are clever enough to capture the winds that blow around our planet for our own power, purpose and benefit, somehow in a very ignorant and arrogant way, we also assume that we can capture the Divine wind of God for our own power, purpose and benefit. What floundering fools we are! For the pleasure and mission of God the Holy Spirit is not to be taught, bought, bound or bent to our nationalistic and denominational designs, but in His wildness, to both corner and capture us and then carry us in His smiling teeth, to the waiting feet of Jesus the Savior of mankind, our Oh so very good Shepherd.

> *When winds take forests in their paws, the universe is still.*

This Holy Spirit cat like deliverance of us to the Master is the most Holiest of moments in the universe. I tell you that all of heaven stands still when our mouse-like forms are laid before the waiting feet of Jesus by Gods great Holy Cat! Yes, God the Holy Spirit is the Great Cat on the prowl and not any man's dog on a leash.

He Fumbles at your soul
As players at the keys
Before they drop full music on
He stuns you by degrees
Prepares your brittle nature
For the ethereal blow
By fainter hammers further heard,
Then nearer, then so slow
Your breath has time to straighten
Your brain to bubble cool
Deals one imperial thunderbolt
That scalps your naked soul

When winds take forests in their paws
The universe is still.

Divine Possession, by Emily Dickenson 1830-1836

Listen: "*After these things I saw four angels standing at the four corners of the earth, holding the four winds of the earth, that the wind should not blow on the earth, on the sea, or on any tree." Rev 7:1-2 NKJV*

Pray: Father put Your great cat out tonight! Come O Holy Wind of God and in Your mercy and according to Your own goodness, by the shed blood of Christ my Savior, come blow through the alleys of my sleeping mind. Come prowl the dark corners of my heart and then Great Holy Cat of Christ, come corner me, come tire me out and come stare me into quaking stillness. O let the universe be still this night! Let the sun and stars, the moon and the mountains that tickle the hanging under-belly of the moonlit, blue-lit sky, all be quiet this Holy hunting night. O Holy Spirit, will You please take all my dark forests in Your powerful and pleasant paws? Will You nip me, bite me, gently shake me, to a reverential sleep, and then dangling from Your delightful and ever smiling jaws, in my dreams, will You carry me off to Jesus and lay me prostrate at His waiting, loving feet, that in my waking, I might be truly blessed once more. Amen and let it be so.

Night-Whisper | **HOPE**

Independence day!

My, oh my! What fireworks we can launch into our skies! What flashes of thunder, what bright dripping rainbows, what crackling, whizzing, popping whistling colors can we momentarily spread above our heads like a neon lit, dancing Indian war bonnet, all thrown up in rejoicing, into the slowly rotating skies! However, beyond this faint and passing flicker of manufactured and expensive, deeply unsatisfying and quickly passing joy, yes, light years beyond the spitting sparkle of earthly celebrations, out there amongst unnamed galaxies, beyond Andromeda, beyond Ambartsumian's Knot, beyond The Bear's Paw even, God's fireworks still flash forever greater, and burn forever brighter in the cosmic confidence of an eternal wonder that pleasures Him alone. God is always watching His own fireworks, and eating His own toffee apples with the angels.

Genesis 3:22-24
"Then the LORD God said, 'Behold, the man has become like one of Us, to know good and evil. And now, lest he put out his hand and take also of the tree of life, and eat, and live forever' - therefore the LORD God sent him out of the garden of Eden to till the ground from which he was taken. So He drove out the man; and He placed cherubim at the east of the garden of Eden, and a flaming sword which turned every way, to guard the way to the tree of life." NKJV

For thousands of years we have not been allowed to attend this singing show of seraphic sentinels, all bursting and blasting glory across His universe. No, not since we took our own independence from Him on that fateful day, for since that fall of man, since that day of independent tragedy, an angel with a flashing, flaming sword, for our protection, has in constancy, stood before the gates of the everlasting pleasure park and shouted, *"Stand well back now! Stand well back, for you cannot get past the Kings guard, for now you will be hurt!"*

The sense of loss that lies within us regarding this eternal exclusion from Gods never ending fireworks party is unspeakably profound, for despite our prized and boasted independence, we are so very, very lonely. So much so, that we have tried to reproduce the pleasures of His firework park in our own fires sexual, in our own fires financial and in our own fires successful, only to have found them to be under fueled, burning ever low, always flickering to ember and to ash, in the ever coming cold light of all our independent days. All forced Independence Day celebrations from a faithful and loving Father, will leave us feeling forever lonely. A testimony to this is that we rarely, oh so rarely, lift our heads to His fireworks forever in the sky, for when we do, we remember, yes we remember our pain. Let me ask you, apart from today my American friends, when was the last time you gazed into God's firework filled heavens? When was the last time you looked up and over the fenced out pleasures of His fun filled fields, of His sealed and gated parks of pleasures? When was the last time you allowed the sound of giggling seraphs, the whooping cries of angel glee, of rushing roller coasters filled with chanting cherubim, all shouting glory, while you were moved in anticipated excitement over the distant music of waiting, whizzing Wurlitzers and the hum of hidden, pumping and powerful living engines all generating light, the sounds of which, all landed gently upon your listening ears? When was the last time such a looking and a listening brought the smell of heavenly toffee apples and cotton candy, hot dogged mustard and buttered pop-corn, and allowed them to creep up your spiritual nostrils and tickle the taste buds on the back of your tongue making your mouth wet in watered longing? When was the last time you looked up?

Then, gazing out of the window and up and over the gates of God into the dark night skies, which are always lit with the wonders of the fireworks of the Father, which are always proclaiming an eternal Sunday, an everlasting fun day, to those holding a ticket to ride, a ticket to hide, a ticket to ever and always live and abide, in Jesus.

Tonight, on this celebrated but lonely Independence Day of ours, on this dreadful and rebellious 4th of July, let us turn off the light, draw back the curtains and lie still under our cool cotton sheets. Then, gazing out of the window and up and over the gates of God into the dark night skies, which are always lit with the wonders of the fireworks of the Father, which are always proclaiming an eternal Sunday, an everlasting fun day, to those holding a ticket to ride, a ticket to hide, a ticket to ever and always live and abide, in Jesus. Yes Christian, you rebel now returned, let us open our senses tonight, to the sights and sounds, the smells and light touches of the world beyond us, the world to come, even our heavenly home of eternal rejoicing.

If you have your ticket friend, then you have great cause to look and listen with expectant longing into all the pleasures of God wrapped up in Christ Jesus for you. So, tonight, I say again, look up! Gaze beyond the pathetic and passing thunder flashes of man's celebrations and peer beyond them into deeper heavens, whilst allowing expectant hope to walk hand in hand with longing, and take you home with you to bed. I tell you, in this continued mess of our earthly rebellion, God's firework party has already started popping. You shall be going to it. It shall be great. May your friends and loved ones and all your hearts desires, be found around the warm and welcoming Holy fires of God most high.

Listen: "For we know that the whole creation groans and labors with birth pangs together until now. Not only that, but we also who have the first fruits of the Spirit, even we ourselves groan within ourselves, eagerly waiting for the adoption, the redemption of our body. For we were saved in this hope, but hope that is seen is not hope; for why does one still hope for what he sees? But if we hope for what we do not see, we eagerly wait for it with perseverance." Rom 8:22-25 NKJV

Pray: Lord, please forgive us of our days of independence and have mercy on our long lost nights of loneliness. Lord tonight, let me listen to the music of Your spinning spheres. Lord tonight, in my dreams let me look upon Your fantastic fun factory, yes, O my Father, let me gaze again upon Your waiting joys for me, for us, together. Lord tonight, please fill my sleeping senses, with pleasure beyond measure. Lord tonight, take me through Your gates, take me hungry to Your table and give me candied apples, all Your toffee apples of delight. Lord tonight, in Your grace and in Your mercy, for all of us I pray, make the bitter bitten apple, ever sweeter in Your day. In Jesus name I ask it, Amen.

Night-Whisper | **TRUTH**

'Cleansing the corners,' or, 'How to deal with Night Terrors'

I grew up with a great fear of the darkness. As a young boy, up until the age of eleven, I lived in a house which I was convinced was haunted. I still remain somewhat convinced.

Exodus 10:21

"Then the LORD said to Moses, 'Stretch out your hand toward heaven, that there may be darkness over the land of Egypt, darkness which may even be felt.'" NKJV"

A combination of strange dreams, white, blue balled lightening appearing and disappearing through the wall on a very stormy night; a consistent malevolent and dark shadowy apparition in the hallway entrance to my bedroom and its ever open door; the feeling of something hidden in the wardrobe or of something lurking menacingly underneath my bed together with the truly felt clawed-scratching across the souls of my in bed feet, all led many times to screaming tears of terror and the desperate running from my place of unrest, to that of my parents bed in the middle of the night. I hated that house and greatly feared the coming on of night.

Because of my childhood hauntings then, I have always been aware of shadows, of ill-lit corners and the seeming darkness lurking therein. It is as though the night and absence of light gives a doorway, if you will, an opportunity even, for malevolence to manifest itself and then wait for the shadows to lengthen toward you, so they might finally grab you, envelope you and drag you down to tortuous hell. In my mind, even today, doors and corners, entrance ways and the cornered gathering points of protective walls, all need my special attention, especially when it's dark!

I remember that my earthly father spoke to my fearful tears from his own observational pain when he often tried to quiet my haunted shaking, saying, "Son, the dead can't hurt you, only the living." It is not true of course but that's for another day. His point then, however, was that there was nothing hidden in the shadows that was not living and breathing and therefore that could possibly do me harm. Like I said, despite his kind encouragement, it is just not true. Suffice to say, that in the seen and unseen worlds, in the physical and the metaphysical, in the material and the spiritual realms, there is often the need for the reclaiming and cleansing of a space that has been cracked and contaminated by a dark intrusion into our own space-time. Such unclean places, offer shelter to malevolence that is undoubtedly out to hurt you.

Friend, there are rooms in your spiritual house that are possessed by darkness and when that place is the place where you seek rest, is the place where you seek renewal, is the place where healing should happen, is even the place where a conduit should open up to heaven and the angels of God should be felt to ascend and descend with messages from the Throne, filling your dreams with morning manna, but are replaced by the long shadows of darkness which now intrude upon it, then great is the trouble in the bed of your heart and great is your fear in the hungry night! For what should be a place of safety and blessing to you, has now become a place of watchful tension, a place where the teeth of your soul are set on edge, where your soft souls are taunted and scratched by the toe nailed claws of a beast unseen. Yes, your inner sanctum has now become a sullied place of expectant fear, a sojourn in the valley of the shadow of death. So tell me, the place where you sleep tonight, where you rest your head and heart each night, is it a place of blessing for you? Or, is your inner self most devilishly haunted there?

Why are you watching wickedness? Why are you contemplating cruelness? Why are you soaking in the sickness of so called entertainment?

If this is the case, then it is time to anoint your dark corners and to say to them, "Let there be light." It's time to halt the swampy pooled gathering of dribbling darkness accumulating in the corners of your mind. "How is this done?" you say. Well, this is done by always bathing your brain in warm, life colored light. It's time to make no place, to make no space for the gathering of darkness. Why are you watching wickedness? Why are you contemplating cruelness? Why are you soaking in the sickness of so called entertainment? Meditate and wash your mind with the light of God's good word.

As well as bathing your brain in light, , it is also time to make all your doorways clean, even to anoint your entrance steps with Holy oil so that those that are seeking access whilst carrying a blessing, are met with a warm welcome and a strong amen from your spirit! And in such an anointing, also protect your doorways, especially against those who might seek to carry through them any false thing, any dark word and deposit it especially into your holy, inner chamber.

Yes, to those curse carrying beings, may a 'hard halting' hit their forehead and may rebound curses debar them from access through your anointed doors! Make sure your doorways are covered in the blood, anointed with the oil of sanctified obedience. So, wash your ears, your eyes, your mouth, your nose your hands and your feet, with the waters of obedience to the word of God.

If a land and its cities can be covered with such felt nastiness of darkness dear friend, then how much more can the comparatively tiny inner sanctum of both your heart and home be overcome and enveloped by the same?

You know. I have seen entire cities enveloped in felt darkness. Yes, I have stood above a city, on the top of watching of hills and seen the spiritual darkness cloak it like a choking smog. Felt darkness is a terrible thing. If a land and its cities can be covered with such felt nastiness of darkness dear friend, then how much more can the comparatively tiny inner sanctum of both your heart and home be overcome and enveloped by the same?

Tonight, if you are plagued by a fearful and felt darkness then you have gotten both problems and places that need your good attention. Indeed, you have problems and places that need a shining light, that need *the* shining light Himself. Friends, with the Holy Spirit of God, prayerfully take Jesus to the corners of your mind and heart, and light them up in all conquering, reclaiming love of God. Let the shed blood be proclaimed there. Let the light of His Word now dwell there in all His fullness. Do this, and I promise you, that the terrors of your night, shall never come again.

Listen: "By the way of the sea, beyond the Jordan, in Galilee of the Gentiles. The people who walked in darkness Have seen a great light; those who dwelt in the land of the shadow of death, upon them a light has shined." Isa 9:1-2 NKJV

Pray: When You arrive O Lord, angels sing "Glory!" When you arrive O Lord, golden gifts of anointing and sweet smelling savor are brought by kings from the land of day break. When you arrive O Lord, darkness flees away, healings happen, peace is restored, life and renewal, hope and resurrection all follow hard on the souls of Your mighty stepping feet. O Lord, I give you this dwelling place tonight, this holy bed I lay in now and this inner sanctum of both my head and of my heart, and ask that Your light be ever present here. O Lord, teach me in the morning how to sweep and clean, how to wash and cleanse, how to open and how to close, in Your Great Name I ask it, amen and let it be so!

| Vol | 01 | Q3 | NW00188 | July 06th |

Night-Whisper | **COURAGE**

When 'Amzi' looked longingly over his trailing flowered wall

Today in 1854, Amzi Clarence Dixon, that is, AC Dixon, was born on a plantation in Shelby, North Carolina. Amzi and his brother Thomas both followed in their father's footsteps as Baptist preachers. Whilst the life path of Thomas zigzagged its way into preaching, politics, law and lecturing, it is his writing that is has now fallen very far behind the racial acceptances of today. Indeed, Thomas Dixon even advocated white supremacy, especially in the form of the Ku Klux Klan. His brother Amzi, on the other hand, was a straight career preacher, a "pulpiteer" of power and eloquence, a graduate of the Southern Baptist Seminary, even pastoring such famous churches as Moody Bible Church and Spurgeon's metropolitan tabernacle. I am sure having Thomas as a physical and spiritual brother was an ever-present challenge for old AC Dixon! There's a couple of lessons there for us for sure, but not for tonight. No, tonight I want to suck on some of Amzi's comments from his sermon entitled *"The Raising of Dry Bones"*.

Ezekiel 37:1-4
"The hand of the Lord came upon me and brought me out in the Spirit of the Lord, and set me down in the midst of the valley; and it was full of bones. Then He caused me to pass by them all around, and behold, there were very many in the open valley; and indeed they were very dry. And He said to me, 'Son of man, can these bones live?' I answered, 'O Lord God, You know.' Again He said to me, 'Prophesy to these bones, and say to them, O dry bones, hear the word of the Lord!'"
NKJV

Regarding Israel of old, decay and disintegration surely did ride on the coat tails of sin. Ezekiel's vision of a valley of dry bones was truly all that was left of them and that is where Ezekiel dwelt. In the valley of dry bones. Amzi says this,

"The temptation is for us to seek the garden with its flowers rather than the valley with its bones. The prophet also responds when God's hand sets him down in the midst of the bones. Dwelling with the bones is more trying than just going to them on a temporary mission. To have bones for neighbors and companions may not be pleasant. We have a taste for the company of living people. But unless we are ready to respond to the hand of God which would lead us to the bones and make us dwell among them, we are not prepared for the work of raising them to life. The work cannot be done at a distance. The millions who throng the streets, crowd the theatres, drink in saloons and revel in dance halls, shunning the church as they would the pest house, cannot be reached by the pastor in his study making eloquent sermons for his cultured congregation, nor by the Christians who meet in parlors, halls and churches for fellowship and Bible study. Thank God for the men and women who gladly respond to the hand of God leading them to the most sinful and hopeless."

> *We need to preach the Word of God to dry bones and to do this, the hand of the Lord will take us and push us, shake us and place us, right there in the middle of those valleys of dry bones and command, no, demand, that we should preach His word to them. It's as simple and as scary as that.*

Amen! I believe this last statement of Anzi's was quite revolutionary for his time and I tell you what, the Southern States of America and in most Southern Baptist Circles down there, his statement is still a revolutionary one today!

We need to preach the Word of God to dry bones and to do this, the hand of the Lord will take us and push us, shake us and place us, right there in the middle of those valleys of dry bones and command, no, demand, that we should preach His word to them. It's as simple and as scary as that.

So where has God's powerful hand been leading you today? As for Amzi, despite his powerful message, he was nevertheless placed in the flower gardens of cultured congregations and the pansy'd parlors of plump pastors' wives. Yes, Amzi could only preach about such a courageous and honored placing in the valley of dry bones! I wonder tonight if despite his honored pulpit, Amzi often stood on his tippy toes and peered over the wall and looked longingly down into the valley of dry bones and wished he had both the bottle and the mettle to be permanently placed amongst them. How about you?

Listen: *"Thus says the Lord God to these bones: 'Surely I will cause breath to enter into you, and you shall live. I will put sinews on you and bring flesh upon you, cover you with skin and put breath in you; and you shall live. Then you shall know that I am the Lord.'" Ezekiel 37:5-6 NKJV*

Pray: Give us the willingness O Lord, to be placed amongst the long gone dead and the faith and courage to speak Your word to them. Allow us then O Lord, the tenacity to stick around to see you rattle them together and put life both on them and in them and all around them dear Jesus. Amen!

Night-Whisper | **HOPE**

Prepared packages & Doorstep gifts

Last night we went to our friends for a meal. As is our custom in the United Kingdom, we appeared hungry on their doorstep clutching a gift and last night, the gift was wine. On other occasions it might be flowers or even chocolates, no matter really, for the purpose of these gifts is not really to contribute to the meal, no, because these doorstep gifts are almost always received with smiles and an "Aaah, thank you so much" and then are often laid aside by the recipients for later and private use! No, these gifts are given to honor the received invitation to dinner, to up front and immediately say to the hosts: "Thank you" and "We value this time, this space, this meal and all your careful preparation".

Hosea 14:1, 2a

"O Israel, return to the Lord your God, for you have stumbled because of your iniquity; take words with you, and return to the Lord."

Now, it isn't really a problem if you turn up to a dinner invitation without a gift, yet I have observed that such a doorstep gift goes a long way in putting the waiting parties at pleasant ease with their long awaited guests, even in oiling the gears of conversation and especially in opening up some smiling dialogue. A prepared package, you see, a doorstep gift, goes a long way to make a pleasant evening.

Israel had most certainly blown it with God. In the most dreadful of ways, they had betrayed Him and dishonored Him. Looking at their dire situation, humanly speaking there appeared to be no going back. It was hopeless. Sin had tripped Israel up and thrown them face down in the mud, where they had then engaged in smiling orgies with their neighbors, openly and fearlessly cavorting even before God's watching and horrified, hurt and angry face. Humanly speaking, there was no coming back from this.

Yet God here in Hosea holds out hope of a restored and renewed relationship with Himself, even an invitation to dine again with the offended King of ages and look, the beginning of that restored and renewed relationship was for Israel to turn up at God's door with a gift, with a package, even a package of prepared words, a prodigals doorstep gift.

The right words, at the right time, go a long way in oiling the gears of conversation and especially in opening up some smiling dialogue. Yes, a prepared package of right words goes a long way to ease the hurt of a broken heart and make no mistake about it, God's heart here, was most thoroughly broken.

> *.A prodigals doorstep gift of repentant words.*

Some of you tonight and all of us at some time will have to go and knock on someone's most greatly hurt and offended door. Maybe even God's! When you do, be sure you to take words with you. A gift of words, a prepared package of the right words, for the right time. A prodigals doorstep gift of repentant words.

Listen: "O Israel, return to the Lord your God, for you have stumbled because of your iniquity; take words with you, and return to the Lord. Say to Him, 'Take away all iniquity; receive us graciously, for we will offer the sacrifices of our lips. Assyria shall not save us, we will not ride on horses, nor will we say anymore to the work of our hands, You are our gods. For in You the fatherless finds mercy.'" NKJV.

Pray: Lord, our sinful actions always in the end, seemingly orphan us. Yes, we become bastard children. Unkempt, wild, hard and hurt, seeking satisfaction from anything and anyone but You. So, wallowing in our wantonness, our sin is become an open sewer for all to see. Please, take away all our stinking sin and receive us undeserving sinners, with Your great and unmerited favor and we shall thank You for it, Yes oh God, we shall sing Your praises for it! For no-one else can save us, especially not our own acquired prestige, pride and power. No, we shall not bow to those damnable liars anymore! We have orphaned ourselves from You great King and all we can do is come with these doorstep words, placing them at Your gracious feet, waiting for Your most kind response, for we have heard and we believe, that You, the great God and Father of mankind, are merciful to the fatherless. We lay these words at Your door, even at Your most gracious feet, and now wait patiently for Your goodness to be show toward us through Jesus Christ our Lord. Amen.

| Vol | 01 | Q3 | NW00190 | July 08th |

Night-Whisper | **CONFIDENCE**

'Real yeast for the bread of victory,'

or, 'When the Rats needed a Ferret to function'

By the summer of 1942, the Allies were in trouble throughout the whole of Europe. The German attack in "Operation Barbarossa" had pushed the Russians far back into their own land and much of western Europe, seemed now to be in the full control of the Nazis. To compound these dark matters even further, in the battle of the Atlantic, German U-boats were having a major effect on the supplying of Britain and the war, which was being fought in the desert of North Africa, was also slipping through the Allied hands like the dry desert sand. Indeed, if the German Afrika Korps under Rommel had ever got to the Suez canal, it would have broken the arms of the Allie's supply routes. The psychological and factual blow of losing the Suez Canal to the Nazis would have been incalculable, especially as this would have given them near enough free access to all the oil in the Middle East.

Revelation 1:17c, 18

"Do not be afraid; I am the first and the last. I am He who lives, and was dead, and behold, I am alive forevermore. Amen. And I have the keys of Hades and of death." NKJV.

The bottle-neck battle of El Alamein then, was to be the last stand for the Allies in North Africa to stop the Nazis reaching the Suez Canal. Though the leader of the German forces on the ground, Field Marshal Rommel, was much respected by his own men and even the Allied forces, the Allie's very own commander, Auchinleck, was not respected by his own forces never mind the Germans! On top of this, thus far in the war, Winston Churchill, being without even one victory to his name also faced the threat of a vote of "no confidence" in the British parliament. Auchinleck then, was speedily replaced with a well-tried and popular leader. Well, at least popular amongst the troops, if not amongst his peers! The new British General was described as being, *"As quick as a ferret and about as likeable!"* Nevertheless, by ensuring the co-operation of all arms at his command, including the air force, coupled with the use of a first-class logistical back-up machine and in the issuing of clear-cut orders, the 'ferret' engendered great morale which became the force that turned the war around! Just before the Battle of El Alamein, this general met privately with his commanding officers and encouraged and motivated them by saying:

Here we will stand and fight.
There will be no further withdrawal. I have orders, that all plans and instruction dealing with further withdrawal are to be burnt, and at once! The great point to remember is that we're going to finish with this chap Rommel once and for all, It will be quite easy. There's no doubt about it, he's definitely a nuisance. Therefore we will hit him a crack and finish him.

"Monty"- 1st Viscount Montgomery of Alamein.

If you are a leader, then communication, organization, co-ordination and clarity of objective are vital in achieving any victory. However, all of these vital ingredients of victory will be like trying to bake bread without yeast if you have not got the ability to inspire the confidence in the achievement of your objective. The Ferret had the ability to inject the yeast of inspiration into his commanding officers and his troops and that my friends, made all the difference in the world! Indeed, it is said that once Monty took charge of his 8th Army, 'the Dessert Rats,' as they were known, had hardly no sickness or absenteeism whatsoever. Imagine that! The Rats needed a Ferret to function!

> *The Ferret had the ability to inject the yeast of inspiration into his commanding officers and his troops and that my friends, made all the difference in the world!*

The last book of the Bible, the Revelation of Jesus Christ, is the yeast that makes the bread of life. Christ's victory, His majestic Lordship, His all-conquering capacity is clearly and awesomely portrayed before our open ears and open mouths! So, if you are in need of inspiration tonight, inspiration tomorrow and inspiration on your third day, then read the book of the Revelation of Jesus Christ and once you've done that, read it again! For without this yeast of inspiration, there shall be no overcoming of sickness, nor of despondency nor of death. No, there shall be no rising in your life! Read the book of Revelation!

Listen: *"Then he said to me, 'These words are faithful and true.' And the Lord God of the holy prophets sent His angel to show His servants the things which must shortly take place. 'Behold, I am coming quickly! Blessed is he who keeps the words of the prophecy of this book.'" Revelation 22:6-7 NKJV*

Pray: Lord, I "knead" inspiration tonight! So, teach me how to delight myself in Your majestic greatness, and hear all Your most encouraging words of victory! For it is in Your magnificent name I ask it, amen and let it be so.

| Vol | 01 | Q3 | NW00191 | July 09th |

Night-Whisper | **DANGER**

The devil's garden and operation light-foot

One of the curses of the late twentieth century, the removal of which was championed by the late Diana, Princess of Wales, is the anti-personnel mine. Even long time after wars are over, AND peace is made and battles and heroes are ALL forgotten, the anti-personnel mine is the gift that just keeps on killing!

Psalms 18:29

"For by You I can run against a troop, by my God I can leap over a wall." NKJV

Last night we looked briefly at the leadership philosophy of General Montgomery as he faced his great adversary at El Alamein, the German Field Marshal, Erwin Rommel. It was in fact Rommel who laid an estimated 3 million, mostly anti-tank mines, around his defensive positions and named the whole defensive entanglement of barbed wire and mines, "The Devil's Garden". Most of these mines are still in position today and still killing people. Imagine that.

Attacking Rommel, Montgomery launched "Operation Lightfoot" with the largest artillery barrage since WWI. It is said that the sound of it made the gunner's ears bleed! Remember, The Devil's Garden was made up predominantly of anti-tank mines, allowing advancing infantry to run through the minefields. Hence the name, Operation Lightfoot! Unfortunately, many of these mines were hard wired together, such that when one exploded, it triggered the explosions of numerous other ones. Even if you were light on your feet, the Devil's Garden was still a most dreadful place of death.

At the fall of man, the world of course became the Devil's Garden. Full of flesh ripping and soul-destroying barbed wire, it is also very well mined. The church of Jesus Christ, like Monty's infantry, is advancing light footedly through the Devil's Garden down toward the tall black gates of hell. Well, some of us are anyways, and we always find at last, often times despite the advancing carnage, that according to Christ's words, the gates of hell have not prevailed against us!

In the Devil's Garden, comparatively speaking, the infantry get away lightly against the hidden mines, whilst it is our "big guns" that have the problems. Oh and we like our big guns don't we? And, the truth is, we need them, for they are truly God's provision to help us punch through some of the most heavily and brutally defended position of the enemy. Yet for our Christian big guns especially, the Devil's Garden is a most dangerous place, as the vast majority of its millions of mines are there specifically and only, to take out these big guns of ours. We all agree that there is no more devastating and disillusioning a site, than to see a Christian big gun fall, to see them and their ministries, them and their churches, them and their futures, them and their families and all who follow after them, explode into a dead and ineffective, million little pieces.

> *There is no more devastating and disillusioning a site, than to see a Christian 'big-gun' fall.*

We prayer engineers, we discerners of mines, we sappers all, must make sure that we most prayerfully and carefully, remove the mines in front of our advancing big guns. Warn them of their possible presence and even mark a way for them to go through them. The need for sappers in the Kingdom of God is an evident and ever pressing necessity. If you are a big gun reading this tonight, if you want to be one even, then you had better halt your advance until God provides you with a few prophetic pathfinders who are light on their spiritual feet, often on their knees and willing to make a way for you to pass through the Devil's Garden so you might fire accurately upon your target. If you are a sapper tonight, then make sure you are indeed light on your feet and also heavy on your knees, most regularly and carefully going before your big-guns and marking a way for them to go. For victory and the minimization of casualties, both sappers and big guns must work and walk together.

Listen: *"Therefore I run thus: not with uncertainty. Thus I fight: not as one who beats the air." (1 Corinthians 9:26-27 NKJV)*

Pray: So Lord, please protect our big guns from being blown up, either by their won sinful stupidity or by the enemy of our souls.. Help us be faithful in marking the mines lain before their pounding tracks, and please Lord, help our big-guns listen. in Jesus name we ask it, amen and let it be so..

Night-Whisper | **GRACE**

Of pleasure and pain

I was a latch key kid. Both my parents worked and not only did I come home each night to an empty home but in the mornings, I was daily left to take care of myself in an early morning tradesman's, hurried and hastily vacated house.

Jeremiah 15:18

"Why is my pain perpetual and my wound incurable, which refuses to be healed? Will You surely be to me like an unreliable stream, as waters that fail?" NKJV

My father always left me some money hidden in my morning shoes or at the bottom of a clean pair of socks, just enough to by some sweet candy for later on in the lonely day. The early morning comfort of sugar, however, was just too much of a temptation for a little child and so each day, I would trot five minutes up the road and into the newsagents for some company, which was for me, my morning comic, the pages oozing with the fresh smell of printers ink and bursting fat with the dancing antics of 'Dennis the Menace and 'Desperate Dan.' To accompany this paper fix of friendship, I would also purchase a long dark bar of chocolate to dip in my hot and waiting cup of three-sugared tea. I did this every day and not surprisingly, it was only at the age of twelve, when I started to have my first real dental issues.

The pull of sugar has remained with me for the rest of my life, as has the consequent dental destruction. Yes, sugar has comforted me but has also cost me dearly. I have paid for it in cuts and crowns, root canals, antibiotics, vast amounts of mercury poisoned amalgam, braces and bridges and no doubt in the future, in implants implacable! Most of all however, I have paid for my passing pleasure, my white crystalled comfort, by being in seeming constant dental pain. Tell me, apart from sea-sickness, is there any worse pain than that from an impacted and infected chipped and fissured molar? Poor sweet baby, if you have toothache tonight, I am so sorry for you. These words to follow my preamble might not comfort you too much tonight then, so I hope you will at least find the first part of the testimony of Romeo to a healer's drugs, to be oh so true for you! *"O true apothecary, thy drugs are quick."* Tonight then for those of you with toothache, may your doctors drugs be quick, for the night in its quietness, seems only to lengthen the passing of time and amplify the presence of the pulsating pain of teeth gone wrong.

In both the seen and the unseen realms, which we inhabit God has made us to be sentient beings, experiencing comfort and closeness, distance and fear, pleasure and pain. Like us all, maybe more than us, Adam and Eve were also created jam packed full of tingling and touching, testing and tasting nerve endings of every kind. So much so, that eastward in a place called Eden, even within the very boundaries of the garden of God, I am sure you could hear shouts of "Whoopee!" and other happy chants of "Hallelujah and Praise God," as well as the many cries of "Ooowees, Yikes and Ouch!" Oh yes! I am sure Adam "mmmmm'd" and drooled over the best of fruit, and also that if Adam had hit his thumb with a hammer, that it would glow red in throbbing pain as he did the famous "one hand shaking oooo-aah dance!" Yes, even in God's economy, if an angel were ever to accidentally fly into a window, I am sure both its ego and its wings would all be painfully broken!

> *There will be some kinds of necessary pain in the age to come. For where there is pleasure, there is also pain.*

Do you see the rule here? For where the sensation of pleasures can be most wonderfully felt, then so can the presence of pulsating pain. God has made us sentient beings and intends us to remain so.

For me then, there is no doubt that in the resurrection and in the restoration of all things to a fuller and fitting glory, that there will be the presence of the policeman of pain, telling us of the hurt and warning us of the danger of continuing to do that with produces pain. I am also sure however, and this is most important, that unlike these times under this failing sun, in the resurrection and in the restoration of all things to a fuller and fitting glory, any restorative growth as the result of the healings of painful hurts, will not be trying, will not even be painful in itself, but rather, will be a most pleasurable experience! Yes, I believe there will be some kinds of necessary pain in the age to come. For where there is pleasure, there is also pain. Do you see the rule here?

Having said all that, I am also most convinced that the deepest of pains, that is, the diseases of the body, the diseases of the mind and of the heart, will not follow us to heaven. The pain of loss, the pain of absence and loneliness will all be gone, never to return again. The pain of guilt and the pain of shame, the pain of condemnation, the pain of accusation, the pain of hopelessness, even the deep pain of the midnight darkness of debilitating depression, shall all be gone, never to return again. For where these things remain, they would turn even heaven into a living hell. This cannot be so.

Believe me when I tell you that the healing of these deeper pains to a permanent removal is in every way, most wonderful, in every way most marvelous and in every way to me, the most miraculous of all the wonders of a healing heaven. Yes, I truly believe that He shall remove once and for all time, those deeper and most dreadful of sin related pains!

> *Yes, diseased pain is a dreadful portent that we shall one day die. Do not ignore such pain. No, try and fix it, but above all, always let it lead you to an eternal cure in Jesus.*

Meanwhile, this side of the restoration, all of us shall experience the pain of an eating rot. Even buxom beauties, all set in shining, smiling and whitened teeth; with strength bound up in tight and toned up muscle and tanned and supple skin, shall all begin to sag, and soon, yes, so very soon indeed, they too shall be eaten by the worm of death, which by the way, always begins its meal as breath and hope dance together in our mortal bodies in an embrace of fond futility. Yes, diseased pain is a dreadful portent that we shall one day die. Do not ignore such pain. No, try and fix it, but above all, always let it lead you to an eternal cure in Jesus.

Tonight then and on the morrow, may you always find a great dentist and a good doctor, an insightful psychiatrist and a kind psychologist. May you always have the money to pay for their services but may the day come sooner rather than later, when in all your pained diseases, you seek an eternal cure for the eternal problem of death which lies within you. May you soon, so very soon, find a Curer for your souls and with them, find the cure Himself. May the presence of Jesus, deliver you now, or at the least, dull your diseased pains until He delivers you from them forever!

Lastly, before you sleep tonight, thank God with me for dentists and for Novocain, for doctors and for the helps and healings of every kind that we can now find so comparatively easy under this quickly setting sun.

Listen: *"And God will wipe away every tear from their eyes; there shall be no more death, nor sorrow, nor crying. There shall be no more pain, for the former things have passed away. Then He who sat on the throne said, 'Behold, I make all things new.' And He said to me, 'Write, for these words are true and faithful.'" Revelation 21:4,5 NKJV*

Pray: O Lord, let there be for those in diseased pain of every kind tonight, a gentle touch of Jesus in their long and painful night. Indeed, my Lord, we pray for those in pain, that You would grant Your beloved sleep. For those O Lord, who must, however, travel through the night with this terrible and painful companion, may You strengthen them with both Your presence and Your preserving power, so that they may never be eternally hurt. Please Lord, for their sake and even for our sake, rid them of this great robber of their joy, this mocker of Your redemption, this pisser on their peace, this eating worm of death, this most dreadful eating pain. We ask O Lord that you do this both for them and for us. Finally father, my imagination fails me in the wonder of the removal of even the remembrance of such deep diseased pain. Yet I long for that day, yes Lord I thank You tonight for that certain day a coming, when under the Son of Your love, You shall banish this pain of sin forever to the pit of hell! Lord thank You, that somehow, even someday soon, You shall make us truly well and truly whole once more. Amen.

| Vol | 01 | Q3 | NW00193 | July 11ᵗʰ |

Night-Whisper | FACE

The face of grace

Before the channel tunnel existed, thereby connecting Britain with France, the only way to get across the English Channel to so furious a continent, was by ferry.

2 Corinthians 4:6

"For it is the God who commanded light to shine out of darkness, who has shone in our hearts to give the light of the knowledge of the glory of God in the face of Jesus Christ." NKJV

My parents were not wealthy and did not possess a car, so when my mother wanted to visit her daughter, who was married to a British soldier then billeted in Germany, we would catch the train to Dover and board the night ferry to the Belgian sea port of Ostend. It was always a night ferry we travelled upon, simply because travelling at night was the cheapest way for many of us poor folks to cross the English Channel!

I remember my father, an old sailor himself, striding with certainty around the rolling decks, his duck feet spread at 45 degrees keeping him in perfect balance whilst other land legged people toppled and fell against the hard cold rusty metal of an old ship in great need of repair. My father had this strange gait about him even on the land, walking feet spread apart, as though the very earth itself at any moment might just begin to tilt and sway and have him over. It's a genetic propensity for sure, for both myself and my son have exactly the same gait.

When on these ferry crossings, beginning at the bow, my father would walk me round the ship, pointing out with fond and familiar knowledge, all the accoutrements of such vehicles that were fitted once in the now dead Scottish shipyards to travel the vastness of God's impenetrable deeps. Last of all of course, we would arrive at the stern, the British merchant flag flapping in the cold middle watch spray, the pale moon riding up and down on the horizon of my wide and tired, gazing eyes and the black sea all churned up into phosphorescence light by the diesel grind of the low frequency elephant grumbling propeller blades. I remember it now, the moon shining pale in the midnight sky, a faint halo stopped short and diminished just inches from its poor shining and the sea, alive with shimmering white, its cut waves all scurrying like white rats released into the black distance, as the ship made its way to a foreign port afar. If we would listen, even death and life would speak to us of light and love in the face of Christ Jesus. Allow me to explain.

You see, the moon of course is dead. The only light it gives is that which it reflects from the sun, that pale and reflected blue moon light which shines so very little in our darkness from its poor dead and pox marked face. The sea however, is alive and the churning of large ship blades produces a phosphorescence of luminescent light. Do

> *The forgotten world these two witnesses speak of is the world of God, which is indeed, a world of light.*

you see that? These two marvels, one above and one below, are but poor pointers to a forgotten world now most clearly proclaimed and published, even sung abroad by these two crying and most competent ambassadors of life and lip. The forgotten world these two witnesses speak of is the world of God, which is indeed, a world of light.

In this material realm, it was God who commanded light to shine, to manifest itself in material form. It is this same God who also caused the rising of the morning sun on that first of days, who from then until now, like an obedient puppy, day after day, comes scampering to the rear of the daily life of our own ship as it grinds its way slowly on to a foreign graveyard port, until in the morning of our own resurrection when God again, according to His own perfect will, shall command a rising, a shining, an epiphany of a paradigm shift if you will, which like an expectant Apollo spacecraft, waited for by ground crew with dry and baited breath, shall slowly appear from the dark side of our moon to gaze with awe and thankfulness on the blue and shining planet of our heavenly home, hung against the silver spotted and infinite depths of space. Yes, like the shining of the morning sun, which is an emergence from deep darkness, the rising of the Son of God in our hearts, is a rising from the dead, a coming round from the dark side of the moon, bringing a crackle of a communication upon a long blackout and bursting us into open conference with the Father, Son and Holy Ghost and all the happy community of all the saints in light. This shining of the Son in our hearts is in all understandings, the rising of warm life on once cold dead hearts that will find its maturity in the resurrection of our bodies.

This shining resurrection light from the Father, is the knowledge of the awesome Majesty and Splendor of God, which is never to be quenched, never to be diminished, never to be exhausted, and is all the time bursting forth in the face and from the face of the Savior, the Sent one, the Supreme Commander of all things. This light is contact. This light is community. This burning, this bright source of the ever shining luminescent outpouring of the everlasting love of God, is to be found in totality in but one place, and that place is the face of grace, and that place, that face of grace, is nothing else but the face of Christ.

For thinking on the love of God so late at night, musing on the Master with open and thankful hearts, will so mightily push back our soul on the bow of His morning, that on our waking, we will be let loose like a blazing comet, to burn across the heavens of our own coming day.

It is not idolatry to think on Christ's face. It is not idolatry to prime our dreams with loving light and to so fill our subconscious darkness with rays of warmth so that our spirit would blaze against our closed eyelids, making them chatter with flickering heavenly REM sleep! For thinking on the love of God so late at night, musing on the Master with open and thankful hearts, will so mightily push back our soul on the bow of His morning, that on our waking, we will be let loose like a blazing comet, to burn across the heavens of our own coming day.

Tonight then friends, on your dark shop, sailing through the night, look at the moon and sea, and think upon the life and light to come. Meditate upon the face of Christ. Think upon the face of grace.

Listen: *"The four living creatures, each having six wings, were full of eyes around and within. And they do not rest day or night, saying: 'Holy, holy, holy, Lord God Almighty, who was and is and is to come!' Whenever the living creatures give glory and honour and thanks to Him who sits on the throne, who lives forever and ever, the twenty-four elders fall down before Him who sits on the throne and worship Him who lives forever and ever, and cast their crowns before the throne, saying: 'You are worthy, O Lord, to receive glory and honour and power; for You created all things, and by Your will they exist and were created.'" Revelation 4:8-11 NKJV*

Pray: Because when I think about You Lord, how You saved me, how You raised me, how You filled me up with the Holy Ghost, how You healed me to the utter-most. When I think about You Lord, how You picked me up and You turned me around, how You placed my feet on solid ground, it makes me wanna shout, "Hallelujah, thank You Jesus, Lord you're worthy of all of the glory, and all of the honor, and yes it makes me want to shout it out, Hallelujah! Thank You Jesus, Lord you're worthy of all of the glory, and all of the honor and all of the praise!"

"When I think about the Lord" Lyrics - Rita Springer

| Vol | 01 | Q3 | NW00194 | July 12th |

Night-Whisper | COURAGE

The glorious twelve

Today in Northern Ireland is the controversial and colorful celebration of the Victory of William III of Orange over King James VII of Scotland and James II of England, whose green and pleasant land, in 1690, was made red with blood at the Battle of the Boyne. Here, at the instigation of parliament, James throne was taken from him, chiefly by the courageous actions of the irregular Cavalry of the Enniskilleners, and the elite troops of William himself, the Dutch 'Blue Guards.' A most colorful confrontation indeed!

1 Corinthians 9:26
"Thus I fight: not as one who beats the air."
NKJV

It is written concerning William III that "danger acted on him like strong drink, opening his heart, loosing his tongue and taking away all appearance of constraint, as he thrust himself time and time again into the very heart of battle, inspiring his troops and mortifying his on-looking commanders as musket shot struck the pistol in his very own hand and even more blew off the heel of his boot!" William, at the head of the Eniskilleners leading them into battle is reported to have shouted at them, *"Gentlemen I have heard much of you. Let me see something of you!"* It is this phrase I wish to consider us tonight.

In the year of our Lord, 2015, as I edit this Night-Whisper, the Church of the Living God in The British Isles plummets like a shrieking Boeing 747 in a seeming irrecoverable nosedive toward the hungry ground and the great teeth of its ever rising rocks. Meanwhile, inside the plastic coated fuselage, economy class Christians are still wining and dining, singing and clapping, rolling in the aisles waving their legs in the air as they take their holiday excursion to another Big Day out. Meanwhile, in first class, well robbed bishops and blinged up Evangelists are all talking about money and how in the name of peace, they might slaughter truth without making it scream so loudly. It doesn't matter, for short time now, the whole thing will be obliterated by the hard palate of the waiting landscape, as it explodes into the waiting earth. No matter, for the watchers and the waiters shall soon fill in the crater and build a Mosque upon it, for the Bishops have already signed over the deeds and given them the keys.

I'm sick of seminars and webinars, of conferences and cafe bars, where the incessant talking drones on in complete irrelevancy to the plummeting catastrophe about to come upon us. I am sick of all the talking. Tonight, we do not need any sectarian war, we do not need any religious confrontation of bomb vests and bullets, but we do need another gloriously committed twelve good men and another King Billy to stop all the talking and lead them into action! William is a conquerors name, it always has been. I fear the William lining up to lead Britain will only lead us into Babylon.

> *"Gentlemen I have heard much of you. Now let me see something of you!"*

Forget the so-called "Glorious Twelfth!" Do you want to be apostolic? Do you want to be part of another glorious twelve? Well, if you do and if any real men are truly listening tonight, then maybe you might hear your own all conquering King, Himself both wounded and bloodied in battle, cry to you from atop his great white charger as it's hoofs claw the cold still air, saying to you, "Gentlemen I have heard much of you. Now let me see something of you!" God we need to see some Eniskilleners rise up and take the field once more!

Listen: "Only be strong and very courageous, that you may observe to do according to all the law which Moses My servant commanded you; do not turn from it to the right hand or to the left, that you may prosper wherever you go. This book of the law shall not depart from your mouth, but you shall meditate in it day and night, that you may observe to do according to all that is written in it. For then you will make your way prosperous, and then you will have good success. Have I not commanded you? Be strong and of good courage; do not be afraid, nor be dismayed, for the Lord your God is with you wherever you go." (Joshua 1:7-9 NKJV)

Pray: My Great Commander, grant me less mouth and much more action and allow me to rub shoulders with other warriors of action and passion, amen and let it be so.

| Vol | 01 | Q3 | NW00195 | July 13th |

Night-Whisper | **BLESSING**

Paraskevidekatriaphobiai

Apparently it was Dr. Donald Dossey, a psychotherapist specializing in the treatment of phobias who coined the term "Paraskevidekatriaphobiai," to describe the morbid fear that some people have regarding Friday 13th. Undoubtedly, some of you in the future are reading this, maybe late on a Friday night somewhere. What kind of a day have you had? After all, some people say that belief in the special existence of bad luck on Friday 13th is "the widest held superstition in the Western world."

Isaiah 2:6

"You have abandoned your people, the house of Jacob. They are full of superstitions from the East; they practice divination like the Philistines and clasp hands with pagans." NIV

About.com, commenting on what it calls this "urban legend" of bad luck on Friday the 13th says that it looked at a study published in the British Medical Journal in 1993 entitled "Is Friday 13th Bad for Your Health?" About.com goes on to say that, "Its authors compared the ratio of traffic volume to the number of automobile accidents on two different days, Friday the 6th and Friday the 13th, over a period of years. Incredibly, they found that in the region sampled, while consistently fewer people chose to drive their cars on Friday the 13th the number of hospital admissions due to vehicular accidents was still significantly higher than on "normal" Fridays. Their conclusion, says About.com, is that *"Friday 13th is unlucky for some. The risk of hospital admission as a result of a transport accident may be increased by as much as 52 percent. Staying at home is recommended."* Ha! Interestingly, Dr. Donald Dossey says that 8% of Americans are in the grip of this particular phobic condition and that friends, at the time of my writing in 2008, means some 21 million folk. Imagine that!

These Paraskevidekatriaphobics, and you may be one of them, are simply victims of superstition. Victims, picked on. Victims, pecked on by black crows, caw'ing fear in the ears of your soul and clawing out your former sensible eyes before black cats, spilt salt, cracked mirrors and other not so magnificent means of stupid self-cursing.

Admittedly now, the roots of some superstitions, like walking under ladders for example, are rooted in common sense. After all, if you walk under a ladder something heavy might just fall on your head! Look for the sensible answer in some of your superstitions for it is amazing how the light of reason can dispel the most unwarranted but deeply held superstition.

The presence and the blessing of God with us and upon us, should both trump and squash any cursing that might have been placed upon us!

However, what about my friend's father, I mean what on earth was that all about? For he was a strong man who never the less held a morbid fear of Friday the 13th who in turn died of a heart attack on Friday the 13th, on the 13th hole of a golf course at 13:00 hrs? Well frankly, I have no answer, except that certainly there are some things on this earth that we do not understand, yes, that is a certainty. The one thing I do understand though, and that most thoroughly, is that focused fear can be a gateway for all kinds of crippling and debilitating diseases, disorders, disasters and even demons! Superstition can lead us to be so emotionally full of dread, so intellectually anticipating of disaster that it puts us on the wrong foot, it leaves us imbalanced and consequently, it leaves us open to a successful attack from the enemy. I am aware of this in my own life.

The Scripture clearly teaches us that when the blessing of God rests upon His people, He makes them a fear and a dread to their enemies, yes, He makes them a fear and a dread to both the seen and unseen beasts stalking the land of their sojourn. You see, yes, you do see that don't you? We have it the wrong way around! The presence and the blessing of God with us and upon us, should both trump and squash any cursing that might have been placed upon us! That magnificent blessing, seen especially in His abiding presence with us, releases us from fear; yes, it releases us from dread and all the other seeming consequence of violated superstitions. You need to see that and in seeing it you must not therefore give any place whatsoever to the superstitious doctrine of demons.

Tonight my friend, my simple encouragement to you, is that you deny the dread of the day and then go to bed! Yes, treat superstition with the disdain it deserves and then in your dreams, bathe in the blessings of God the great, and God the good, for He is in your neighborhood, tonight.

Listen: *"The LORD of hosts, Him you shall hallow; let Him be your fear, and let Him be your dread." Isa 8:13 NKJV*

Pray: Father God, I am sorry for my sins and the sins of my family, both those now present and those gone well before. Father God, I am sorry for the sins of my community and the sins of my nation, both those now present and those gone well before. Father God, I am sorry for all curses and lies I have placed upon myself and placed upon my family, my community and on my nation. Lord Jesus Christ, according to the economy of Your Kingdom, as a Royal priest before Your throne, I bless those who curse me, I bless my family, I bless my community, I bless my nation. I believe Your word O Lord and so I also count myself blessed with every spiritual blessing in the heavenly places in Christ Jesus both this night dear Lord and forever more. Therefore, my mighty God, in Your great name I now slip the shackles of superstition and make You my fear and make You my dread, upon the alter of this my peaceful bed, tonight. Grant me restful sleep O Lord, and courage for the coming day. Amen and let it be so.

Night-Whisper | **PREACH**

Of pig sties and palaces

The grey dawn broke over the residence of the Selina, Countess of Huntingdon. However Job like in her life's experiences, this illness looked as though it could be her last. Her personal chaplain, George Whitfield, who had preached in all of her houses to most of her noble friends, now moved purposefully towards the window. Cracking it open, the voices below of thousands of admirers came prayerfully to the end of their petitioning hymn:

Acts 16:14,15

"Now a certain woman named Lydia heard us. She was a seller of purple from the city of Thyatira, who worshiped God. The Lord opened her heart to heed the things spoken by Paul. And when she and her household were baptised, she begged us, saying, 'If you have judged me to be faithful to the Lord, come to my house and stay.' So she persuaded us." Acts 16:14-15.

"Uphold this star in thy right hand
Crown her endeavors with success;
Among the great ones may she stand,
A witness of thy righteousness,
Till many nobles join Thy train
And triumph in the lamb that's slain."

Eighteenth century England was a hard and brutal world to live in. Alcohol and poverty proved a malevolent mix for the masses of the lower classes and there was many a highwayman still roaming the heaths along roads into London. Poverty, inequality and drunkenness became a heady cocktail for violence. However, it was not only Whitfield and Wesley that feared not the mobs whilst loving the masses and preaching Christ to the forgotten and poverty stricken. No, Selina, since her conversion, had become very active and compassionate amongst the poor as well, visiting them and praying for them in their sickness, and with such a love and concern that when they died, they left their children to her as a legacy that they might be cared for by the Countess!

However it must be remembered that not only did Selina care for the lowly, but also for the high and the mighty as well. Selina was a regular visitor to the Royal Court, even appealing at one point directly to the king concerning the lifestyle of the then Archbishop and his wife. Her witness was indeed, to both pig sties and palaces. However Selina was more than a kind benefactor. She was a woman of great vision, zeal, courage, continuance, sacrifice, understanding, and discernment.

The upper class did not mingle with the minions in education, society, health or amenities. The Evangelical preachers call to conviction, confession and repentance may have been well understood and received by the much poorer masses, but on the whole, the rich nobility rejected it. Indeed, the then Duchess of Buckingham did not believe that people with "blue blood" had to listen to such humiliating truths. Sneering at the then growing sect of the Methodists she wrote, *"Their doctrines are most repulsive and strongly tinctured with impertinence and disrespect towards their superiors, in perpetually endeavoring to level all ranks, and do away with distinctions. It is monstrous to be told that you have a heart as sinful as the common wretches that crawl the earth."* It took a woman of courage like Selina to place the claims of Christ before such arrogant pomposity. Selina was aware of the blind danger associated with her rich estate for she remarked many times concerning herself that she *"Thanked God for the letter M in 1 Cor 1:26 where it says, 'For you see your calling, brethren, that not many wise according to the flesh, not many mighty, not many noble, are called.' The M thankfully indicated not many rather than not any!"*

> *It is monstrous to be told that you have a heart as sinful as the common wretches that crawl the earth.*

"It is estimated that through the tireless efforts of the Countess of Huntingdon, no less than 200 chapels and mission stations were opened and it is recorded that in 1828, forty years after her death, there were some 35,000 people regularly attending these places of worship, cared for by 72 officiating ministers." Though at the time Oxford and Cambridge were still the only places where men could train for the ministry, Trevecca house near Talgarth in Breconshire was set up by the Countess and had more than 150 preachers passing through it, dispatching them all over England and even to the Americas! Indeed, Missionaries sent to the southern state of Georgia in 1772, though there primarily to preach to the Indians and set up a college for the native Indian nations, nevertheless, became instrumental along with Whitfield, in the conversion of many African slaves then in the south. Following their emancipation from slavery, some 2000 are reported to have left for Sierra Leone in 1792. At least half of these were associated with the Countess of Huntingdon's Connexion of churches and indeed, a group of Connexion churches still exist today in Sierra Leone and are in fellowship with the remaining few Chapels still left in England.

Paul had his Lydia, but Whitfield had his Countess. Maybe today, many of you Pastors are still in need of some godly and powerful patronage? Possibly we should be praying that more fish shall be caught, and found to have money in their mouths, mercy in their gills and influence at their fingertips!

> *Possibly we should be praying that more fish shall be caught, and found to have money in their mouths, mercy in their gills and influence at their finger tips*

The story is told of a bishop who complained about the Countess's Ministers who had created some kind of sensation in his diocese. His majesty offered a solution to the Bishop saying, *"Make bishops of them - make bishops of them!"* The prelate replied: *"That might be done, but please your Majesty, we cannot make a bishop of Lady Huntingdon."* At that point the Queen interposed, *"It would be a lucky circumstance if you could, for she puts you all to shame."*

Listen: *"Therefore, holy brethren, partakers of the heavenly calling, consider the Apostle and High Priest of our confession, Christ Jesus, who was faithful to Him who appointed Him, as Moses also was faithful in all His house. For this one has been counted worthy of more glory than Moses, inasmuch as He who built the house has more honour than the house. For every house is built by someone, but He who built all things is God. And Moses indeed was faithful in all His house as a servant, for a testimony of those things which would be spoken afterward, but Christ as a Son over His own house, whose house we are if we hold fast the confidence and the rejoicing of the hope firm to the end." Hebrews 3:1-6 NKJV.*

Pray: Oh Great Apostle Jesus, may we be like You, faithful in all our appointments. Lord, whether our calling be to pig sties or to palaces, may You be clearly seen in us. In all our works for You then Lord, enable us through the provision of great and godly benefactors, in Your great name we ask it, amen and let it be so!

| Vol | 01 | Q3 | NW00197 | July 15th |

Night-Whisper | **CHOOSE**

Could this be your finest hour?

I went to meet a friend of mine who was arriving at St Pancras station from Paris. There, overlooking all the comings and goings of all the busy, head down fast moving folk, is a nine meter high bronze sculptor by Paul Day, called '*The Welcome.*' This stunning piece itself is based on a drawing of the artist embracing his French wife. However, in my opinion, '*The Welcome.*' pales into insignificance before probably one of the greatest work of arts ever produced by this same artist, which I later strolled by later that same day. Yes, there alongside the River Thames, on the Victoria embankment, commemorating the halting conflict of the aggressive, rampant Nazi forces, is the majestic and moving, Paul Day, Battle of Britain monument.

It was two weeks after the fall of Paris in June 1940 when the then Prime Minister, Winston Churchill, stood and addressed the house of commons in what history now calls, his "Finest Hour" speech. The prefix of Churchill's spectacular and rousing speech, acknowledges what Alexander Cadogen, the then Permanent Undersecretary at the Foreign Office called, a most "miraculous" and "marvelous" event whereby, the defeated British Expeditionary Force, trapped and defeated on the wet dark shores of Dunkirk, waiting for destruction under the mighty jackboot of Hitler were able to be removed by an armada of small boats,

Joel 2:15-17

"*Blow the trumpet in Zion, consecrate a fast, call a sacred assembly; gather the people, sanctify the congregation, assemble the elders, gather the children and nursing babes; let the bridegroom go out from his chamber, and the bride from her dressing room. Let the priests, who minister to the Lord, weep between the porch and the altar; let them say, 'Spare Your people, O Lord, and do not give Your heritage to reproach, that the nations should rule over them. Why should they say among the peoples, "Where is their God?"'*" *NKJV.*

back to the safer shores of England. The destruction of this defeated army never happened, because for unknown reasons even today, Hitler halted and never forced home his victorious advantage. Indeed Churchill said, "During the last few days we have successfully brought off the great majority of the troops we had on the line of communication in France; and seven-eighths of the troops we have sent to France since the beginning of the war - that is to say, about 350,000 out of 400,000 men - are safely back in this country. Others are still fighting with the French, and fighting with considerable success in their local encounters against the enemy. We have also brought back a great mass of stores, rifles and munitions of all kinds which had been accumulated in France during the last nine months. We have, therefore, in this Island today a very large and powerful military force. This force comprises all our best-trained and our finest troops, including scores of thousands of those who have already measured their quality against the Germans and found themselves at no disadvantage. We have under arms at the present time in this Island over a million and a quarter men."

> 70 years ago we had a nation that knew God, knew His word and knew His promises. Today, we have nothing. How can we call a nation to a God they do not know

Make no mistake about it, this was a mighty miracle. This miracle came about because of one reason alone and that is that on May 26th, the church finally called the whole nation to a national day of prayer. The nation's churches, overflowed. As I write this night in 2008, I am undecided as to which side of the thin red line of destiny we are on. It's a close call, for if the *church* mobilized itself even on the morrow, in courage and sacrificial conquest, I am not sure if it would be just in time, or frankly just far too late to save our land. In any event, we are in need of a Spiritual Churchill to once again come and steel our hearts to fight. The great problem we have is that nearly 70 years ago we had a nation that knew God, knew His word and knew His promises. Today, we have nothing. How can we call a nation to a God they do not know. Editing this Whisper, now in 2015, I know which sod of the red line we are on. The wrong side. It is 'over' for the legacy church in Britain. Doctrinally compromised and spiritually corrupt, Christ is spewing it out of its mouth. The nation is like one long Nightmare of a Jeremy Kyle show, and its populous is dumbed down and dogging around with whatever demon is presenting itself.

The remnant, (are you out there?) and God help us it is a remnant of what was once a Christian nation, must begin to stir itself up and lay hold of God once more. From what I have seen of the remnant however, we are all very soon to be wearing the Devil's insignia. I say again that unless we stir ourselves up to lay hold of God and beg Him to do us good, then at the very best, we shall be reduced to fighting an underground Guerrilla war, hiding and huddling whilst many of our brethren are thrown into prison, waiting and praying until someone else, at great cost, eventually comes and rescues them. Each of us needs to decide which side of the line of destiny we are and make our plans and decisions accordingly. Only a bloody revolution will save the legacy church. I see no revolutionaries. Only an unprecedented turning to God of the people of this nation will prepare us from the judgement which is coming. Note that I did not say save us from it. No. We shall not be saved from it. However, by the grace of God, if we turn to Him, we might just be saved through it.

Listen: *"What General Weygand called the Battle of France is over. I expect that the Battle of Britain is about to begin. Upon this battle depends the survival of Christian civilization. Upon it depends our own British life, and the long continuity of our institutions and our Empire. The whole fury and might of the enemy must very soon be turned on us. Hitler knows that he will have to break us in this Island or lose the war. If we can stand up to him, all Europe may be free and the life of the world may move forward into broad, sunlit uplands. But if we fail, then the whole world, including the United States, including all that we have known and cared for, will sink into the abyss of a new Dark Age made more sinister, and perhaps more protracted, by the lights of perverted science. Let us therefore brace ourselves to our duties, and so bear ourselves that if the British Empire and its Commonwealth last for a thousand years, men will still say, 'This was their finest hour.'" (The Prime Minister – Winston Churhill)*

Pray: Great and Almighty God, soon bring us each and every one to places of sober choosing and places of fighting, in Jesus name I ask it, amen and let it be.

Night-Whisper | **APPREHEND**

The clarity and change of the ramrod of correction

Last night, I made reference to Winston Churchill's "Finest Hour" speech and I shall refer to it again tonight. For within that most magnificent of speeches, lies another admonition of vital importance for the remnant of local legacy churches and mission organizations of the present day.

Philippians 3:12-14
"Not that I have already attained, or am already perfected; but I press on, that I may lay hold of that for which Christ Jesus has also laid hold of me. Brethren, I do not count myself to have apprehended; but one thing I do, forgetting those things which are behind and reaching forward to those things which are ahead, I press toward the goal for the prize of the upward call of God in Christ Jesus."
NKJV.

In his speech, Churchill, whilst touching on an explanation as to why only three British Divisions were left to stand with the then fallen French army, says at last, *"I am not reciting these facts for the purpose of recrimination. That I judge to be utterly futile and even harmful. We cannot afford it. I recite them in order to explain why it was we did not have, as we could have had, between twelve and fourteen British divisions fighting in the line in this great battle instead of only three. Now I put all this aside. I put it on the shelf, from which the historians, when they have time, will select their documents to tell their stories. We have to think of the future and not of the past. This also applies in a small way to our own affairs at home. There are many who would hold an inquest in the House of Commons on the conduct of the Governments and of Parliaments, for they are in it to during the years which led up to this catastrophe. They seek to indict those who were responsible for the guidance of our affairs. This also would be a foolish and pernicious process. There are too many in it. Let each man search his conscience and search his speeches. I frequently search mine. Of this I am quite sure, that if we open a quarrel between the past and the present, we shall find that we have lost the future."*

Did you hear Winni's final remark? *"Of this I am quite sure, that if we open a quarrel between the past and the present, we shall find that we have lost the future."* I am becoming increasingly convinced that as we are now many hours after midnight, Winni's final comment in that particular section of his "Finest Hour" speech spawns three important points towards personal revival, local church revolution and "church national" repentance and change.

First then, we need to truly see the dire situation that we are in. There is a strange blindness in the church at large today, caused I think by the closing lids of a demonic sleepiness. It's so bad, that if we ever do get fully on our knees, it's still only a heavenly cattle rod placed up our stuck up rear end which will finally lift our heads and electrify and brighten our eyes! We need this ram rod electric shock to fully take in our most dreadful and urgent of positions. Your leaders, yes, it has been your leaders who have failed to keep your eyes clean friends. Shame on them! Now, the good shepherds need to sew your eye lids open. LOOK! Those of you who dare look, must now pray for the urgent ramming of this rod of sparking illumination upon the rest of the sheep, so that we might finally give some standing and shouting, butt clutching attention, to the plans and present conquests and victories of the enemy. We need to get off our backs, crawl on to our knees and finally leap to our "star jumping" feet. Only a Holy Spirit cattle rod up the rear end will do this. Yes, it's time to stop laughing and start weeping and we can only do that if we shocked off backs and forced up onto our feet. Picnics! Bloody picnics and Big day outs! We need shocking into action. Shame on you blind sheeple for being complicit in your own upcoming trip to the slaughterhouse. Shame on you leaders who have kept your sheep's eyes matted with silly effeminate love songs. Shame on you!

> *Of this I am quite sure, that if we open a quarrel between the past and the present, we shall find that we have lost the future*

Secondly, we must be presented personally, locally and nationally, with some strategies for victory. These will be commanding strategies, these will be different, daring and faith filled strategies, sacrificial strategies, all new and all fresh! They need to be, for there is one thing that we can be absolutely confident about and that is, everything we have tried thus far has failed abysmally. The new must come. But where are the commanders in the field? O Lord, send us some fighting general once more.

Thirdly, in terms of failed strategies, pitiful power bases, bickering, bitchiness and bald faced blandness, we must personally, locally and nationally, thoroughly let go of all these past hindrances, for I tell you, if we continue to clutch anything associated with past failures, we shall foster continual arguments between the present and the past and we shall never lay hold of our future. Never!

Make no mistake about it, the final arrival of clarity and command, if they are acknowledged, accepted and apprehended, will bring with them such a profound and shaking change to all of our structures, directions, patterns, partnerships, resource allocations, systems, styles, plans and personnel, that they will shake us to our core! It will be a bloody revolution and its long, so very long overdue. Such a revolutions is probably the only chance of the recovery of any possibility of victory. How else can we stand in the coming judgement?

> *It will be a bloody revolution and its long, so very long overdue.*

Finally, may I say that if the letting go of the past and laying hold of the future fails, if upon going through the judgement we do indeed find ourselves to be destroyed, then , at least we can go down fighting. Yes, at least we can go out with a sword-wielding shout, instead of an abattoir's whimper. Even so tonight, *"Of this I am quite sure, that if we open a quarrel between the past and the present, we shall find that we have lost the future."*

Listen: *"Therefore let us, as many as are mature, have this mind; and if in anything you think otherwise, God will reveal even this to you. Nevertheless, to the degree that we have already attained, let us walk by the same rule, let us be of the same mind." Philippians 3:15-16 NKJV*

Pray: Lord, bring that very particular rod of correction tonight and ram it where the sun doesn't shine! Wake us up O Lord and in the waking send us leaders, send us movers and send us shakers, in Jesus name we pray, amen and let all be so!

| Vol | 01 | Q3 | NW00199 | July 17ᵗʰ |

Night-Whisper | ASCEND

The mighty mountain of the moral majority

In 2004, aged 95, just four weeks before his death, Alistair Cooke, after 58 years of writing "Letter from America," the longest running talk radio show ever, put the finishing touches to letter number 2,869 whilst he lay dying of bone cancer, propped up on pillows in the same New York apartment he had lived in for 50 years.

Genesis 17:1

"And when Abram was ninety years old and nine, the Lord appeared to Abram, and said unto him, I am the Almighty God; walk before me, and be thou perfect."
KJV.

Cooke, in his final letter, makes reference to the 'Lewinskian' fall President, Bill Clinton, remarking that, *"In all the 12-year concern about Saddam's intentions this fear never failed to haunt the White House - the fear of an overnight Saddam attack and either the outbreak of a whole Middle Eastern war or the death of the state of Israel. President Clinton fretted over this problem as much as anyone and had plans to go into Iraq to enact, on his own if must be, 'serious consequences,' when Miss Lewinsky became a figure of fate, as significant as Napoleon's mistress, Madame Waleska. By the time Clinton was ready to mobilize an American or allied force he didn't possess the moral authority to invade Long Island."*

Regarding the whole and necessary issue of "moral authority," I came across this definition on the internet, here it is: *"Moral authority is having the personal credibility with your target group that makes your words persuasive to them. Moral authority is achieved when your target group perceives that you have these two qualities: integrity and compassion."* I like that. You see, the real magnificence of a mighty '"moral majority" does not bear the marks of a pompous religious pressure group but rather, it bears the marks of Christ! The marks of the great Shepherd of the sheep. The bloodied brow, the slapped face of the rejected words of truth. The broken and pierced hands and feet. All these scars have been received by the disciples of Christ, chiefly, by being true to their Master and His message. In all these trials, these damaged disciples have been found to be constant in care and the very embodiment of kindness in terms of expressed compassion towards the folks they are leading. Yes, Integrity and compassion, those two things my friends, is where the power of any "moral majority" is going to come from.

> *Integrity and compassion, those two things my friends, is where the power of any "moral majority" is going to come from.*

Yes, a leader must possess a moral majority. He must exude an impartiality in terms of fairness in love, provision of goods, protection of lambs and practicality in leading and yes, these must be exhibited towards all those folks he is leading. Such worked out, worked at integrity and compassion will provide leaders with the necessary credibility to set both the pace and the direction of change. For such a broad ranging fairness will be indicative of compassion, and such plodding persistence in the same unalterable direction, despite persecution and suffering, will be indicative of a true integrity. I tell you, if you can make the steep ascent to the mountain-top of the moral majority, then the earth will be yours my friend, and everything in it.

Alistair Cook had many friends, two of which were ancient actors, Humphrey Bogart and Lauren Bacall. Whilst on a train journey, it was Alistair who burst into their carriage asking the question *"Was it Christ who said, 'Be Ye Perfect?'"* For a brilliant and an educated man, the son of a Methodist Minister, Cooke should have known the answer to that question. I suspect he did and that is was in fact a relevant question for the contemplation and consideration of both Bogart and Bacall. "Are we commanded to be like God? Full on integrity and compassion."

Like many of you leaders tonight, you too know that answer to that question but for whatever reason, you have failed to climb the steep ascent of the mountain of the moral majority. Unless you begin to ascend that mountain, you shall not lead your people into the promised land. Yes, if that plane of impartial compassion and persistent integrity leaves the ground and you're not on it, you'll regret it. Maybe not today. Maybe not tomorrow, but soon and for the rest of your life. Never Bogart impartiality, compassion or integrity. Oh, and if you have arrived at the top of the mountain, don't Lewinsky your valuable prize. Now there's' a couple of hip descriptive terms to look up!

Listen: *"Keep my soul, and deliver me; let me not be ashamed, for I put my trust in You. Let integrity and uprightness preserve me, for I wait for You." Psalms 25:20-21 NKJV*

Pray: Lord, deliver me from self-righteousness and blind religious pomposity but oh my God! Lead up the rough ridges of consistent integrity and the steep cliffs of impartial compassion, that I might ascend mountain of the moral majority, yes, that I might lead your people well, in Jesus name I ask it, amen.

Fighting for life

The telephone rings and the Father begins the awkward conversation with his son. Apparently, the girl is pregnant and not a believer in God. However, she has chosen life, she has chosen to keep the baby and she won't even be tested for Downs Syndrome; indeed, no offer or hint of a quick end to this very personal problem is even contemplated. The father is angry, disappointed but nevertheless, impressed and thankful for the fact that life has been chosen and chosen in the face of great difficulty, for the new family has no roof, no job and no prospects in the new city they have moved to. Life with all its difficulties has been chosen. Now what?

Psalm 10:14b

"To you the helpless commits himself; you have been the helper of the fatherless." ESV

They are together, at least for today. Who knows what the future will hold. Will the pressures of want, push them even closer or drive them further apart? Thinking about the question the father thinks he already knows the answer, for joy and want, are only good neighbors in the movies; real life is not soft and cuddly, it is like a meat cleaver to any relationship that is birthed on the financial chopping block; it is sharp and dreadfully divisive. Surely they know this? Yet despite all its inherent difficulties, life has still been chosen. Now what?

The thought crosses the Father's mind as to how much easier it would have been to get an abortion. A simple procedure, some repentance at a later date maybe, you know, when they've got on their feet a bit, financially speaking that is, maybe got a job, a place to live, a steady income, and spent some time getting to know one another. The father is feeling guilty that such a thought should ever cross his mind but his heart and wallet are already hurting. However, despite the pain, life has been chosen with all its difficulties, with all its baggage, with all its financial burdens, all its late nights, all its cumbersome meetings with angry future "in laws;" yes life, with all its ducking and all its diving, all its mess and bloody surviving. Life has been chosen. Good grief! Now What?

Common and confusing, culturally mixed messages don't make choosing life easy. Society at large is living in the land of contradiction, spending millions each year on heart transplants and launching helicopters and lifeboats to rescue rich blondes and their prancing poodles who having spilled their "champers" on shiny new decks, have slipped off tall yachts around the Isle of Wight on Cowes week! Whilst at the same time, to save a few bob and a few bucks, we are pulling the plug on those forgetful wrinklies of the bed wetting variety, that have become an ever growing burden and rancid smell on the rest of polite and hardworking society; and to mix it up just a little more, if a sad man, a bad man, a mad man, attacks a pregnant mother and the child in her womb is lost, then that same mug is in prison for manslaughter; (or is it child destruction now?) whilst, if the mother should decide, with sterile suction or long sharp knitting needles to terminate and poke out the life of her own son or daughter in the warm but now salt ridden waters of her womb, whilst the human abattoir sells the uncrushed baby organs on for profit, she shall be cosseted and caressed for doing "the wise and selfless thing!" Even the doctor who slips out the head of the sad vagina before scissor slicing the back of the babies neck with surgical shears, and in the so doing is paid for severing the spine of the future before a cry is heard, well even that doctor is honored and thanked. It's alright, we've renamed the child as 'Fetus, Embryo, 'Not yet human,' Garbage, Scientific materiel, Savior Sibling.' Aye we have called it everything but what it is. A baby.

> *It's alright, we've renamed the child as 'Fetus, Embryo, 'Not yet human,' Garbage, Scientific materiel, Savior Sibling.' Aye we have called it everything but what it is. A baby.*

Society is sick and this devilish disinformation is meant to confuse the possessors of life to grotesquely, for personal comfort, societies ease and prudent and practical cost cutting, give up the same, you know, babies, children, life and future, give them up without a fight! It is a miracle then, when amidst all this confusion, amidst the lies and disarray, people still choose life! Hip hip hip hooray!!!

Pastors must rejoice at such choices and one day at a time, must journey such life into He who is the light of life, the only God eternal, our Lord and lovely Savior, Jesus the Christ. More than ever the charge of the shepherd is to grow up and engender a loving and living community of the saints that can righteously and graciously walk in truth and love, humility and mercy before the unwashed and the seemingly unashamed. God help the church and the society who are the subject of the cries and complaints of those unmarried mothers who have chosen life, and of their subsequent and fatherless little offspring, who have asked for help with life and got no help at all! For I tell you the truth, God will take up their case of life, even if we refuse to. In all practicality, the Church of God must now fight for life! Are you fighting for life?

Listen: *"You shall not mistreat any widow or fatherless child. If you do mistreat them, and they cry out to me, I will surely hear their cry, and my wrath will burn, and I will kill you with the sword, and your wives shall become widows and your children fatherless." Exodus 22:22-24 ESV*

Pray: Lord, teach us how to stand with those who choose life. In Jesus name we ask it, amen and let it be so.

Owned and loved by the Lord of the sword

Donning his priestly robes, the sword smith, after days of prayer and fasting approaches the finishing of his task. The fire is hot, the hammer and anvil are ready, together with the primeval elements of metal, wood, water, earth and air. His task is to complete before him what he considers to be a spiritual entity; a multi-heated many folded, million layered, highly and uniquely individual, flexible, functional, sharp and sure, weapon of war. For sure, every civilisation has seen the making of swords as a spiritual act producing an end product of both a common and yet highly unique character. It's not unusual.

Romans 5:3-5

"And not only that, but we also glory in tribulations, knowing that tribulation produces perseverance; and perseverance, character; and character, hope. 5 Now hope does not disappoint, because the love of God has been poured out in our hearts by the Holy Spirit who was given to us." NKJV.

King Jesus, walking among the lamp stands holding in His hand the seven stars, has coming out of His mouth a sharp double-edged sword. This is the sword of the Spirit, the very Word of God. Certainly at the very least, the sword is an emblem of spiritual power, prowess and character. Christ the Master Sword Smith, the Lord of the Sword, is specialised, unrelenting, fine and focused when producing a sword of character. Yes, God is at work in us blades, producing common and yet uniquely individual characteristics, the cascading colours of which, will be unashamedly borne by us for all to see throughout eternity.

The source of those fine and distinguishing, individualistic markings of Christian character, is in fact "working tribulation." Working, I say, in the sense of it being a repetitious, purposeful, and applied heat and beating pressure. All martial arts have the "Kata" of training: you know, that repetitious exercise of position, movement and application; and in the same way, "trials and tribulation" are worked into the life of the Christian by the Master Sword Smith. It would appear that the Lord of the Sword, is producing weapons of war, through his own very own "Kata of Working Trubulation."

Yes indeed, the Lord of the Sword is at work in your life through trials and tribulations, for in the same way a fine sword is hammered and beaten, made hot and cold, folded and broken, pressed into purposeful multi-layers of strength, absorption, flexibility and sharpness, we too, through trials and tribulations of various kinds, experience this same kind of enfolding and applied, persistent spiritual pressing. The pressure of pain, the pressure of need, of lack, of fear, though all are common to man, in the Kata, that is the "Kata workings" of God the Holy Spirit, they are enfolded into our life in the hot fires of crucified and crucibled afflictions. When this happens, the Kata workings of God, produce an increasing tempered endurance; that is, a constancy of obedient direction, despite the difficulties of applied trials, which may be set before us. In each fold of the metalled sword, in each beat of the hammer, in each dimming of the light to examine the colour of temperature and the settled state of worked in character, yes, in each swing of the weapon and test of its balance, the Master Sword Maker is looking for perfection! If more of the character of the piece needs to be worked in, or drawn out to produce the assured, tried and trusted, purchased, pressed and proven character that is required by Him, then be assured, that the Lord of the Sword will take it back to the heating and back to the quenching, the beating and the folding. In all the precise practice of perfectly placed, persistent pressure, the Lord of the Sword, will not let up, until the individual completeness of His desiring is seen to form both in and on the blade.

> *In all the precise practice of perfectly placed, persistent pressure, the Lord of the Sword, will not let up, until the individual completeness of His desiring is seen to form both in and on the blade.*

Christian character then, this side of heaven at least, is not to be seen as a settled state, but rather, is that which bubbles up in the revelation of all our crucibles of experience in both trial and in testing. Christian character then, is a work in progress, for it is the tried and tested, pure ore of continuous development. Note as well, that in all pressing and preparation, the sinful scum, resulting from affliction rising to the surface in our lives, all needs continually scraping away! It would appear that this is a process, which every Christian blade will go through to be made fit for the Master's use. Yes, the crucible will be continually reheated, and the blade has continuous pressure applied, so as to eventually produce a pure and the shining sword. I am both daunted and encouraged by this process and find it helpful in two major ways.

First, that we don't become discouraged by seeing people pass through various trials and then failing! Providing their journey continues, the crucible will be re-heated and that scum will eventually be scraped away. The Lord of the sword is unrelenting in this and he shall do His work both thoroughly and well.

Problems then, are a sign of God's continued sanctification process.

Secondly, that the continuance of trials in a person's life, is in fact a sure sign that God intends to produce pureness of character. Problems then, are a sign of God's continued sanctification process.

May I finally say tonight, that if there have been no pressings problems in your life as a Christian, no pressures and no beatings, then maybe you should ask yourself if you are in fact owned and loved by the Lord of the Sword?

Listen:

>When God wants to drill a man,
>
>And thrill a man, And skill a man
>
>To play the noblest part;
>
>When He yearns with all His heart
>
>To create so great and bold a man
>
>That all the world shall be amazed,
>
>Watch His methods, watch His ways!
>
>How He ruthlessly perfects
>
>Whom He royally elects!
>
>How He hammers him and hurts him,

And with mighty blows converts him

Into trial shapes of clay which

Only God understands;

While his tortured heart is crying

And he lifts beseeching hands!

How He bends but never breaks

When his good He undertakes;

How He uses whom He chooses,

And with every purpose fuses him:

By every act induces him

To try his splendor out--

God knows what He's about.

(Author Unknown)

Pray: O Great God, grant me mercy in Your great and purifying fire. Amen.

| Vol | 01 | Q3 | NW00202 | July 20th |

Night-Whisper | **POWER**

Playing cards with Dr Vomit

I used to work in the downtown heat of northern Miami, the city of Hollywood to be precise. So anyway, when I used to drive down past our church I always took a good look underneath the covered entrance way situated at the front to the building for this shaded area always seemed to attract a very weird variety of wild life from the local area and many times from far, far beyond. Sometimes they would be people from Boston, taking a picnic from the heat having just been robbed at the local greyhound bus station, (interestingly everyone with a tale to tell me had just been robbed at the local greyhound bus station! They've closed it down now), a family changing their car radiator with a distraught Romanian gypsy in tow and in desperate need of prayer, or someone just out of prison, or someone else maybe carrying a sick child, needing money, or... well you get the picture. The covered entrance way of that downtown church….my goodness!

Acts 19:11-15

"Now God worked unusual miracles by the hands of Paul, so that even handkerchiefs or aprons were brought from his body to the sick, and the diseases left them and the evil spirits went out of them. Then some of the itinerant Jewish exorcists took it upon themselves to call the name of the Lord Jesus over those who had evil spirits, saying, 'We exorcise you by the Jesus whom Paul preaches.' Also there were seven sons of Sceva, a Jewish chief priest, who did so. And the evil spirit answered and said, 'Jesus I know, and Paul I know; but who are you?'" NKJV.

One particular day though I bumped into Dr Vomit. She was a middle-aged woman calling "Bill and Hughie," on the hot sidewalk, leaving splashes of speckled coloured sputum on all the cars driving by. So, I swung round and called to her, "Hey can I help you ma'am? Can I call 911?" She looks up sweaty, with sick dribbling down the side of her mouth and says, "No thanks I'll be just fine." I don't believe her so I get out of the car and walk up to her.

"Really my dear what's wrong and how can I help?"

"No honest, I'm fine, I'm a doctor." and with that she wretches more black sputum into the road.

"What's happened?" says I.

"El Presidente! Happened!" (Now, El Presidente was the awful and smelly, South American supermarket on the corner...). "Yeah, El Presidente and their #$#@@ rice and black beans! That and those *%6#$%'s in that family that I put away! They're messing up all the people around here again with all that tarot card crap and screwing their minds up!"

> "No honest, I'm fine, I'm a doctor." and with that she wretches more black sputum into the road.

She shook a shook a dirty finger at me with a piece of vomit still sitting precariously on her well-chewed nail. "Yeah, they live just round the corner there, the whole bad family; watch out now! They'll mess you up as well, they're bad."

So, by now I'm a bit confused but knowing the nature of the multicultural community round here I says, "What, do you think they've put a curse on you?"

"No! I'm Doctor Willow. I'm a doctor they can't put a curse on me. They just can't!" By now she's started puking again, quite nonchalantly into the side of the road. "No you can't help me, I'll be OK, but watch out for them, they'll put Buddhism on yer!" And with a wave of her hand and a final puke she turns and staggers off into the distance. The passers-by are treading carefully but apart from that, no one is really phased by what they have both seen and heard. It was North of Miami and it was hot. It was most abnormally normal.

Dr Willow? Ah yes, I think I remember that she came by our church stall at the local city open air expo and gave me one of her business cards. "Dr Willow" it read, "Reiki Healer". Now, I have dealt with the plush and proper forms of Reiki healing before but with poor old Dr Willow all jacked up on fear, mutual cursing, black beans and bad rice, well, the flow of universal energy wasn't doing her much good right then I can tell you!

It was evident that this particular lady was very ill indeed. No intellectual presentation of the Gospel of choice would even begin to get her attention. For her and the family she had previously "put away," now roaming around with a pack of tarot cards and a big bag full of lies, yes it was obvious that only a direct encounter with the living and powerful, resurrected Lord Jesus would be able to begin to rescue and redeem this particularly pitiful and puking practitioner and all her sworn enemies.

The enemy today no longer keeps his cards close to his chest. Right now, in this post modern, post Christian and increasingly Pagan age, they are on the table face up for all the world to see. For Christians of course, even for two thousand years God's cards have been on the table and all bear this title, "The Gospel - The Power of God to Salvation!" So then friends let's play! We'll beat him hands down. We always have. We always will.

> *For Christians of course, even for two thousand years God's cards have been on the table and all bear this title, "The Gospel - The Power of God to Salvation!" So then friends let's play! We'll beat him hands down. We always have. We always will.*

Listen: "Then the man in whom the evil spirit was leaped on them, overpowered them, and prevailed against them, so that they fled out of that house naked and wounded. This became known both to all Jews and Greeks dwelling in Ephesus; and fear fell on them all, and the name of the Lord Jesus was magnified. And many who had believed came confessing and telling their deeds. Also, many of those who had practiced magic brought their books together and burned them in the sight of all. And they counted up the value of them, and it totaled fifty thousand pieces of silver. So the word of the Lord grew mightily and prevailed." (Acts 19:16-20 NKJV.)

Pray: Lord, the devil is making a power play today for the souls of lost men and is seemingly winning. His bondage is no both open and blatant. We ask You our Jesus, that Your church will make use of the power You have so readily granted us. So come Lord, follow the preaching of Your word in all mighty signs and wonders, amen!

Night-Whisper | **SPRINGS**

Of borders, boundaries and particular blessings

In the Bible, the possession of your "lot" in life is never expressed in terms of a pessimistic and determined, destined destruction but rather, is a precious picture, pregnant with peace, a peace which is full of desire and open to delightful development. In our text for tonight then, the word "lot" is used in a figurative sense regarding destiny, and it bears no negative connotation whatsoever! Yes this lot has boundaries, and yes this lot will be constantly infringed upon by our enemies, but it is a vast lot, a lot that is open for Divine development and more than that, it contains your inheritance and all the possibilities and variations thereof.

Joshua 15:1

"So this was the lot of the tribe of the children of Judah according to their families." NKJV.

Now regarding the tribe of Judah, Joshua 15:20 goes on to say that, "This was the inheritance of the tribe of the children of Judah according to their families" and in so doing, begins to list the cities within their vast and delightful borders of destiny. The word "inheritance" here focuses on both the present occupancy and the future gifting to descendents of the heirlooms if you will, all of which are contained within the vast borders of their delightful destiny, which is also always open to Divine development. For here lies a multitude of charming cities, all ready for present occupation, all ready to be passed on to their blood inheritors, the future blessed benefactors of all their present bounty. Do you see that?

I am taking our texts tonight, and I believe legitimately so, to be a metaphor for our own personal lot in life, our destiny if you will. For we are each an undiscovered country, that only if we would search, some gem would glint our eye, some seam of preciousness would marble the black hard rock within and when correctly mined, could then be burnt to bring forth the warmth of other's hearts, even thine, and if fired, then fashioned, this treasure could deck the neck of kings! If cooked by the great chef, would grace our tables in the midst of our enemies and amongst them we could feast together! Oh taste and see, Oh search and see, that the Lord is Good!

So, within the delightful borders of our destiny, there are vast cities of inheritance. Gifting's of every kind, great gardens, good roads, centres of development and areas of great industry. From these cities spring horses and chariots, spring warriors and artisans, spring seeds and with the seeds, all manner of tasty delights. Yes, do you see your destiny tonight? Do you now possess your inheritance? Do you know how to?

So, my friends, tonight. It is time to begin to take a good look at your personal lot and see it as a delightful destiny. Reclaim the lost cities for they are your inheritance, and your inheritance to your blood offspring. -

The cherry on the top of this great "knickerbocker glory," is found in Joshua 15, where amidst the details of the overwhelming and delightful borders of destiny and the vast cities of personal and progenetic inheritance, God has planted another blessing for us in terms of crystal waters, even rivers of it! These rivers run beneath the broad meadows and wait to spring up where we will. Yes, in the interjected and important, most marvellous story of Achsah, the little ankle bracelet of Caleb, we see here both our need and opportunity to receive the blessing and then ask for more! Achsah, (Joshua 16:16-19) in effect says to her father, *"Since you have given me such a great destiny, give me also springs of water! Give me more!"* She says, *"According to my courage, mix my faith with your grace and give me also springs of water!"* In response, the Scripture tells us that she received a double portion of both upper and lower springs. Imagine that!

So, my friends, tonight. It is time to begin to take a good look at your personal lot and see it as a delightful destiny. Reclaim the lost cities for they are your inheritance, and your inheritance to your blood offspring. Live in the cities of your destiny, prospering in them and from them. Then see what you still lack for present development and future prosperity and go to your Father and ask for it. Beneath your rich red earth, lay vast and flowing rivers of grace and provision. So, open your mouth wide and He shall fill it! Go on, once you've had a good gander at your lot, surveyed the ground, go gush to God for a more bountiful blessing saying, "Give me also, springs of water!"

Listen: "'What do you wish?' She answered, 'Give me a blessing; since you have given me land in the South, give me also springs of water.' So he gave her the upper springs and the lower springs." (Joshua 15:18-19 NKJV)

Pray: Holy Spirit, walk me through the land of my inheritance, show my cities and the possible lushness of Your Divine development, then my Father, in the name of Jesus, give me also springs of water, that I may overflow!

| Vol | 01 | Q3 | NW00204 | July 22ⁿᵈ |

Night-Whisper | **DESTINY**

The re-naming of the shrew

Whatever you think of Gideon, he was, upon the receipt of our text for tonight, both a hiding and a quivering before the rampant Midianite swarm! Nevertheless, it was to him that the angel of the Lord appeared with a description of Gideon's character and action, that as far as we know, bore no resemblance whatsoever to either his past or present condition! Even so, he was, according to the angel, and therefore could be and would be, nothing less than a mighty man of valour. How wonderful.

Judges 6:12

"And the Angel of the Lord appeared to him, and said to him, 'The Lord is with you, you mighty man of valour!'" NKJV.

I love the way that God consistently calls into being those things which are not! Well, not yet anyway. Especially people. So Jacob the twister is called Israel, Prince with God, yet frankly, you don't get a glimpse of this until many years later, even on his death bed when he is praying and prophesying over his sons. So with Saul. Saul the accessory to murder and I suppose the instigator of the murder of a multitude of others, Saul the Paul, though immediately commissioned as an apostle to the Gentiles, did not for many years first fulfil that calling. Yet he was an apostle, even in the quiet and studious repentant years of preparation! God tells and God calls it and so it sure shall be.

So when God gives new names to projects and to peoples, to dreams and to visions, they most thoroughly encapsulate much, much more of what those things shall be, rather then what they at present are. Indeed, their future shall resemble little to their present, never mind their past. Yes, with both a new name and a Divine declaration, a hope and a future can be birthed by such prophetic proclamation. Yes, with a name and a declaration, God can change a shrew into a samurai and a mouse into a magnificent knight. Go ask Reepicheep!

Listen: "And I also say to you that you are Peter, and on this rock I will build My church, and the gates of Hades shall not prevail against it. And I will give you the keys of the kingdom of heaven, and whatever you bind on earth will be bound in heaven, and whatever you loose on earth will be loosed in heaven." (Matthew 16:18-19 NKJV.)

Pray: Lord, call me forth, to a resurrected life and a designated destiny of a proclaimed path. In Jesus name we pray, amen.

| Vol | 01 | Q3 | NW00205 | July 23rd |

Night-Whisper | **REFRESH**

Enjoying the best of beers with Jesus the thirst quencher!

Some people drink to drown their sorrows, to numb the pain and to forget. Some people drink for relational inclusion, for the smoothing of a social awkwardness and the facilitating of relational dexterity. Some people drink to bathe in the social sunlight of that short window of nimble numbness before drunkenness takes a hold. Some people drink because they are thirsty and sometimes, but not too often, some people drink to live, yes some people drink because they are happy, because they are celebrating! I tell you tonight, that there is no more refreshing a drink, than a drink which celebrates life and bathes your lips in laughter to so stretch out, your smiling jaws in joy!

Isaiah 12:3

"Therefore with joy you will draw water from the wells of salvation."
NKJV.

It was the 'bursting forth" - the Gihon spring, that fed the waters to the pool of Siloam, the pool of peace and quiet rest. It was from this same pool that on the eighth day, the day of Holy convocation, the day of the solemn assembly, yes, on that last great day of the feast of tabernacles, that the priests in procession, accompanied by psalms of joy and sounding trumpets, would take a golden vial filled with water and mixed with wine, and pour it on the sacrifice of the alter. I wonder if it was here, at that High priestial pouring, that Jesus, the High Priest of Heaven, stood and cried out concerning the Spirit whom those believing in Him would receive, saying, "If anyone thirsts, let him come to Me and drink. He who believes in Me, as the Scripture has said, out of his heart will flow rivers of living water." (John 7:37b-39a NKJV)

In the Scriptures, wells, streams, fountains, rivers, springs, are all used as being emblematic of the abundant fullness and richness, of all the mercies, which God has provided to the needs of the flock of His pasture. The idea in our text for tonight then, is that we should drink deeply of all the free mercies of salvation; of all the springing up, overflowing, refreshing waters of salvation, given to sojourning sons, pilgrimaging in a dry and thirsty land, even a parched land; and that we should drink of these with joy unspeakable and full of glory!

I tell you tonight, that when God becomes the water source of our strength, of all our salvation and of all our songs of joy, then all our drinking shall be of the happy kind, bathing in His most bountiful of blessings, even in all the prosperity of the adopted son's of God, through Jesus Christ our Lord.

> *I tell you tonight, that when God becomes the water source of our strength, of all our salvation and of all our songs of joy, then all our drinking shall be of the happy kind, bathing in His most bountiful of blessings, even in all the prosperity of the adopted son's of God, through Jesus Christ our Lord*

In your heart, at the centre of your being is a day beyond the day of rest, it is an eighth day fountain of living water! Bubbling up within you and flowing out of you. If it's not happening folks, then ask for the Holy Spirit. If You have Him, then make sure He has you. If He has You, and there is still no happy flow, then unblock your wells, that springs of living water may gusher up within you.

Listen: "From there they went to Beer, which is the well where the Lord said to Moses, 'Gather the people together, and I will give them water.' Then Israel sang this song: 'Spring up, O well! All of you sing to it' - the well the leaders sank, dug by the nation's nobles, by the lawgiver, with their staves." (Numbers 21:16-18 NKJV.)

Pray: O LORD, I will praise You; though You were angry with me, Your anger is turned away, and You comfort me. Behold, God is my salvation, I will trust and not be afraid; "For YAH, the LORD, is my strength and song; He also has become my salvation." Therefore with joy we will draw water from the wells of salvation and tonight we sing, "Praise the LORD, call upon His name; declare His deeds among the peoples, make mention that His name is exalted." Amen! (taken from Isaiah 12:1-4)

| Vol | 01 | Q3 | NW00206 | July 24th |

Night-Whisper | **DECLARE**

Something salvific?

In 2008 at the Lambeth Conference, the ten-year gathering of Anglican Bishops, both male and undecided, one liberal theologian there, whilst chatting to a reporter remarked that *"He regarded Jesus as uniquely the son of God. But he said 'have other religions encountered God working on earth? Yes. Has God done something salvific (opening the way to ultimate "salvation") with them? Yes.'"* Unfortunately, this kind of statement, especially when made in a multi-faith environment, does little to clarify the total uniqueness and absolute necessity of the declaration of the Gospel of Jesus Christ to all people.

1 Timothy 2:4-5
"Who desires all men to be saved and to come to the knowledge of the truth." NKJV.

Of course it must be acknowledged, that in other faiths where revealed truth has been received through the declarations of the tri-fold declarations of conscience, creation and the Word of God then, it is absolutely right and proper that this should be honoured and acknowledged. Even so, I like the way one Roman Catholic theologian approached what has been called Inter-Faith dialogue when he says, *"The distinction between theological faith and belief in the other religions, must be firmly held. If faith is the acceptance in grace of revealed truth, which 'makes it possible to penetrate the mystery in a way that allows us to understand it coherently,' then belief, in the other religions, is that sum of experience and thought that constitutes the human treasury of wisdom and religious aspiration, which man in his search for truth has conceived and acted upon in his relationship to God and the Absolute."* In other words, other religions, though they might contain some revealed truth, are not built on revealed truth, but rather, on the aspirations of a human search for truth.

Remember tonight, that when the Scriptures tells us that "Jesus Christ is the way the truth and the life and that no man comes to the

Father but by Him," that this is an absolute metaphysical assertion. In other words, Jesus is the only way to God.

Through my lips, so very often, the declaration of this metaphysical assertion sounds nothing short of arrogance. However, it is also true that whenever a truth is checked for fleas, the doctrinal vet will always get his fingers nipped. Indeed, I have yet to come across a humble nit nurse. Even so, despite the failings of our sinful selves, this one way truth is so asserted toward us in the Scriptures that it is not open to debate but merely, open to declaration. Indeed, this all engulfing, cornerstone and capstone nugget of ultimate revelation demands a declaration, for there is a pursuance in its declaration and the power of Almighty God behind it.

> *For the Christian, even in all his fallen arrogance, dialogue must simply become the means of further declaration.*

For the Christian, even in all his fallen arrogance, dialogue must simply become the means of further declaration.

Listen: "Who desires all men to be saved and to come to the knowledge of the truth. For there is one God and one Mediator between God and men, the Man Christ Jesus, who gave Himself a ransom for all, to be testified in due time, for which I was appointed a preacher and an apostle - I am speaking the truth in Christ and not lying - a teacher of the Gentiles in faith and truth." (1 Timothy 2:4-7 NKJV.)

Pray: Oh power of God to Salvation, O freedom declaration of Your inheritance of the nations, come dance upon our lips in commanding declaration, in Jesus name we pray, amen.

| Vol | 01 | Q3 | NW00207 | July 25th |

Night-Whisper | **GOOD**

Praying for pagan neighbours

As I write tonight's Whisper, I am living in a beautiful terraced house. Bounded by the road at the front, on the left and right and rear, we are surrounded by our neighbours. It is surprisingly quiet considering the fact that we live on the same old anthill! I breakfasted out in the garden this morning and the quiet of the day was broken by a very intrusive builder, his radio blaring and his small dog, yapping like David Coleman, after yet another Scottish soccer defeat against England. You could see the curtains twitching, feel the annoyance rising and almost hear the tut, tut, tutting coming from behind the slam shut widows. It reminded me that there is something intensely practical about being a good neighbour, and in the heat of the rising annoyance, I reminded myself that rarely would a man die for a neighbour, but on many an occasion you might like to kill them!

Romans 15:1-4

"We then who are strong ought to bear with the scruples of the weak, and not to please ourselves. Let each of us please his neighbour for his good, leading to edification. For even Christ did not please Himself; but as it is written, 'The reproaches of those who reproached You fell on Me.'" NKJV.

St Alban is the first British Christian martyr ever recorded and frankly, it was being a good neighbour that led to his death. The story goes that sometime in the third century when England was under the iron studs of Rome. Christians were then being persecuted by the empire and a priest who was maybe called "Amphibolus" fleeing persecution passed through the Roman town of Verulamium, where a pagan citizen of Rome, a former Roman soldier called Alban, took him into his own home and hid him from his pursuing persecutors. A good non-Christian neighbour who could not abide the injustice of such vicious persecution of Christians. Moved by the piety and reality of Amphibolus, Alban himself becomes both his convert and his disciple.

Later of course, as in all good stories, the wicked Roman Governor becomes aware of the presence of the fugitive priest and so sends the local guard to arrest him. Alban here turns hero, in that he exchanges his "free man" cloak with the priestly cloak of Amphibolous, thus allowing the priest to escape out of the city whilst Alban offers himself, takes his place. Of course, in good medieval money making fashion, the story is further embellished with miraculous happenings and further sacrifice, as Alban's first executioner refuses to perform the act of decapitating Alban and instead becomes a Christian, whilst the second executioner who finally removed Albans head, literally has his eyes drop out after the act is performed! I tell you, in mad medieval England, I'd pay money to hear that story and see the bony relics!

> *It's time me thinks, to pray for both our present and our future neighbours!*

There are of course two miracles here. The first is the miracle of the good pagan neighbour. Some of you wish right now here in the present you had some good pagan neighbours, I just know you do! I am also sure that in the future, there may also be a need for Christians to still have some good pagan neighbours, who might just be willing to protect them from the terror of persecution. Alban my friends, was a pagan miracle of the God he did not yet know! Think about that.

The second miracle is that Alban was rewarded in two ways. First by benefiting from the heat of the fire which he had brought to the hearth and heart of his house and secondly, that through the thankful prayers of Amphibolous, his insightful instruction, and shining example, Alban is finally convicted and converted to a "count the cost" Christian!

It's time me thinks, to pray for both our present and our future neighbours!

Listen: "By this we know love, because He laid down His life for us. And we also ought to lay down our lives for the brethren." 1 John 3:16 NKJV

Pray: Lord, do good to us through our neighbors and do good to them through us. In Jesus name we pray, amen.

Night-Whisper | **EFFORT**

Snakes and ladders

Snakes and Ladders is a child's game and I am sure that many of you have played it and also remember that there is no better feeling than landing on that square with a ladder and a fast track to victory.

1 Timothy 4:7

""But reject profane and old wives' fables, and exercise yourself toward godliness." NKJV.

Today in the Christian church, through one outpouring or another, there have been a multitude of fast track Jacob ladders placed on the squares of many a Christian life that has led to deliverance, victories and conquering of many kinds. Tell you what, I wanna get me some of that!

The problem is that although some of these many manifestations are clearly seen in the Scriptures and I say some, I have never seen them responsible for movement towards the chief end of the work of the Holy Spirit in us, that being the sanctified life which has Christ formed in us. Never!

The passionate and persistent pursuance of a Godly aggression, a fierce determination to become the Athletae Dei, the Athletes Of God, is rarely found on lazy and obese Christians. Indeed, I wonder if often times our outward obesity might picture our lack of spiritual athleticism towards the disciplines of the spiritual life. Solitude and silence, prayer and fasting, worship and study, fellowship and confession, humility and acts of mercy, community, etc.

As Dallas Willard has said, *"We must stop using the fact that we cannot earn grace (whether for justification or for sanctification) as an excuse for not energetically seeking to receive grace. Having been found by God, we then become seekers of ever fuller life in him. Grace is opposed to earning, but not to effort. The realities of Christian spiritual formation are that we will not be transformed 'into his likeness' by more information, or by infusions, inspirations, or ministrations alone. Though all of these have an important place, they never suffice, and reliance upon them alone explains the now common failure of committed Christians to rise much above a certain level of decency."* I like that. It's very Scriptural.

The present Charismatic Evangelical games of Snakes and Ladders are on the other hand, rather open themselves to the judgements of being, non Scriptural and I watch with baited breath, to see if those ladders which so many folks have seemingly fast tracked up on, actually morph themselves into some very slippery snakes, that in the end, will leave these laughing and twitching folk, far farther back than when they first begun.

We shall see, time will tell.

Listen: *"Therefore, my beloved, as you have always obeyed, not as in my presence only, but now much more in my absence, work out your own salvation with fear and trembling." (Philippians 2:12-13NKJV.)*

Pray: So work in me O God, both to will and to do Your good pleasure. Train me O Holy Spirit, in the Gymnasium of life, that Christ would be so thoroughly formed in me, that it would be to eternal praise and honor to You, great Lord and Father. Amen.

| Vol | 01 | Q3 | NW00209 | July 27th |

Night-Whisper | **COURAGE**

Order no 227

On this day in 1943, the monster Joseph Stalin, issued Order no 227, the "Not one step backward" order, declaring that, "Panic makers and cowards must be liquidated on the spot. Not one step backward without orders from higher headquarters! Commanders who abandon a position without an order from higher headquarters are traitors to the Fatherland."

Hebrews 10:37,38

"For yet a little while, and He who is coming will come and will not tarry. Now the just shall live by faith; but if anyone draws back, My soul has no pleasure in him." NKJV

If you're fortunate you can catch courage. You can be inspired to stick it out even in the most dreadful of circumstances, drawing your strength from the steadfastness of other brave souls around you. It's tough, but courage can be taken up into yourself by osmosis. Slowly, steadily, surely.

Cowardice on the other hand, spreads like wildfire. It's easier to catch than the common cold, ten times as nasty and who can measure the depth of self-loathing destruction, that for years to come, still festers in such a rotten and a running heart.

Our text for tonight sends not a dictator's communiqué but nevertheless a clear message to troops whose chief motivation is the pleasing of their captain. He says, "those of you who cower, shrink, withdraw, keep back yourself, be half-hearted, half-committed, live a one foot in, one foot out kind of Christianity, well, I shall take no delight in you." Tell me now my brethren is there any worse thing a soldier of Christ could hear? Wouldn't being shot on the spot be far better?

Some of you need to get a grip tonight. Some of you need to become wholehearted tonight. Some of you, tonight, wish you could just be taken out and shot, yes, some of you wish you could just be put out of your yellow bellied misery. Enough of this! Death is not the answer, no, an overwhelming sense of His displeasure toward You, is a far greater judgement and may I say a far greater solution. For everything within our new man wants to please Him. Yes the great vacuum like void of His displeasure will draw what little courage we have to the very surface of our lives. If you are a double minded Christian, then such words should surely shock you back to the courage of counting the cost? Surely! However, in this Laodicean age of blind paupers, all yellowed with deceitful riches and the cares of this world, all saddled with niceness and a good pension plan, if this is you and these words do not move you from yellow to red, then I suspect you are not a Christian at all, but rather a feigner of faith, a faker, a fruitless tree, a false prophet, even a blind leader of the blind and all your riches shall lead to ditches all full of cissies with certificates of every kind, all blind leaders of the blind. These words from the Captain of our Salvation never worry the illegitimate but the child of God however, seeing themselves lost in Laodicea, is shamed by them, moved by them, changed by them.

> *I am thankful to be able to tell you that there is always a comeback for cowards.*

I am thankful to be able to tell you that there is always a comeback for cowards. By our confession, our repentance, yes by His grace and strength, we can once again feel His pleasure, we can once again stand and not draw back.

Meanwhile on the morrow, let us be wise and let us engage in osmosis, making a decision to surround ourselves with people of strength and courage.

"I am going to my Father's; and though with great difficulty I have got hither, yet now I do not repent me of all the trouble I have been at to arrive where I am. My sword I give to him that shall succeed me in my pilgrimage, and my courage and skill to him that can get it. My marks and scars I carry with me, to be a witness for me that I have fought His battles who will now be my rewarder." Heard from Mr. Valiant for truth on his crossing the river to the City of the Great King.

Listen: "No one engaged in warfare entangles himself with the affairs of this life, that he may please him who enlisted him as a soldier." 2 Timothy 2:4-5 NKJV.

Pray: Lord, grant strength to us Your people, yes Lord, give us good courage, that we might please You and feel Your pleasure. Lord let us never take but one step back, amen.

Night-Whisper | **SOLID**

'Wibbles,' rubber valves & novelty Christians

Well, I see the inflatable church was in the news again today. The original church designed by a British company, was some 47x47x25 feet, and included a blow-up organ, altar, pulpit, pews, candles and "stained glass" windows. Blow-up vicar is extra.

There are quite a few of these inflatable churches now scattered throughout the world, and are used by various denominations. They are primarily novelty items used for quirky weddings or bizarre funerals, or worse still, they are used Evangelistically to take church to the beach, or wherever else the scantily clad but spiritually minded may be lying in the sun, all covered in factor 8, all begging God to send church to them because they can't be bothered to get dressed and pay a visit. I'm sorry, but part of me says, "Let the lazies burn!" Remember, the Lord said, "Those who seek me with all of their heart shall find me." He did not add that, "And for those of you struggling at the beach, my own bouncy house is just left of the bouncy castle. Oooh and do remember to take your shoes off please. Just hate that sand!" We have taken our most presumptuous desire to make God more accessible to new depths.

Romans 1:18-23

"For the wrath of God is revealed from heaven against all ungodliness and unrighteousness of men, who suppress the truth in unrighteousness, because what may be known of God is manifest in them, for God has shown it to them. For since the creation of the world His invisible attributes are clearly seen, being understood by the things that are made, even His eternal power and Godhead, so that they are without excuse, because, although they knew God, they did not glorify Him as God, nor were thankful, but became futile in their thoughts, and their foolish hearts were darkened. Professing to be wise, they became fools, and changed the glory of the incorruptible God into an image made like corruptible man — and birds and four-footed animals and creeping things." NKJV.

Anyways, this innovative product was exhibited at the Ideal Churches exhibition in Sandowne Park (how fitting.) The sales blurb said that it was "well received", especially after it was dedicated by an Anglican vicar from Tamworth. Those Pelicans, God bless 'em! If they're not arguing about what gender they can have sex with, they're blessing bouncy castles! The world and his wife has gone mad and the established church has got its underpants on its head, pencils stuck up its nose, and is stood in the religious market place offering two for one on any deal whilst dribbling the word, "Wibble!"

The inflatable bouncy church is not innovation my friends, but rather it is devastation. This is a real church catastrophe of cataclysmic proportions. Don't you know that blow-up churches produce blow-up Christians? In other words, when the church is brought to you lest you should be too inconvenienced to go to it, it reinforces a whimsical and novel kind of Christianity, and shows its clown faced ministers of accessibility to be painted with a brown nosed, mealy mouthed, pleading pitifulness. These plastic air filled monstrosities are emblematic of what we are doing on a much grander scale in our overly seeker-sensitive gatherings. My friends, we are, at best, producing novelty Christians. We are collecting husks of people, empty shells, and then wondering why they crumble in the way.

> *The answer to the phenomenon of the blow-up Christian, the inflatable church-goer, is not to pander to their flesh, but to proclaim the message of fleeing the wrath to come, whilst praying passionately for the redemption of their eternal souls.*

The answer to the phenomenon of the blow-up Christian, the inflatable church-goer, is not to pander to their flesh, but to proclaim the message of fleeing the wrath to come, whilst praying passionately for the redemption of their eternal souls.

In the coming days, all blow up Christians will most surely get blown away so please examine yourselves tonight and should you find any rubber valves on your own body, you need to be very worried. indeed.

Listen: *"Now we know that whatever the law says, it says to those who are under the law, that every mouth may be stopped, and all the world may become guilty before God." Romans 3:19-20 NKJV*

Pray: Lord call Your people and then make them solid and lasting. In Jesus name we ask it, amen.

Night-Whisper | **FORMATION**

How not to become a cold turkey Christian

2 Corinthians 12:1-8

"It is doubtless not profitable for me to boast. I will come to visions and revelations of the Lord: I know a man in Christ who fourteen years ago — whether in the body I do not know, or whether out of the body I do not know, God knows — such a one was caught up to the third heaven. And I know such a man — whether in the body or out of the body I do not know, God knows — how he was caught up into Paradise and heard inexpressible words, which it is not lawful for a man to utter. Of such a one I will boast; yet of myself I will not boast, except in my infirmities. For though I might desire to boast, I will not be a fool; for I will speak the truth. But I refrain, lest anyone should think of me above what he sees me to be or hears from me. And lest I should be exalted above measure by the abundance of the revelations, a thorn in the flesh was given to me, a messenger of Satan to buffet me, lest I be exalted above measure." NKJV.

It was Dallard Willard I believe, who called the formation of Christ in His disciple as "The Daring Goal of The Christian Life". I believe that. For this side of heaven, the seemingly un-closable gap between our real and stated position with Jesus in the high and well sanctified, most holy and happy heavenlies, and our experience of that same position while we walk down here on earth, makes for a very tough journey and is the cause of so much mocking laughter both from within the church and without, especially in the cold light of pain, sin and loss. Yes, it is only the solid formation of Jesus in the centre of our selves, in the middle of the way of our earthly sojourn, which shall remove such laughing from the rear of our ears forever. Indeed, the formation of Christ in us is the only way to close the gap of our position in Christ with the facts of our experience here under this setting sun.

Formation and maturing takes time, that and a great deal of spiritual chiselling. The time and pain from moving from a seemingly observed apparition to that of an experienced acquisition of "Christ in us the hope of glory", is the very journey which we are on. Yes, like it or not, in terms of our spiritual formation, we are on a journey of both time and pain. All of us of course, especially in the dark and lonely valleys of such a spiritual journey, long for a short cut, long for a fast track, a by pass if you will, of such formational difficulty. Unfortunately, there is none. Let me say it again: "there is none".

Whilst of course spiritual formation cannot take place this side of heaven without the combination of time and chiselling pain, that and whole lot more besides I might add, there is however, a blessing which is so full of grace and preciousness, which is so dear to us that, when we get it, we often mistake it for the longed for holy grail of "fast track" spiritual formation! The blessing I refer to is of course, the special visitations of the manifest presence of God.

Yes, as the Holy spirit continues His unrelenting task of forming Christ in us for the glory of God the Father, we are sometimes privileged to have the special visitations of the felt and manifest presence of "Christ in us, the hope of glory". Some of the physical manifestations of that manifest presence in us, are often so powerful and so precious, that they become in our lives, land marks of directional change, even forming the very feathers of flight for our pointed arrows of now purposeful direction. This is wonderful, this is a precious blessing, but I say again and my friends do not be misled here, it is not spiritual formation!

If there ever was a downside to the special visitations of the manifest presence of Jesus in our lives, it is that for so many of us, we can become spiritual sugar junkies, hopelessly hooked on the energetic excitement caused by the release of spiritual charged endorphins that such visitations

> *If there ever was a downside to the special visitations of the manifest presence of Jesus in our lives, it is that for so many of us, we can become spiritual sugar junkies, hopelessly hooked on the energetic excitement caused by the release of spiritual charged endorphins that such visitations often bring with them.*

often bring with them. There is danger here of course, for there are a multitude of spiritual drugs which can produce such a similar high. Do not mishear me now, but dare I suggest that the devil is often a dealer in such diverting drug use. I tell you, that if the highs of His presence, continues to be experienced without the depth of His continued and daring spiritual formation, then you have been deceived and my friend, you have become a junkie instead of a disciple and the cold turkey of your recovery, shall either make you, or shall break you.

> *Remember tonight then , that such precious and often times, vital visitations, may change our trajectory and may somewhat sooth our way, but they shall never, and I mean never, "fast track" our journey of spiritual formation.*

Often times, the rigours of our journey demand nothing short of the manifest presence of God in our lives, in all His various ministries! However, these times are not the tools, neither are they the goal of our spiritual formation but rather, they are the sometimes booster rocket blessings of fresh inertia, appearing in our being and ultimately manifesting themselves in our changed and refocused direction.

Remember tonight then , that such precious and often times, vital visitations, may change our trajectory and may somewhat sooth our way, but they shall never, and I mean *never*, "fast track" our journey of spiritual formation. In light of this, don't become a cold turkey kind of Christian forced to always be seeking spiritual highs! The devil's a great drug dealer in this kind of rubbish. Press on daily in all the providences of God, knowing that it is Christ who works in you both to will and to do His good pleasure. Have faith in this great fact.

Listen: "Concerning this thing I pleaded with the Lord three times that it might depart from me. And He said to me, 'My grace is sufficient for you, for My strength is made perfect in weakness.' Therefore most gladly I will rather boast in my infirmities, that the power of Christ may rest upon me. Therefore I take pleasure in infirmities, in reproaches, in needs, in persecutions, in distresses, for Christ's sake. For when I am weak, then I am strong." (2 Corinthians 12:8-10 NKJV)

Pray: On this our journey dear Jesus, feed us with sufficient grace! And now and then O Lord, take us to heaven that we might feast with You on words inexpressible. In Your great name we ask it, amen.

| Vol | 01 | Q3 | NW00212 | July 30ᵗʰ |

Night-Whisper | RESPECT

Forever young

We have been living in a throwaway society for some decades now. Indeed, speedy advances in technology, already makes those items we purchase off the shelves today, virtually redundant on the morrow. So much so, that most design processes and manufacturing materials, now come pre-packaged with a very limited lifestyle and a lot of built-in redundancy. Thus we consistently make way for the new.

Numbers 11:16-17

"So the Lord said to Moses: 'Gather to Me seventy men of the elders of Israel, whom you know to be the elders of the people and officers over them; bring them to the tabernacle of meeting, that they may stand there with you.'"
NKJV

I am afraid the same approach is being adopted in the church, and it's an attitude which is especially adopted by the generationally focused, emerging churches. It would appear by their rhetoric and action that in consistently making way for the ever new and rising stars, they are throwing away the older folk and I have experienced at first hand how that throwaway age is getting younger by the year!

Should Christ wait a little while before coming to get us, then it will be very interesting to see how the rising demographic of politically powerful, lobbying old aged baby boomers, will shape the cultural landscape once again. The church will need to respond to this enormous aging crowd in practical loving and caring ways. Only older Christian people can do this. Only they can care enough to do so.

Today in 1965, president Lyndon Johnston signed Medicare into American law providing health care for each American over the age of 65. The cost of this care will continue to rise at an astronomical rate, fuelled interestingly enough, by our ability to cure disease and keep the aged alive and kicking that much longer. Nevertheless, this throwaway culture of ours, this youth-focused, age-redundant society will most subtly require that old people exit the scene more quicker than before to make way for the newer models. I have three comments on this challenge tonight.

First, may I encourage us older folk to try and stay young in our spirit. Exercise yourself in continual creativity. As much as you can, keep looking to the future. Bring all your experience, the good and the bad, to bear upon your creations of the present that will flower in the future. Even if that future is not yours to rejoice in. Create. Stay young in this.

> *Even the emergent churches will one day lose their teeth and one day remove the hip from worship.*
>
> *Think about that.*

Secondly, exercise your power. Whilst it is healthy to always apprentice and at some point step aside for the younger, *do not* be pushed aside. Be young in your spirit, be as strong as you can, continue to create and don't let the younger bucks antler you out of the way. Bear your arms, show 'em your scars and keep on fighting the good fight. There is *more than* enough work for younger folk to be apprenticed into, to be released into, to be resourced into without you stepping aside just yet. Don't be bullied. Don't be shoved around.

Thirdly, the church needs to make plans now, about how to evangelise, care for, honour and respect an increasingly elderly population. How we honour and respect our elderly, says much about not only our depth and breadth and spread of mercy but much more about our vision. We must remember that their life of service is not a limited one and though the outworking of this fallen world in their bodies, will, despite new knees and replacement hips, bring a slowing down of their frame, it is not God who has built redundancy into their being!

Tell me tonight, what kind of vision have you written into your personal law and into your church law regarding both the harnessing and release of powerful older folk into their own personal destinies. Even the emergent churches will one day lose their teeth and one day remove the hip from worship. Think about that.

Listen: "Then I will come down and talk with you there. I will take of the Spirit that is upon you and will put the same upon them; and they shall bear the burden of the people with you, that you may not bear it yourself alone." (Numbers 11:17-18 NKJV)

Pray: Lord, grant to our older folk, youthfulness of heart to go with their years of wisdom, strength of body to continue the fight and courage to lead Your people, further up and farther in. In light of forced redundancy and a throw away society, give us older folk some gumption to keep going Lord, in Jesus name I pray, amen.

Night-Whisper | **WISDOM**

Down the transsexual toilets

In my first of three thoughts on sexuality, tonight I would like to focus on the rising problem of sexual identity issues, especially amongst young boys, which is on an ever–steepening, rising curve. The advance in medical technology and expertise has made physical re-alignment surgery increasingly common. Indeed, sex-change surgery has become such a speciality of the Thai health industry, that it has become a relatively inexpensive procedure; so much so that patients are travelling there from all over the world to get the operation. As I write today in 2008, the challenge for the country of Thailand is that up to 20% of boys in their secondary schools, some as young as twelve years of age, are so camping in it up in school and talking about their plans to get transgender surgery as soon as they are legally allowed, that the school authorities have built a third set of toilets, such that now, the schools have male, female and transsexual toilets.

Genesis 1:27, 28a

"So God created man in His own image; in the image of God He created him; male and female He created them. Then God blessed them" --- *NKJV*

A Thai campaigner for transgender rights, male to female, commenting on the rising weirdness, remarked that, "Maybe the numbers of gays, of people with sexual identity issues, might be the same as in other countries but because Thai society and culture tend to be very sweet, very soft, and the men can be really feminine, if we tend to be gay, many of us tend to be transgender." Interesting.

On the whole, I believe that it is our fallen society, which through its manipulation of mass media, both generates these unnatural tendencies and then continually propagates the growth of these unnatural inclinations by political means, legal means, and further cultural manipulation which all go to foster an atmosphere of acceptance. Meanwhile, with this literal emasculation of society, diseases such as AIDS and the marketed dis-ease of male pattern stupidity, together with the subsequent destruction of family life, all take us ever closer to the precipice of moral madness, the decimation of society and ultimate population destruction. Yes, it is a serious as that.

The church now has to face the financial cost of political correctness and growing legal challenges. If it does not, then it to shall go the way of camp old Cain and mince its way into utter feminisation. The Anglican and Episcopalian denominations in 2009 are a present picture of this and make no mistake about it, the coming and long overdue complete Anglican split, is not so much about the authority of Scripture as we are led to believe by embarrassed conservatives that have not had the bottle to get out of this religious Sodom, but rather, it is about sexual infiltration in the church and cultural manipulation of by homosexuals with an agenda.

> *The church now has to face the financial cost of political correctness and growing legal challenges. If it does not, then it to shall go the way of camp old Cain and mince its way into utter feminisation*

Even so, grace and truth must sleep together, for they are marriage partners. Therefore, just how does a church graciously minister to those folks from a country where 20% of the population and rising, have had their todgers tacked back, and through hormones and surgery, have grown a couple of breasts? Indeed, how will the church in the U.K. and the U.S.A. minister to "lady boys" and "fem men" in our own countries! It's an ever-increasing problem that's for sure, for there is no coming back from the hormone and scalpel train wreck, which is transgender surgery. We need to really think this through as we reach out to our fellow sinners with God's love.

We now live in an age where women are men and boys are frightened. If you are a Christian tonight, then you have to help shape and formulate in the wisest of ways, legal plans and practical protection for your congregational futures and finances. More than that, somehow we all need to learn how to preach the Gospel to people who have travelled the transsexual road and try and imagine the shape and direction of a journey of sanctification and spiritual recovery which they will have to undertake. My goodness, we need the anarchy of God's grace to come and sort out this most agonizing of messes. I'm sure you agree with that!

Listen: "You shall not lie with a male as with a woman. It is an abomination." (Leviticus 18:22-23 NKJV.)

Pray: Lord, we need wisdom. Lord, we need grace. Lord, we need protection. Lord, we need men to men and women to be women and strong models for both. Have mercy upon us O God and assist us to walk with great grace and great truth in these most complicated of matters. In Jesus name, we ask it, amen.

PAUSE FOR PRAYER | 66CITIES

Well, I do pray that the first month of this quarters Night-Whispers written with you in mind, have prospered you spiritually and pushed you on a little farther down the road in knowing, obeying and immediately following the commands of the God of the whole Bible. This is my desire.

I am Victor Robert Farrell and I am the author of Night-Whispers. I also have the privilege of being the President of The 66 Books Ministry and I want to tell you a little bit about our major project which is: 66Cities. I believe one of the problems with the rapid moral decline of the West coupled with the influx of other religions, has been the compromise of the local church. It is as though we leaders have watered down the wine of the Gospel with the methods and culture of the world and have done so to such an extent that all we are left with is an anemic and slightly rose colored, fluoride-filled cup of poor tepid mouth wash. It is good for nothing except to be poured down the drain. This compromise I speak of, was to stop speaking about the God of the whole Bible and to such an extent that Christians were left in a strange kind of idolatry, worshiping the God of a cultural constructed Christianity, and so much so, that when these same Christians came into contact with the real God of the Bible, He troubled them and offended them. Indeed, they were embarrassed by Him and wanted Him excluded from their parties. The world of course, found more substance in the other gods, especially that kind of unbiblical Trinitarian spirituality which allowed science and hedonism to mate with the X factor of their own particular choosing.

We at The 66 Books Ministry intend to preach the Gospel of Jesus Christ and the God of the whole Bible, from each of the 66 Books of the Bible in the 66 most influential cities of the nations of the world. That's 16,500 cities in an annual and ongoing basis. To make this happen we are prayerfully raising up teams of proclaimers and 'prayer rangers' to go into these cities. We see this is a true prophetic witness to the glory of God. Indeed. This is the main reason why we are doing this: that God the Father and God the Son may be seen and Glorified in the power of God The Holy Spirit. We hope and pray, that many will see the Father, trust in the Son and be saved by the power of the Holy Spirit as well. Brethren, **we covet your prayers as we do this.** Check out WWW.66Books.TV

Night-Whisper | **GAIN**

Cutting the cost and the cost of cutting

In my second of three thoughts on sexuality, tonight I want to look at this passage in Isaiah 56. In this text, a eunuch is not a transsexual, neither did bearing the title of 'Eunuch' necessarily mean that you had been mutilated in that way. In other words, being a eunuch did not necessarily mean that your testicles had physically been taken away. The term and title of "eunuch" you see, could also be used figuratively. Here in Isaiah however, I believe it us used quite literally!

Isaiah 56:3-5

"Nor let the eunuch say, 'Here I am, a dry tree.' For thus says the Lord: 'To the eunuchs who keep My Sabbaths, and choose what pleases Me, and hold fast My covenant, even to them I will give in My house and within My walls a place and a name Better than that of sons and daughters; I will give them an everlasting name that shall not be cut off.'" NKJV

This act of mutilation (this radical cutting of permanent destruction) was sometimes done voluntarily. Yes, it was a voluntary practice even in the early history of the church, but more often than not, it was done purposefully and as an act of domination and forced servitude. Today, we would call this an act of abusive, forced domination and servitude. This text refers to those people upon which this violation has been inflicted. Nevertheless, such violent actions and the resultant large group of people who had been put under the knife at a very early age, who had on the whole been robbed of their dangly bits, now had become so common that God particularly addressed them here in this text from Isaiah.

In that cultural context where children were seen as a sign of blessing from the Lord (when mine were teenagers I would have contested that viewpoint most energetically) and where children were seen as being a cultural comfort and a sign of personal continuance, for the eunuchs then, *not* to be able to father children, having no children, was an opposite sign of God's blessing, even a sign of cursing, seemingly saying that they were not to be able to share in the covenant blessing as it expressed itself in both cultural comfort and personal continuance.

These words to eunuchs in Isaiah 56 are from the mouth of the God of all comfort, who says to them in effect, *"You please Me! And you do this by keeping my covenant and my Sabbaths and by consistently choosing to live to please Me. Thank you! I am sorry about 'your bits' your lack of 'home', your lack of personal comfort and personal continuance but don't worry, you won't lose out! No, even better than that, 'Mi cassa essu cassa,' and also, I shall give you an unforgettable and everlasting name. Yup, you might have had yer bits cut off, by I shall make sure, your name, the full embodiment of who you are and who you shall become in me, that is, all you ever hoped to be, yes that, will never be cut off! So in light of this, don't lose hope, don't give up honouring, obeying and pleasing Me, for in that, there is great reward, even if it not yet stood before you on two legs!"*

> *"...honour Me in the keeping of my laws, then I shall bless you, and bless you way beyond your capacity. You will by no means lose out in following Me."*

Yes, our text for tonight is for those who have seemingly been robbed of the blessing of the covenant by the loss of the cultural comfort and personal continuance, which a pair of testicles might have brought them. What a word of encouragement for folk so abused. Hallelujah!

The general application of this promise here is very clear then for us all I believe. *"Whatever your condition, whether you have been robbed by others, whether you have robbed yourself, whether sin, situation or circumstance has robbed you, if you now begin live to please Me,"* says God, *"To honour Me in the keeping of my laws, then I shall bless you, and bless you way beyond your capacity. You will by no means lose out in following Me."*

Listen: "Then Peter said, 'See, we have left all and followed You.' So He said to them, 'Assuredly, I say to you, there is no one who has left house or parents or brothers or wife or children, for the sake of the kingdom of God, who shall not receive many times more in this present time, and in the age to come eternal life.'" (Luke 18:28-30 NKJV.)

Pray: Lord, restore to me all that I have trashed, all that I have been robbed of, all that I have lost. Father, let Your redemption rule in my life, yes in all its fully redeemed and fantastic fullness. In Jesus name I ask it, amen.

| Vol | 01 | Q3 | NW00215 | August 02ⁿᵈ |

Night-Whisper | **PREPARE**

Of genitalia and gender, or the lack of both!

In my final of three thoughts on sexuality, may I say again tonight, that these texts about eunuchs, do not speak directly to transsexual issues but rather, they speak directly to sexual celibacy, both as a gift and as a practice. Let me explain.

Matthew 19:8-12

"He said to them, 'Moses, because of the hardness of your hearts, permitted you to divorce your wives, but from the beginning it was not so. And I say to you, whoever divorces his wife, except for sexual immorality, and marries another, commits adultery; and whoever marries her who is divorced commits adultery.' His disciples said to Him, 'If such is the case of the man with his wife, it is better not to marry.' But He said to them, 'All cannot accept this saying, but only those to whom it has been given: For there are eunuchs who were born thus from their mother's womb, and there are eunuchs who were made eunuchs by men, and there are eunuchs who have made themselves eunuchs for the kingdom of heaven's sake. He who is able to accept it, let him accept it.'" NKJV.

In our Bible text for tonight, the response of the blokey disciples to the instructions of Jesus here regarding marriage and both its demands and difficulties, placed next to divorce and all its inherent and serious repercussions, is one of, "Bloomin' Nora! Best not even go there then!" Jesus immediately responds to them by highlighting the great difficulties of such a fearful and negative statement. "Unless the gift of celibacy has been given" He says, "....you will never be able to not get married." In other words, in us all, there is a driving imperative for physical union. Now, as sex outside of marriage was never even contemplated by Jesus, it is the good sex drive as expressed within marriage then that He is talking about here. So in effect then, JESUS goes on saying, *"You can't give up sex, unless celibacy has been given to you and accepted by you as a gift."* Jesus then highlights celibacy in this text, by describing three classes of eunuch, that is, the three classes of men who have no testicles, and in terms of procreation then, have no real capacity for sexual intercourse in marriage, which is what He is actually talking about.

"For there are eunuchs who were born thus from their mother's womb, and..."

Jesus acknowledges that there are *natural* Eunochs, and please note here that I use the word natural somewhat reluctantly. Even so, here I believe Jesus is referring primarily to an involuntary but natural and literal absence of male genitalia. This happens! And Jesus here seems to see this as an opportunity for such folk to better embrace the focused Kingdom life. I do not think Jesus here is referring to those folks who are born inter-sexed or androgynous. I will deal with that later.

> *Origen and many others in the early church, who stupidly chose to mutilate their manhood and all its underlying passions, so as to live what they considered to be a more holy and a more pure life.*

"there are eunuchs who were made eunuchs by men,..."

Jesus acknowledges that there are *artificial* eunuchs. This is the involuntary removal of male genitalia, so that the dispossessed might better serve the robbers. For without testosterone they would have less strength to rebel, and as there would be no children born to them, then there was little chance of future blood vengeance, and certainly no chance of the implantation of their seed placed into the women of put into their charge. Jesus acknowledged the existence of this type of person. They were a people without sexual choice. Their condition was imposed upon them. Even so, again Jesus here seems to see this as an opportunity for such folk to better embrace the focused Kingdom life.

"and there are eunuchs who have made themselves eunuchs for the kingdom of heaven's sake."

Jesus acknowledges that there are eunuchs by *choice*. For sure, the choice Jesus refers to here does not lead to a transsexual turning. No, this choice must not lead to mutilation, as His reference was not to literal castration here but to a figurative one. Though I acknowledge that a literal interpretation and subsequent wrong choice was made by Origen and many others in the early church, who stupidly chose to mutilate their manhood and all its underlying passions, so as to live what they considered to be a more holy and a more pure life. By the way, Origen later repented of this early and fanatical choosing of losing. No, this is a figurative choice which Jesus is talking about in this part of the verse, and it is not a choice rooted in the drives of gender confusion, or of cultural manipulation or of the fleeing of right or wrong sexual urges. No, this is a positive choice (though not for me, for I cannot accept it) of laying aside the passions of procreation and recreation for the sake of the Kingdom of God. That is, to forsake the many energies, passions, and personal time enjoyed in personal relationships and then to refocus that redeemed energy, time and passion, putting it to good use for the Kingdom, seeing it blossom in terms of a closer relationship with God, in terms of the conception and creation of Kingdom dreams, Kingdom peoples, Kingdom processes, Kingdom procedures and Kingdom products of every kind!

Yes, we do need to acknowledge the presence of many folks in our world, whose human "firmware" has been damaged both by drug use and the out-workings of original sin.

"He who is able to accept it, let him accept it."

Like I said, I personally am not able to accept it. However, I know of some who are, though not that many, for sure. The apostle Paul had the gift of celibacy. Now listen, for often times, being single and waiting to be married is like living the eunuch life! This is not so much a choice but a necessity. It is only for a period of time however, until marriage most happily occurs. Without the gift of celibacy this kind of waiting singleness can become a nightmare unless the Kingdom of God is sought most thoroughly during the time you are waiting and seeking to be married.

Being not able to accept being a eunuch, I am also very fortunate not to have had this challenge of "castration" imposed upon me in terms of the foul physical, selfish actions of others, or in terms of the out workings of this particular manifestation of sexual death through one of the by products of the presence of original sin. No, I have a whole bunch of other emasculating challenges to battle against! Neither have I had to accept the damage imposed upon me by the side effects of various drugs intended initially to do good. I am chiefly talking here of the effects of Diethylstilbestrol, though not totally so. Yes, we do need to acknowledge the presence of many folks in our world, whose human "firmware" has been damaged both by drug use and the out-workings of original sin. In these cases for sure, medical technology can aid gender assignment or even gender re-assignment, but it can *never* justify sin and continuing to live in sin. When local churches increasingly become presented with such emasculated folk, then each case of broken humanity must be judged by the local church leadership, in grace, in truth, in clarity, and with the gingerness of a cat with big paws walking through an overpopulated minefield.

> *There is also a continuing demonic design to destroy the image of God. Remember, "Male and female He created them."*

Unfortunately there are still three things the church cannot allow itself to let its guard down on.

First, that there is also a continuing demonic design to destroy the image of God. Remember, "Male and female He created them." Yes, the attempted destruction of this Biblical gender differentiation through the addition of another gender consisting of the blending of the male and female, is manifested both in the terrible side effects of certain drugs like Diethylstilbestrol, as well as in present political and legal action against the church. We must graciously then, but with great clarity and strength, be prepared to fight in this gender related Biblical barley field.

Secondly, that there are greedy money grabbers 'disguised' as transsexuals and homosexuals, who hoping to make a swift and substantial buck, will bring lawsuits against people making such a stand in the Biblical gender barley field. When this happens, be sure this is not a transsexual or a gender issue. It is a greed issue, a theft issue and therefore needs addressing as such.

Thirdly, that there is a need to put in place, local church constitutional guidelines and practices that are *redemptive* in root and flower, to so guide local bodies of churches in dealing with such rising and challenging matters.

These are challenging days into which we wake, challenging nights in which we lay our weary heads. Let's walk wisely. Let's not mince in anyway. That means walking Biblically, that means walking in grace and truth and in strength and courage.

Listen: "Our Father in heaven, hallowed be Your name. Your kingdom come. Your will be done, on earth as it is in heaven. Give us this day our daily bread. And forgive us our debts, as we forgive our debtors. And do not lead us into temptation, but deliver us from the evil one. For Yours is the kingdom and the power and the glory forever. Amen." (Matthew 6:11-13 NKJV)

Pray: Lord, this celibate life is certainly no gift to me. Though I cannot accept it, I pray tonight for those who have accepted this strange gift. Strengthen them O Lord, and fill up in them all that is lacking in procreation peace and prosperity, that your Kingdom through their efforts would come all the quicker and all the more, in Jesus name we pray, amen.

Night-Whisper | **COURAGE**

Hic sunt dracones or hic sunt remuneror

I was watching a TV programme one night which was talking about the next manned space mission which would encourage NASA to leave its present fascination with the exploration of low earth orbit. It was called Mars Direct.

Numbers 13:33

"There we saw the giants (the descendants of Anak came from the giants); and we were like grasshoppers in our own sight, and so we were in their sight." NKJV

Dr Robert Zubrin seems to be the remaining and main proponent of an early and low cost mission to Mars. He is above all a passionate proponent of what he considers to be a journey of human necessity. As NASA has recently and most unceremoniously rejected his ideas and has decided instead to revisit the moon by 2020, it is evident that Zubrin holds little respect for what he considers to be NASA's lack of vision and courage! Indeed, when commenting on what NASA referred to as the "unknown and incalculable dangers" of such a mission to Mars, Zubrin made reference to the practice of early cartographers, that is, map makers, who when being similarly unsure and uncertain of what lay beyond their knowledge and understanding, wrote "Hic Sunt Dracones" on their maps, or "here be dragons"! "NASA," said Zubrin with some disdain, "NASA are simply populating their maps with dragons!"

God has the distinctly uncomfortable habit of encouraging us to step out into the unknown. God, like some intergalactic faith junkie, is always demanding that we please Him with our walk of faith, for "Without it," He says, "You just cannot please me." Now the problem with walking by faith is it never gets any easier. Yes, once we get comfortable in our faith walk, once we believe God and see God is coming through for us, He seems to make the next faith exploit that much more demanding, challenging, gambling and dangerous! Unfortunately with our tiredness comes fear of loss, and in our fear of loss, we write on all our own maps, "hic sunt dracones" and further, for wisdom's sake of course, we refuse to move from the spot. Yes, in marking our own maps with dragons, we destroy our very own faith missions of the colonisation of all our promised lands. Tell me, have you become a scaredy cat instead of a roaring lion? Meeeow... What a pitiful position to be in. Maybe we should rather die trying than rot quivering. At least there is more honour and self respect in that kind of exploit. Would to God we were rid of all our pussy cats in the church! Yes indeed, would to God our belly was full of fire instead of fur balls. My God! Where are the men that used to run to meet all their Goliaths?

> *In marking our own maps with dragons, we destroy our very own faith missions of the colonisation of all our promised lands.*

Listen: "He laid hold of the dragon, that serpent of old, who is the Devil and Satan, and bound him for a thousand years; and he cast him into the bottomless pit, and shut him up, and set a seal on him, so that he should deceive the nations no more till the thousand years were finished. But after these things he must be released for a little while." (Revelation 20:2-3 NKJV.)

Pray: Lord, deliver us from crippling and compromising fear. Where we have wrote on the maps of Your calling "hic sunt dracones" please forgive us, and provide us with a great eraser to undo the devilish lie and write instead, hic sunt remuneror - there be rewards! In Jesus name I pray, amen.

Night-Whisper | **CLEANSE**

Of socks and sweat

In Europe it is of course the Finns who keep wiping the floor with all contenders concerning their ability to "sauna sit" for the longest of times! The Finns consistently get the top three places in the annual world championship sauna sitting competition, braving steamy temperatures of 110 degree Celsius and above. Finland is a very cold country and the winter cold snaps they get there increase sauna use to such an extent, that the whole nation has to ration their energy supplies. Let me tell you now, that's way too cold for me!

John 13:7

"Jesus answered and said to him, 'What I am doing you do not understand now, but you will know after this.'"
NKJV

Many years ago, having done a brief study of the Yurok Indians of North America, I became fascinated with the use and the spiritual implications of the hot rock, male communal sweat lodge. Now, although that sounds like an ad you'd find in the *San Francisco Herald*, there is nothing seedy or untoward here. Nope, apart from the guys just getting together to have a good natter, the main use of the sweat lodge was to cleanse their skin and also purge their bodies of impurities. I sat in a sauna a few weeks ago with a guy who'd been out on the town over the weekend who remarked that he could "still taste the booze" in the sweat which was oozing out of his pores. It works!

Now for the Yurok and other North American Indians, this physical action of communal sweating, of group sweat therapy, obviously became for them a metaphysical act as well as a physical act, in that they felt that they were also cleansed from the evils of their sin and the sin of others, all of which had sullied their soul and that consequently, they also purged from their spirit all the collected impurities and repercussions of bad spiritual walking.

Now, there is nothing better for getting things off yer chest, for gaining instruction and wisdom and even for making you and the community feel a little better, yes, there is nothing better than talking things out in a hot communal setting, in a womb-like setting of fire and water, light and dark, animal skins, plants, earth and ancient rocks. Yes, this can do an awful lot for natural grounding, for the settling of the soul and the unloading of baggage. Yes, I'm up for that! At the end of the day, it's all good psychology, it's all good psychotherapy, and a whole lot cheaper than you'd be paying a professional, that's for sure.

There is something to be said for same-sex communal sweating, and it appears to me that God in His good providence often turns the heat up in our lives to facilitate such communal sweating. My suggestion as that men and women in the church have their sweat-boxes built, honoured and used, in preparation for such times.

> *There is something to be said for same-sex communal sweating, and it appears to me that God in His good providence often turns the heat up in our lives to facilitate such communal sweating.*

The Christian sweat box has one very distinct rite which is carried out before entering the steam. Gently, tenderly and with great respect, those with most maturity, those with most authority in the gathering, gird themselves with a towel, stoop down to undo the shoelaces and then slip the leather from the seated participant. Then, after rolling off their sweaty socks, with the coolest and clearest of fresh spring water, they wash the dirty and dusty feet of all those about to enter, all that cleansing heat. Along with the cleansing, such action also brings instruction. Think about that. He who has ears to hear, let him hear.

Listen: "And supper being ended, the devil having already put it into the heart of Judas Iscariot, Simon's son, to betray Him, Jesus, knowing that the Father had given all things into His hands, and that He had come from God and was going to God, rose from supper and laid aside His garments, took a towel and girded Himself. After that, He poured water into a basin and began to wash the disciples' feet, and to wipe them with the towel with which He was girded." (John 13:2-5 NKJV.)

Pray: Jesus, wash my feet. Jesus, help us to wash one another's feet. Jesus help us fully enter all our providential communal sweat boxes with joy, where by the actions of Your Spirit and the application of the blood of Jesus we might be cleansed and purged, helped and instructed, envisioned and empowered, made ready to do Your full and perfect will. Amen and amen!

| Vol | 01 | Q3 | NW00218 | August 05th |

Night-Whisper | **SOBER**

The most terrible loss of a load of old bulls

Regarding the questions as to whether or not elephants have good memories, an American reporter in Chicago recently recorded the following incident at the Chicago Zoo:

Titus 2:2-3

"Guide older men into lives of temperance, dignity, and wisdom, into healthy faith, love, and endurance." (from THE MESSAGE)

"In 1986, Mike Hogan was on holiday in Kenya after graduating from Northwestern University. On a hike through the bush, he came across a young bull elephant standing with one leg raised in the air. The elephant seemed distressed so Mike approached it very carefully. He got down on one knee and inspected the elephant's foot and found a large piece of wood deeply embedded in it. As carefully and as gently as he could, Mike worked the wood out with his hunting knife. The elephant gingerly put down his foot. The elephant turned to face the man and with a rather curious look on its face, stared at him for several tense moments. Mike stood frozen, thinking about being trampled. Eventually the elephant trumpeted loudly, turned and walked away. Mike never forgot that elephant or the events of that day. Over thirty years later, Mike was walking through the Chicago Zoo with his own teenaged sons. As they approached the elephant closure, one of the elephants turned and walked over to where Mike and his son were standing. The large bull elephant stared at Mike, lifted its front foot off the ground, then put it down. The elephant did that several times then trumpeted loudly, all the while staring at the man. Remembering the encounter in 1986, Mike couldn't help wondering if this was the same elephant. Mike summoned up his courage, climbed over the railing and made his way into the enclosure. He walked right up to the elephant and stared back. The elephant trumpeted again, wrapped its trunk around one of Mike's legs and slammed him against the railing, killing him instantly. It probably wasn't the same elephant."

For some years now teenage Pachyderms have been roaming in wild and angry packs, seemingly reeking revenge on human settlements in their area. An examination of the increasingly savage problem of young elephants on the rampage, tusking each other to death, vandalising crops and houses and killing human beings, seems to indicate that is linked to the killing of old bulls. In other words, a major problem in elephant herds has been that of absent fathers and the destruction of the secure mentoring of a patriarchal system. Without the strength and leadership and no doubt the giving of a good slap of an old trunk behind large floppy ears, the teenagers have had all boundaries removed and in the end have just gone wild. You will forgive the poor pun.

> *In Western society it is evident that the emasculation of old bulls, by political feminisation and the intentional and continuing dismantling of our own patriarchal system, has also led to the takeover and self-destructive rampage of teenagers.*

In Western society it is evident that the emasculation of old bulls, by political feminisation and the intentional and continuing dismantling of our own patriarchal system, has also led to the takeover and self-destructive rampage of teenagers. Knife crime, gun crime, sex crime, abused and abandoned single mums are all signs of a removed patriarchal system. Our young men have been purposefully and deliberately delivered up to the politically correct knife of emasculation, whilst the old bulls have been killed off. I tell you, for society to continue, this feminisation must come to a fatal end.

There is a call out tonight then, to all seemingly younger folks in the church of the living God. I am afraid that many of you need to grow up real quickly. Where the older bulls have been blown away or have blown it, you in great maturity must now grow up quickly and lead the way in wisdom and patriarchal manliness. If this is true for the young men of our churches, then may I say that it is even more applicable to the young women. You too must grow up and lead the way in Godliness, honour and true love among the sisters.

It's time to rid the world of these chav-like packs of pitiful packyderms! We can only do that by letting men be men, letting them live like men and allowing them to teach the younger blokes. Only men can teach boys how to be men. If this is not honoured in action, then all we can expect in our world is rampage, killing and wild anarchy. I am afraid this is the awful truth.

Listen: "Guide older women into lives of reverence so they end up as neither gossips nor drunks, but models of goodness. By looking at them, the younger women will know how to love their husbands and children, be virtuous and pure, keep a good house, be good wives. We don't want anyone looking down on God's Message because of their behavior. Also, guide the young men to live disciplined lives." (Titus 2:3-6 from THE MESSAGE)

Pray: Lord, help us to be, in the most irreligious and un-pompous of ways, to become the very best of ear flicking mentors. In Jesus name we ask it, amen.

Night-Whisper | **CLEAR**

What grows now, in the furrows of your tongue?

Hosea is the prophet of the broken covenant. His life had been lived in a web of cellophane lies, his heart crippled and scarred by the effects of the cold and creeping paralysing poison of deception, which dripped from the jagged neck of his broken bottle of a marriage covenant, like oozing maggots from putrid sores, upon his open soul and his love for the wife of his youth now all gone way, way wrong. Yes, Hosea's very own marriage to Gomer had been publicly shattered for all the world to see.

Hosea 10:4b

"...Thus judgment springs up like hemlock in the furrows of the field." NKJV.

The prefix to this poetic and powerful picture of a ploughed furrow mixed, maybe, with both wheat and hemlock is this: (Hosea 10:4) "They have spoken words, swearing falsely in making a covenant. Thus judgment springs up like hemlock in the furrows of the field." NKJV

Yes the prefix to our text for tonight was the outworked falseness of their spoken words. In other words, there was no substance in the covenant words of Israel, there was no sanctity in the saying, none, no, none whatsoever! They had rejected the King of Kings, they had broken covenant with Him! If so great a covenant could be broken then, why should they not also break every other lesser earthly covenant they had also entered into. Yes, the fact is that broken words release a fast spreading and corrupting poison, even into the bread of the field, such that a whole nation might be in paralyses, yes, even its very heart, become suffocated in a bondage of lies. Broken covenants, you see, become poisonous to all the relationships in families, communities and nations.

Remember tonight then, that when spoken words lose both substance and sanctity, a cold paralysing death always flowers in the furrows of life, bringing with it a creeping and stupefying, most poisonous death. Let me ask you then, How about your words tonight? Are they mixed with hemlock? Yes in these past days, has your tongue become tainted with the blood of Socrates?

Listen: "But no man can tame the tongue. It is an unruly evil, full of deadly poison. With it we bless our God and Father, and with it we curse men, who have been made in the similitude of God. Out of the same mouth proceed blessing and cursing. My brethren, these things ought not to be so. Does a spring send forth fresh water and bitter from the same opening?" (James 3:8-12 NKJV)

Pray: Lord, horridness crouches at the door of my heart and hemlock flowers upon the fauna of my tongue and in the furrows of my words, death resides and sometimes reigns. Have mercy on me O God and let that pure, clean refreshing spring water, bubble up from deep within me, that by Your power, my words would be granted substance, solidness and surety, in Jesus name I ask it, amen!

Night-Whisper | **SENSE**

Spiritual synesthesia

I have three confessions to make to you tonight. First that I am not a Christian who believes that *some* of the spiritual gifts have ceased after the primary apostolic era. Second, that I am also a Christian who believes in the fact of real signs and wonders following the preached Word and third, that I believe we are probably living in the time of the end. Now let me tell you tonight friends, that such a triple combination of belief, can lead you into giving charlatans all your loose change and hitching your wagon to some of the wackiest, way out, whirling dervish Christian circuses that have ever toured the land! And by the way, there are more and more of these each and every year. Fortunately I am from that great county of Derbyshire, where a good dose of brutal common sense was a free side order with every bag of chips. In all these things then folks, let's speak plainly and let's not be stupid!

Ezekiel 10:14-15

"Each one had four faces: the first face was the face of a cherub, the second face the face of a man, the third the face of a lion, and the fourth the face of an eagle." NKJV.

Now having said all that, allow me to make some spiritual observations about the manifestation of spiritual gifts in the church. Considering something so very important, frankly there are hardly any decent and practical books on the subject available. I think this is a triple testimony to our historical fear of the charisma, our respectable embarrassment of some of them and our utter disdain of that mixed bag of manifesting fruitcakes who rob us blind, and yes, I am talking about of being robbed of more than money! Nevertheless, maybe this brief thought will assist some of you this evening.

In the physical, material world, synaesthesia, literally "with sensation", is a neurologically-based phenomenon in which stimulation of one sensory or cognitive pathway, leads to automatic and involuntary experiences in a second sensory or cognitive pathway. In other words, people may hear what they see, or more commonly maybe, see what they hear, in terms of colour, shape and form. Yes, they may even taste a shape! Two well-known synaesthetes would be the artist, David Hockney and the great composer and musician, Duke Ellington. Both of these guys used their probably hereditary gift of synaesthesia in artistic exploration and expression. Of course, drug use and neurological damage can so traumatise the brain that it might also produce similar synaesthetic mixing of the senses. Yet this is quite different from the natural hereditary and genetic gifting of the same. Well so what?

I am fascinated by the descriptions of heaven in the Scriptures, and so I should be! I am a citizen there and it is my eternal home. What is most wonderful for me however, are the descriptions of the marvellous composite creatures, so special to God, that they surround and seem to live the near the very vicinities of His mighty throne. Whilst no doubt being both emblematic and metaphorical, I believe these creatures are also so very real! The power and the abilities of creatures of such combinational sensory perception must be extraordinary. Again I hear you say tonight, well, so what?

> *It is important for people of spiritual gifting to band with those of the same gifts, for mutual encouragement and for investigation, instruction and correction.*

What I am about to suggest tonight will assist some of you pastors to better counsel your flock and it will also assist some of you folk who think you are going barmy, for it has been my observation, and I just lay this out tonight for your simple consideration, that in terms of spiritual perception, in terms of spiritual "seeing" even, there is a vast amount synaesthesia involved in this type of spiritual gifting, especially for those with the gifts of discernment, mercy and prophecy. I leave the questions of whether or not such a gifting may have physical manifestations, or if such anointing is also spiritually heredity, for another day. Simply to say tonight then, that many of you "seers" in the church, actually experience, and should delight in such experience by the way, this cross-sensory expression of communication. This, to you, will be a most personal and tailored way of experiencing the spiritual realm. I believe in the life to come we shall all bathe in similar but far more intense cross-sensory perception, however, for now, here in the church, some people in comparatively small measure to the future life, already experience this spiritual syneasthesia.

It is important for people of spiritual gifting to band with those of the same gifts, for mutual encouragement and for investigation, instruction and correction. I wonder if many more church organisations should have "schools for prophets" for example, instead of schools for profits? There is safety in this, for heresy happens! In any event, many of you tonight, nevertheless need to see what God is saying in your ear, and maybe allow yourself to feel the colour of both His nearness and instruction. There is strength for the church in such spiritual synaesthesia. So to those of you who experience this may I say to you, "Those who have ears to see, let them taste!"

Listen: "After that you shall come to the hill of God where the Philistine garrison is. And it will happen, when you have come there to the city, that you will meet a group of prophets coming down from the high place with a stringed instrument, a tambourine, a flute, and a harp before them; and they will be prophesying." (1 Samuel 10:5 NKJV.)

Pray:- Lord, may all our "synaesthetic seers" be welcomed in Your church and subject to both Your written word and Your chosen leadership. Give to each of them O God, a good dose of Derbyshire common sense and good friends and pastors to advise and aid them in their journey. Make them a blessing to us all, in Jesus name I pray, amen.

Night-Whisper | **TRAVEL**

Despite disappointments, there are always new beginnings

Tonight, are you maybe going to bed confused? Tonight, are you at the end of your rope? Good! For know this: "All trails come to an end and all ends are really new beginnings." No, this is not some dank motivational little thought in the face of debilitating disappointment, that will never do, that will never edify, no that, will only get you angry. However, you must understand that the last three stations towards the end of all our present rail journeys of seeming un-achievement and failure are always, I mean always, Trepidation, Confusion and Disappointment!

Hebrews 11:13

These all died in faith, not having received the promises, but having seen them afar off, and were persuaded of them, and embraced them, and confessed that they were strangers and pilgrims on the earth. NKJV

Even when we think we have arrived at our own trails end, at the end of our rope of possible fulfilment, at the end of our line of promise, we find upon reflection that we usually have either missed our connection to our goals, or simply, for some unknown reason, have arrived at a dead end, a cul-de-sac in a journey that seemed, at first, to certainly be going somewhere. Yet, despite the scenery outside our window so slowly passing by, our train inevitably rolled onward through those last three stops of Trepidation, Confusion and Disappointment!

If you are feeling a little lost, bewildered and unsatisfied tonight, don't get too depressed, for this coming and mournful and triple grumble of mine, is simply the pressing preamble to an oncoming hunger for Satisfaction and Completion. Yes, we must succeed at something! Anything even! Yet, even when these Chinese food of the senses are sometimes consumed and digested, yes, when we feel satisfied in seeming completion, they will eventually leave us hungry for a fuller satisfaction and definite completion once again, and that pretty quickly as well. Listen to this poem…

Trails End

Lost
I picked up what I thought was
Your red and golden thread
Followed it
Hand over hand
Dragging its
Dew dripping plats
Through my
Wet little fingers

I followed it
Hunched back and looking
Over raging rocks and
Down the slip grass hills
Through the ice cold river up to my
Shivering knees
Along the muddy path and
Through the green specked trees

I followed it
Singing
I followed it
Winging
My way with
Prayers and fastings
I followed it with
Hope and with
Belief
I followed it
Happy with relief
Like four dogs
Hungry for their prey
Straining at the leash

Yet when my face hit the mountain
No rock opened wide in its side, but
There on the floor
Like a dead maggot
Unwriggling
Lay it's yellow and tattered little
End

> *Now, having travelled*
> *The length of the thread*
> *I find*
> *At both ends*
> *There is nothing.*
> *Nothing but*
> *The journey and*
> *The ever changing*
> *Seasons of my soul*

There is some truth in this poem but only some. For friends, at all our present bewildering trail ends, even if it is at the last station of disappointment, there are always three choices left to us when we get there.

The first choice is to either go under and through the subway, or go over bridge above the tracks to the other platform and get the next train back from whence ye came. This choice of returning, of doubling back, might neither be good nor bad, might neither be right nor wrong but it is a choice. Be sure of this though, that when you get on that train of return, although some scenery looks the same, all things have changed, and you especially so. Time and space have both moved on and you with them. Do not be deceived by seeming similarities. Things are different, things are new, even this return journey is a new journey for you.

The second choice is find a seat in the waiting room, plonk down your baggage, stare into your moth filled wallet and then feeling totally spent, begin your wailing and your bemoaning. This choice might neither be good nor bad, might neither be right nor wrong but it is a choice. Be sure though that others shall join you there. Many others still, have been in this same disappointed waiting room a long, long time and in a scary sort of way, are somehow comforted by your arrival there. Misery enjoys company you see. It always has. If you have gone into this waiting room, do be careful not to turn it into a funeral parlour. You are not dead yet! Bite yourself, real hard! Did it hurt? Did it make you smart? There I told you. You are not dead yet! You still have a lot of living to do, so put your emptiness away, get in contact with your Dad and see what He can do. That's the best way to wait.

> *Misery enjoys company you see. It always has.*

The third choice, which though it might not either be good or bad, though it might not either be right or wrong, is I think nevertheless, the best of choices, and it is to go and find the station master. This is the end of this trail, no doubt about it but with His help, with His provision, with His instruction and direction, it will assuredly be the beginning of another portion of your short journey home. Go seek the station master.

Today, you arrived at a destination. If it is the station of joy and satisfaction then eat it and bathe in it, knowing that its taste will soon either dull, or sour and you will be hungry soon again, yes, even the present warm waters of your satisfaction, will soon grow cold. All achievements this side of heaven, still slowly roll on to disappointment. Go seek the station master.

Today, you arrived at a destination. It may be the last station of Disappointment on this leg of the journey. Go seek the station master, He will undoubtedly send you to the trail head station of hope, in the vale of fresh vision, where new vistas and exciting adventures and discoveries await the travelling man!

> *In all your journeying dear friends, remember this, that despite the fact that you never purchased a ticket to disappointment, you shall be here again.*

In all your journeying dear friends, remember this, that despite the fact that you never purchased a ticket to disappointment, you shall be here again.

Don't you see it yet? Almost *all* the legs of all our journeys lead here to this station of Disappointment! Just about every single one of them! That is until your final day when, instead of coming to a steaming halt, your train shall pick up steam and scream through this last stop of disappointment, its whistles blaring in speeding thunder, until it finds itself coming to rest most happily in Jesus, where, in the land of the God of all comfort and fulfilment, your face will be filled with ever-smiling peace, for only in His land of heaven, shall He lay His treasures and wonders of completion and utter satisfaction before your travelling feet.

Today however, you arrived at an earthly destination. What will you do tomorrow?

Listen: *"These all died in faith, not having received the promises, but having seen them afar off, and were persuaded of them, and embraced them, and confessed that they were strangers and pilgrims on the earth. For they that say such things declare plainly that they seek a country. And truly, if they had been mindful of that country from whence they came out, they might have had opportunity to have returned. But now they desire a better country, that is, an heavenly: wherefore God is not ashamed to be called their God: for he hath prepared for them a city."* Hebrews 11:13-16 NKJV

Pray: Master tomorrow, travel close by me and help me to enjoy each moment of my present journey with You, for surely You and this short and ever changing, almost always disappointing ride, are the only constants in my life. Master, this night I choose life and this night I choose new beginnings. Tonight, my station Master, in faith, I lay my head in the lap of Your goodness and on the soft pillows of Your hope. Please prepare me with strength for the coming day, by granting me fresh dreams of hope and vast visions of fruitfulness. Amen.

| Vol | 01 | Q3 | NW00222 | August 09th |

Night-Whisper | **SURFACE**

Dealing with those sounds in the night

Whilst serving at HMS Dolphin in Gosport on the South coast of England, I once remember walking around the weapons lab on base and seeing the insides of a Mark 24 Tiger Fish Torpedo. Wire guided, its electronic wires and innards were at that time hanging helplessly over its surgically opened cylindrical sides like bust intestines! It looked lost, hopelessly long, simply an open pipe waiting to be laid in the earth to carry away our refuse. The torpedo looked dead and useless but of course, it was simply unconscious for now, out of its element, sleeping.

Exodus 10:21

"Then the LORD said to Moses, 'Stretch out your hand toward heaven, that there may be darkness over the land of Egypt, darkness which may even be felt.'" NKJV

The truth is that torpedoes are terrible monsters once they are let loose on their prey in their wet, dark, familiar and often fatal element. During the Falklands War for example, a British Hunter Killer Nuclear Submarine, HMSM Conqueror, let loose three old Mark 8 torpedoes at the Argentinean Cruiser, the General Belgrano and in that single attack, sank the cruiser, killing over 320 sailors.

Bill Budding, the man who fired the torpedoes that sank the General Belgrano on May 2 1982, said that, *"The next day I made myself listen to the tapes of the attack. The sound was like shattering glass. It was horrible."* Again, Steve McIntosh a young sailor on Conqueror at the time and helping with tracking operations remarked that, *"The sound of the explosion could be heard clearly in the submarine. It was like a thud and a hollow clap and a weird tinkling, which was the metal of the ship breaking up."*

Sounds in the night are terrible things to listen too. All those blown apart, screaming, burning, drowning, oil and blood spattered bodies sinking to the cold South Atlantic depths. Yes, your imagination can run wild in the deep dark of your night.

You know, I have seen some of the smallest creatures make the most terrifying of noises. I have seen cats cry like hurting babies. If I hadn't had seen them, then the unknown source of those weird sounds would have frightened me but seeing the source of those sounds, have you got that, seeing the source of sounds, allows you to be fully observational and somewhat calmer in such seeing knowledge, able to be in control and if necessary, to make yourself safe from any oncoming fury that might just follow hard on the heels of such a seen but now clearly understood sound. Ah but if you cannot see the source of the sound, then the monster in your mind gets ever larger. Unseen sounds in the deep dark night, are terrible things to listen to, for your imagination can run wild.

> *If you cannot see the source of the sound, then the monster in your mind gets ever larger.*

Many years ago I was trained to be very familiar with the shape of sounds that hid in distant seas. A submarine sonar operator during the cold war and serving on the old Polaris fleet, meant that I spent months of my life listening, identifying and classifying sounds, which gathered information, in turn assisted others in the placing of some kind of visible structure on the incoming acoustic waves. Serving on the most silent boats of the most secret of services, meant that just about all my sonar experience was passive. In other words, there was no sound transmission and subsequent collected reflection for examination, just listening, just the ever constant listening to the dark sounds of the always deep, dark and distant drowsy night.

Tonight, I want tell you of the three most disturbing sounds I ever heard.

The first was the splash-pop-fizz sound of a Sting Ray torpedo being dropped by an aircraft or helicopter into the water. The second most fearful sound was of that same torpedo turning its own active sonar into search mode. The third and most terrifying sound was that of the now hunting torpedo acquiring its target, as heard in the subsequent increased frequency pulse of its own active sonar. At that point my friend, despite the drama portrayed in *The Hunt for Red Volume 01 | Quarter 04 | October* , in all honesty, it was probably time to put your head between your legs and kiss your bits goodbye! Sounds in the night are terrible things to listen to, for your imagination can run wild.

I need to ask you this evening if you are as familiar with your internal surroundings as much as you are with the contents of your external surroundings? Are you familiar with the source of the creaking sounds of your own rigging as it sails through the night? The squeak of that spiritual wheel, the cries of the hurt prisoners still locked in your brig after all these years? Are you familiar with the crying and creaking sounds of your own soul and the flickering of your own spirits images, projected on the screen of your terrifying dreams, baying for attention and begging for an explanation?

Sounds in the night are terrible things to listen to, for your imagination can run wild.

It is time to surface and to draw close to all your sinking ships dear friends. It is time to identify all the disturbing sounds that have haunted the dark nights of your soul, so that in the end you might posses a knowing, healing and all redemptive peace. Sounds in the night are terrible things to listen to, for your imagination can run wild. Look!

Listen: *"By the way of the sea, beyond the Jordan, In Galilee of the Gentiles. The people who walked in darkness Have seen a great light; Those who dwelt in the land of the shadow of death, Upon them a light has shined." Isa 9:1-2 NKJV*

Pray: When You arrive O Lord, angels sing "Glory!" When you arrive O Lord, golden gifts of anointing and sweet smelling savour are brought by kings from the land of day break. When you arrive O Lord, darkness flees away, healings happen, peace is restored, life and renewal, hope and resurrection of all our wrecks, shall follow hard on the souls of Your mighty stepping feet. O Lord, I give you this my dwelling place tonight, this my holy bed, this inner sanctum of my head and of my heart, and ask that Your light be ever present here. O Lord, teach me in the morning how to sweep and clean, how to wash and cleanse, how to open and how to close. In Your great name I ask that you blow my main ballast and help me to safely surface to Your great morning light, Amen!

Dream word | **REMEMBERED**

Of tear drops and pillows

Today in 1846, the Smithsonian institute was created. James Smithson, an Englishman and illegitimate and unacknowledged son of a nobleman, was born in France and later buried in Italy. Though widely travelled in his lifetime, Smithson however, had never visited the United States! Yet on his death, he left his fortune to his nephew, Henry James Dickinson, son of his brother who had died in 1820, stipulating that, "If that nephew died without legitimate or illegitimate children, the money should go to the United States of America, to found at Washington, an establishment for the increase and diffusion of knowledge among men." Smithson's nephew, Mr. Henry James did in fact die without an heir and subsequently, over half a million dollars in gold came to the United States. A tidy little sum even in those days, that's for sure!

Psalm 56:8

"You number my wanderings; Put my tears into Your bottle; Are they not in your book?" NKJV

Smithson gave over his life to investigating the natural world and was already the embodiment of both a chemist and mineralogist when aged just twenty-two years, he became the youngest elected fellow of the Royal Society of London for Improving Natural Knowledge. Smithson in his lifetime wrote twenty seven scientific papers, one of which was even dedicated to the chemical composition, of a lady's teardrop. Imagine that!

Tears are the liquid produced by the body to both clean and lubricate the eyes. There are in fact three types of tears. The first are basal, produced by the lachrymal system or the tear system. These basically, keep the Cornea continually lubricated. The second type are called reflex tears and are produced in an attempt to flush out the eye in response to any irritation really, from both grit to onion vapours. Isn't God amazing!

The third type of tears are common only to humans and they are called psychic tears, crying tears, that are produced by strong emotional stress, or physical pain. Wikipedia reports that, *"Tears brought about by emotions have a different chemical make up than those for lubrication."* Maybe Smithson wasn't that eccentric in scientific investigations after all!

Certainly the tie between our declarative and emotional memory systems, produces tears. Therefore the source of the cause of these tears, as well as the chemical composition of these same crying tears, have made them to us, special, eventful, honourable even and worthy of a moist and most special consideration.

Tears of sadness, tears of woundedness, tears of sorrow, tears of grief, indeed all the big seas of our tears, cried over the centuries by a billion men women and children alike, are noteworthy, are notable, are not forgotten. In times past, tears cried at funerals for example, were placed in a bottle and then later, the bottle was placed at the graveside as a mark of respect. In the American civil war, it is also reported that ladies left behind and crying over their men folk would save their tears in a bottle and then give them to their returned men as tokens of their love and testimony to their faithfulness.

Tears of sadness, tears of woundedness, tears of sorrow, tears of grief, indeed all the big seas of our tears, cried over the centuries by a billion men women and children alike, are noteworthy, are notable, are not forgotten.

Selling "the saving of our tears" in bottles, or lachrymatory as it is called, is still good business today by the way, and for just a few bucks you can purchase your very own tear bottle and have it shipped straight to your door! Nevertheless, I still think that even our modern day slick business practice, does not take away the honour we all give to all the genuine tears that are cried.

In our text for today, David under the guidance of the Holy Spirit says something so matter of fact, so simple even, that it is both solid in its profundity and supremely comforting in its content. David tells us, that God has got two methods of recording our sorrows. God has both a bottle and a book for the tears of His people! Did you know that the shelves of God's study are full of ten thousand million and millions of sparkling bejewelled bottles and many of them contain your tears. Tears you thought no one saw, tears you thought no one cared about, tears you thought He was indifferent too, tears you thought He had forgotten! No,

He has not forgotten them! For in God's double accounting, not only is there a bottle but there is also a book, and in that book is a ledger of every millilitre of special compound psychic tear, that you have dropped to the ground in your deep distress. Dear friend, beloved of God, every drop is recorded and kept, every single drop.

We can go to sleep tonight then, knowing that He is also truly afflicted with our afflictions and that our sorrows are indeed very precious in His sight and are never to be forgotten by Him.

We can go to sleep tonight then, knowing that God looks at our sorrows with tender compassion and genuine concern. We can go to sleep tonight then, knowing that He is also truly afflicted with our afflictions and that our sorrows are indeed very precious in His sight and are never to be forgotten by Him. So then, regarding your sorrows, let me tell you once more tonight, that God has a double record of them, in both bottle and in book.

Listen: **"Go and tell Hezekiah, 'Thus says the Lord, the God of David your father: 'I have heard your prayer, I have seen your tears'" Isaiah 38:5a NKJV**

Pray: Lord, much of what could never be said, my whole being has wrapped up in a chemical compound, and poured upon Your feet. This, according to Your Word is deposited with You. So then, touch my tears O Lord, wipe them upon Your very own cheeks. Let them drip down My God, and then take Your tongue and taste my most terrible concern, taste all my desperate sorrows, taste all my pitiful pleadings, now flowing in the crease of Your lips, now lake'd in the corner of Your mouth. O Lord, may my tears turn Your taste buds into dancing alters, which are set ablaze by the offered up pleadings of my most desperate outpourings, and then, then may Your tasting be turned to Your telling, and Your sending of comfort and answers, to my most desperate of beds. Tonight my God, I close my eyes and I pray to You and say, "Even so come quickly Lord Jesus, yes even so, come quickly Lord Jesus." Amen.

| Vol | 01 | Q3 | NW00224 | August 11th |

Night-Whisper | **SAVE**

Surf's up!

Not many people might imagine God as the celestial surfer. Not many people imagine the God of heaven, clutching His gigantic board, running towards the crashing waves, His great feet leaving large imprints in the sand, kicking up the granules into the wind as He crashes head long into the surf shouting, "Cowabunga!" and paddling like Billio towards the shivering mass of humanity, all bobbing like lost buoys and screaming for help, pleading for some saviour as the deep begins to suck them down to the cold dark depths beneath. Well allow me tonight, to please paint you a picture of God the great celestial surfer, God the eternal lifeguard, looking out to sea upon those He will save.

Job 9:8

"He alone stretches out the heavens and treads on the waves of the sea."
NIV

On this day in 1911, the Hawaiian Amateur Athletic Union excitedly telegraphed the Union headquarters officials in New York with some astonishing news. The folks in charge there receiving the news however, were quite incredulous and reportedly replied to the telegram saying, *"What are you using for stop watches? Alarm clocks?!"* You see, the Hawaiian AAU had reported that the then swimming record for the 100 yards free style, had been smashed to smithereens in Honolulu harbor! It was in fact Duke Paoa Kahinu Mokoe Hulikohola Kahanamoku, who had taken 4.6 seconds off the record, who by the way, also went on to become a three-time Olympic gold medal winner in swimming!

The Polynesian people and the Hawaiians in particular, invented the art of surfing! In his youth after school, down on Waikiki beach, Duke Kahanamoku used a traditional surf board, constructed after the fashion of ancient Hawaiian boards. His surfboard, made from the wood of a Koa tree, was sixteen feet long and weighed 114 pounds! Between Olympic competitions, Duke Kahanamoku travelled the world giving swimming exhibitions and guess what? Yes, he also incorporated surfing exhibitions into his routine. He was such an advocate and propagator of this ancient art, that today he is now regarded as the father of modern surfing.

Bronzed bodies, long blond straggly sun bleached hair, baggy beach pants, slinky walks and lots of "Hey dude"-ing! might conjure up pictures of the modern surfer but I tell you, that it was an incident in California, in 1925 on Newport beach, that really pictures for us our celestial surfer of a God.

> *"The most superhuman surfboard rescue act the world has ever seen!"*

In heavy and pounding surf, Duke Kahanamoku rescued eight men from a fishing vessel that capsized while attempting to enter the city's harbour. Twenty-nine fishermen went into the water and seventeen perished. However, Duke Kahanamoku, using his surfboard, was able to make quick trips back and forth to rescue as many sailors as he possibly could. Along with him, two other surfers saved four more fishermen. At the time, Newport's police chief called Duke's efforts, *"The most superhuman surfboard rescue act the world has ever seen!"* What a trinity of surfing saviours were seen in California on that most disastrous of Newport harbour days.

Our text today poetically paints for us, the great feet of our great God, treading down the pounding surf. Yes, here in our text for tonight, Job paints for us God, treading down upon the waves of disaster, paints for us God, treading down upon the waves of death, paints for us God, treading upon the hungry waves of justice with the strength of a warrior, bending down His bow to string it in preparation for war, or, like a conquering army marching into the land which they intend to possess, Job paints for us God, treading down with confidence and authority the rising and the revolting of the enemy before Him. In out text for tonight, God like a bronzed and strong, mighty celestial surfer, stands unperturbed, stands with majestic authority, right in the middle of a drowning humanity, lifting and saving, carrying and caring, cosseting and caressing those He has pulled from the deep, delivering them safe to heaven's most beautiful shore.

What storms are you in tonight dude? Stop worrying, for your Mighty God is strong to save and treads with rescuing and conquering authority, upon all the waves of all your mountainous seas.

Listen: ***"But He said to them, 'Why are you fearful, O you of little faith?' Then He arose and rebuked the winds and the sea, and there was a great*** *calm. So the men marveled, saying, 'Who can this be, that even the winds and the sea obey Him?'" Matthew 8:26-27 NKJV*

Pray: But as for me, my prayer is to You, O Lord, in the acceptable time; O God, in the multitude of Your mercy, hear me in the truth of Your salvation. Deliver me out of the mire, and let me not sink; let me be delivered from those who hate me, and out of the deep waters. Let not the floodwater overflow me, nor let the deep swallow me up; and let not the pit shut its mouth on me. Hear me, O Lord, for Your loving kindness is good; turn to me according to the multitude of Your tender mercies and do not hide Your face from Your servant, for I am in trouble; hear me speedily. Draw near to my soul, and redeem it; deliver me because of my enemies. (Psalms 69:13-18)

Night-Whisper | **REMOVE**

A smack on the side of the head

In his book, *A Whack on the Side of The Head, How You Can be More Creative,* Roger von Oech, tells of the origins of the QWERTY keyboard. That's right folks, the very keyboard you have probably been using today! Have you ever thought of why the keys were laid out in that particular way? Well the story goes that in the creation of the early typewriters, the inventor CL Sholes who built the first commercial model in 1868 in a machine shop in Milwaukee, had great problems with the keys continually clogging up! Apparently, those first fast typists would jam up his sluggish machine. In an attempt to stop this happening, Sholes arranged the keys on his new typewriter in such a way as to slow the typist down. Sure enough he did just that and the constant jamming of the early machines was also greatly reduced. Yes indeed, speed might have been reduced but productivity was greatly increased.

I suppose there are two things for us to muse on tonight.

The first is that sometimes it's good to slow things down so you can get things done! What things are you doing in your life that might be done better, might be accomplished more thoroughly, might be more definitely completed, if you just slowed down the process a little! The old adage, that old English idiom of *"more haste, less speed"* is really quite true you know.

Hebrews 12:1,2

"Therefore we also, since we are surrounded by so great a cloud of witnesses, let us lay aside every weight, and the sin which so easily ensnares us, and let us run with endurance the race that is set before us, looking unto Jesus, the author and finisher of our faith, who for the joy that was set before Him endured the cross, despising the shame, and has sat down at the right hand of the throne of God." NKJV

The second thing is that old habits of the past which used to be useful to you in reaching gaols, in accomplishing tasks, in moving forward, may in this new day, in this different time, simply be slowing you down! You may indeed be organising new ideas, new dreams, new goals etc, around some very old ways of doing things and this might well in fact be slowing you down substantially. You may have the heart of a 21st century hotrod, the design of the latest Porsche even but frankly, if you're sticking an old lawnmower engine in it, what's the point?

> *Old habits of the past which used to be useful to you in reaching gaols, in accomplishing tasks, in moving forward, may in this new day, in this different time, simply be slowing you down!*

Maybe tonight, your subconscious mind will come up with a couple of items in your life, a few engines, and some motorised drives, which need your attention in the coming days, by either slowing them down or ripping them out!

So sleep well folks, you've got some thinking to do tonight and tomorrow and then maybe, some ripping work to do for the next wee while!

Listen: *"Now no chastening for the present seemeth to be joyous, but grievous: nevertheless afterward it yieldeth the peaceable fruit of righteousness unto them which are exercised thereby. Wherefore lift up the hands which hang down, and the feeble knees; And make straight paths for your feet, lest that which is lame be turned out of the way; but let it rather be healed." Hebrews 12:11-13NKJV*

Pray: Lord, teach me tonight and enable me tomorrow to un-clog my life. In Jesus name I ask it, amen!

| Vol | 01 | Q3 | NW00226 | August 13th |

Night-Whisper | **MARKING**

Letting God mark your territory

In the early hours of this morning, in the thick darkness before the coming day, the fox who lives in our back garden and thinks he owns the place, decided to very noisily beat the boundaries of his territory, to both proclaim his presence and to protect his claim. A fox's territorial yell is one of the most disturbing sounds in the night that you will ever hear. It is loud, aggressive, disconcerting and troubling. I tell you, it would certainly make me think twice about encroaching upon his territory!

Song of Solomon 2:15

"Catch us the foxes, The little foxes that spoil the vines, For our vines have tender grapes." NKJV.

Now, whatever you think about territorial spirits, I do both from the Scriptures and from my own experience believe they exist. Like the fox you will hardly ever see them and be only aware of their presence by secondary signs of their presence, such as ripped open garbage bags, smelly faeces or leftover bones and feathers on the lawn. If however, you begin to encroach or move upon their territory in any manner that relates to conquering, subduing or removing, then I tell you, like wild banshees, the secret foxes will begin to march the bounds of their territory and noisily proclaim their possession. Oh, and they will bite you!

Most of us Christians are often unknowingly plagued by such foxes. From the mysterious murdering of small dreams, whose remains are laid unceremoniously upon the sparkling dew of our wet morning greens, to the genocidal devastation of all of our chickens of providence, the secondary evidence of spiritual foxes nevertheless abound. When this happens, we need to go fox hunting and when we find them, we need to unmercifully get rid of the infestation of such predator vermin. I am of course now not talking about real foxes!

Spiritually speaking then, getting rid of these little foxes is both messy and time consuming and even when we succeed, even then there is no guarantee that they will not return. There are however, two immensely practical things we can do to help get rid of the foxes and then keep them out. Those two practical things are all about the making of music and the marking of our territory.

First then, we need to mark our own boundaries, our possessions with the fierce proclamation of the victorious possessor. We need to march around our being, around our families, around our ministries, around our churches, around our jobs, around our vocations, around our gifting and our callings, singing Psalms and spiritual songs of declarative and confrontational possession! In the name of our God we need to march and pray with warlike intent, powerfully proclaiming that this land *is ours* and we shall possess it with every ounce of energy within us. We need to be very definite and fierce in this.

> *We need to get some lion poop!*

Secondly we need to get some lion poop! Yes indeed, one of the best ways to deal with real foxes, to get them out and keep them out, is to go down to the local zoo and get a bag of lion poop! Get the poop and spread it on your land. Once the foxes realise, even just through the secondary indicators of a possible larger and fiercer predator on their patch, then they shall up sticks, take the kits and go! Let us then invite our great King, The Lion of The Tribe of Judah, to mark our territory with His very presence. Don't you know that even the secondary indicators of the presence of the King, will cause the foxes to depart? Invite God this night then, to come and most thoroughly make you His possession and so mark all the boundaries of your territory with the steaming proclamation of all His mighty claims. Now if you dare, that will make a very interesting prayer for you tonight!

Listen: "When an unclean spirit goes out of a man, he goes through dry places, seeking rest, and finds none. Then he says, 'I will return to my house from which I came.' And when he comes, he finds it empty, swept, and put in order. Then he goes and takes with him seven other spirits more wicked than himself, and they enter and dwell there; and the last state of that man is worse than the first. So shall it also be with this wicked generation." (Matthew 12:43-45 NKJV)

Pray: Lord, when You have cleansed us, help us always with light and power, hope and victory, grace and truth, mercy and tenacity, to fill our houses with light and love. Meanwhile Lord, great Lion, we invite You to come and mark us with signs of your great possession. In Jesus name we pray, amen.

Built by God and put beside the bulldog

Happily married and healthy, he was in semi-retirement and running two small grocery shops, when the call came to meet Winnie at Croydon airport. For the next eighteen years between 1921 and 1945, Detective Inspector Walter Henry Thompson (who died in 1978) was the bodyguard of Winston Churchill.

The stern, tight lipped figure of Thompson, Winston's shadow, can be seen lurking quietly in the background of most photographs featuring Churchill. During the course of his duties, Thompson lost his marriage in a divorce, his health in a nervous breakdown and nearly lost his life, times without number. All of this happened whilst protecting Winnie from some twenty assassination plots! Winston (Winnie) Churchill believed that over the course of his life, that he had been protected by a supreme being in order to deliver the world from the excesses of Hitler and the Nazis. I personally believe that to be the case, and being the case then, God also used Thompson as one of his mighty tools for preserving Churchill's life. Thompson was built by God for such a time as that.

Benaiah means, "built by God". This mighty man of strength and courage was made chief of King David's bodyguard having proved

1 Chronicles 11:22-25

"Benaiah was the son of Jehoiada, the son of a valiant man from Kabzeel, who had done many deeds. He had killed two lion-like heroes of Moab. He also had gone down and killed a lion in the midst of a pit on a snowy day. And he killed an Egyptian, a man of great height, five cubits tall. In the Egyptian's hand there was a spear like a weaver's beam; and he went down to him with a staff, wrested the spear out of the Egyptian's hand, and killed him with his own spear. These things Benaiah the son of Jehoiada did, and won a name among three mighty men. Indeed he was more honoured than the thirty, but he did not attain to the first three. And David appointed him over his guard." NKJV.

himself after having, in particular, killed an Egyptian over seven feet tall, two fierce warriors, lion like men of Moab and a hungry lion weighing some 300-500 lbs, very angry and cornered in a pit, on a cold and slippy, wet and snowy day. This man's courage was tried and tested in the facing of all kinds of lions. These deeds simply made known to other people, the kind of man he already was. Thus he was charged with the command of King David's bodyguard.

What if the life you really want, and the future God wants for you, is hiding right now in your biggest problem, your worst failure... your greatest fear?

Some of you have been built by God and charged with the protection of His leaders. Protect them. Give your life for them. Some of you leaders know that other people would willingly spend their lives for you. Don't let your stupidity make that spending a cheap price. Some of you fail to face your lions, you run from them instead of running to them! This needs to change, for yes, Benaiah was a lion chaser! As Mark Batterson says, *"What if the life you really want, and the future God wants for you, is hiding right now in your biggest problem, your worst failure... your greatest fear? Go on,"* says Batterson, *"Chase that lion, overcome adversity, unlearn those fears, embrace uncertainty, calculate the risks, seize the opportunity, defy the odds and don't be afraid of looking foolish!"*

A lion is a terribly dangerous thing! However, maybe, just maybe, you are even more dangerous than him. Go on, growl a little! Maybe then God might place even you beside a bulldog!

Listen: "Be sober, be vigilant; because your adversary the devil walks about like a roaring lion, seeking whom he may devour. Resist him, steadfast in the faith, knowing that the same sufferings are experienced by your brotherhood in the world. But may the God of all grace, who called us to His eternal glory by Christ Jesus, after you have suffered a while, perfect, establish, strengthen, and settle you. To Him be the glory and the dominion forever and ever." Amen. (1 Peter 5:8-11NKJV)

Pray: Yes Lord, make us into lion chasers and show us that the gates of hell, shall not prevail against us, in Jesus name I ask it, amen!

Night-Whisper | **FOCUS**

No More Macbeth Mournings

Tomorrow, and tomorrow and tomorrow
Creeps in this pretty pace from day to day
To the last syllable of recorded time;
And all our yesterdays have lighted fools
The way to dusty death. Out, out brief candle!
Life's but a walking shadow, a poor player
That struts and frets his hour upon the stage
And then is heard no more: it is a tale
Told by an idiot, full of sound and fury,
Signifying nothing

Of course this is from the pen of the great bard himself, Mr William Shakespeare, *Macbeth* Act V, Scene V. Here King Macbeth, out of utter despondency, counts his life as nothing, and in so doing of course, counts all life as nothing. It is of course most reminiscent of the lines from our Bible text of for this evening, which have in turn been pulled out from the journal of the richest, most wisest and yet most self-indulgent man that ever lived. King Solomon himself.

Ecclesiastes 1:1-2

"The words of the Preacher, the son of David, king in Jerusalem. 'Vanity of vanities,' says the Preacher; 'Vanity of vanities, all is vanity.'"
NKJV

Age creeps up on you. Young person I say to you again, age creeps up on you. Despite all your creams, wrinkles will still appear like unwanted maggots, crawling and wriggling on the crinkle cut surface of what was once your soft and supple skin. Despite the years of trying to shoo away the birds from your brow, crow's feet will still imprint themselves around your eyes yet they shall never assist you by pecking the smoky cataracts of discoloration from the once clear lenses of light imprinted beauty. Yes indeed and despite all those tens of thousands of abdominal crunches, your belly, your porky little penguin plump balloon, unbeknown to you, has secretly made a pact with gravity and will fall in love with your belt, fondly folding its pink flesh wantonly over the top of the hot brown leather. Despite the alluring sound of this last sentence, getting old is just not that sexy!

Did I tell you that age creeps up on you? Well so does illness and incidents and accidents and all the other soft brown goo. There are days, maybe you have had one today and if not, then just wait awhile, for they shall surely come, yes, there are miserable Macbeth like days, days that make life seem but a walking shadow, a poor player that struts and frets his hour upon the stage and then is heard no more: that make life appear like a tale told by an idiot, simply a passing noise, full of sound and fury, which in the end, as far as you are now concerned, signifies nothing! These miserable Macbeth like days come upon us all eventually, but God help the person who has them day after day, after all the long dark day.

> *There are but two ways that you can stop the dawning of such miserable, Macbeth-like days in your life and they are to both "fear God and focus."*

There are but two ways that you can stop the dawning of such miserable, Macbeth-like days in your life and they are to both "fear God and focus." Let's deal with focus first of all.

Focus. Tonight, number your days. Three scores years and ten might just be yours, and if so, how many of them might you have left? Don't count sheep tonight, count your days. Yes, Focus. Now you know how many you might have left, be sure to choose to enjoy each moment, live in each *now* moment, for the past was once but a *now* moment upon which you built your present and your future, should God grant it, is simply a phantom extrapolation which is built only upon what you shall do in the *now*. Enjoy *now*. Live *now*. Choose *now*.

Secondly, be sure to Fear God. Yes, number your days and focus upon your limited time span, your final destination, your gifts and callings and the living beat of your heart but do it all in the sight of a Holy God!

The apostle Paul went with confidence into his future. How about you? Whoever gives your eulogy at your funeral, will it be told in such a way that your life will be seen to be but a tale told by an idiot, full of sound and fury, signifying nothing! If in all your deathbed dreams, God allows you to listen to such a eulogy tonight, will you feel that you have laboured like a woman in child birth and simply given birth to wind?

Tonight I want you to lie in your coffin, and imagine you are finally at the front of the church, your eyes closed, but your casket lid and crumpled cartilage ears, both open and listening. What will the eulogist say about your life, your loves, your achievements, your *impact*, yes your large cratered impact upon the once blue–lit, wondrous world in which you walked?

> *Tonight I want you to lie in your coffin, and imagine you are finally at the front of the church, your eyes closed, but your casket lid and crumpled cartilage ears, both open and listening.*

Maybe tomorrow, it's time for the comet to begin to change course. Maybe? For tonight it's time to both Fear and Focus. Let's get rid of those Macbeth like mornings and death like evenings once and for all time. Fear and focus friends, fear and focus, that's the key.

Listen: *"**For I am already being poured out as a drink offering, and the time of my departure is at hand. I have fought the good fight, I have finished the race, I have kept the faith. Finally, there is laid up for me the crown of righteousness, which the Lord, the righteous Judge, will give to me on that Day, and not to me only but also to all who have loved His appearing." 2 Timothy 4:6-8 NKJV***

Pray: Lord, tonight may I change any despondency I might carry, for the gifts of faith, hope, fear and focus, so that all my Macbeth like mournings would truly wilt away. In Jesus name I ask it, Amen.

| Vol | 01 | Q3 | NW00229 | August 16th |

Night-Whisper | **RECONCILE**

The reconciliation of Christina The Astonishing

I would not count it as a "feather in my cap" to be regarded as the patron saint of the insane, I would certainly not be pleased to have this accolade on my eternal Curriculum Vitae! This peculiar honour however, falls to a 12th century Belgium woman who has become known as "Christina the Astonishing". No doubt like most medieval saintly tales, there has been shall we say, some imaginative liberty and some maybe not so elegant elaboration placed upon the accounts of her life and of her wild, wild exploits.

1 Corinthians 6:19,20

"Or do you not know that your body is the temple of the Holy Spirit who is in you, whom you have from God, and you are not your own? 20 For you were bought at a price; therefore glorify God in your body and in your spirit, which are God's."
NKJV

Christina was orphaned aged 15 and proceeded to live the life of a contemplative shepherdess. There is no doubt that poverty as well as ascetic mysticism and the consequent mental and bodily ill health following this combination, led to her subsequent demise. It is after her death however, that the accounts of her life get just plain weird! Yes, I said her life after her death, for apparently it was at her funeral, even during the saying of the Mass, that she flew up from her coffin like a bird and perched herself in the rafters. Mind you, if you were ever wake up in a coffin during the saying of a Mass, I am sure me and you both, would do just the same! From this resurrection point onwards, the record of Christina's life now takes on a very Roman Catholic flavour, in that purportedly now having spent some time in both heaven and in hell and also in that most useful and invented of Roman places called purgatory, "Christina the Astonishing", then chooses not to remain with God but rather, to return to earth and publicly suffer the fires and pains of Purgatory before the astonished medieval masses.

Cynthia Large records that Christina found the stench of human sin most repugnant, choosing to perch high in the tree-tops, on the smallest of branches and pray with the birds. Christina's recorded escapades range from throwing herself under mill wheels, to rolling in open fires and sitting inside bakers ovens, either screaming in agony due to the pulverising water, wood and heat, or tortured into terror by the scorching flames, then only to emerge completely and utterly unscathed! We won't even go near her miraculous and virginal breast tonight, suffice to say, that like most Roman Catholic saints and earthly heroes, Christina The Astonishing publicly suffered for the sins of others, thereby filling up the merits which were left lacking in the sacrifice of Christ. Now, this terrifying titillation of the human conscience by Christina was later turned by an over indulgent Tetzel, into a magnificent medieval money maker for the Church of Rome, whose gross extravagance in turn helped formed the blow which struck the wedge of "Sola Fide" (by faith alone) into the very dry wood of the then visible church, splitting it, removing the living from the dead and thereby forming both one Roman Catholic and many Protestant denominations. In many respects I believe, the mad old mystic of Christina The Astonishing greatly contributed to this eventual reformation of the church.

> *We won't even go near her miraculous and virginal breast tonight!*

Christina The Astonishing was either a mystic or a mad woman, or maybe even possibly both. A life so full of terrifying accounts of mental madness, meant both then and now, that the jury is still out on whether she was demonically possessed or divinely inspired! However, there is one recorded and I think most astonishing incident that is worthy of our consideration this night. Again Cynthia Large writes, "It seems that Christina's soul and body coexisted uneasily, as demonstrated in an account told by a priest who secretly trailed after her one day when she entered a church to pray. He concealed himself behind a pillar and observed her bitterly throw herself before the altar and cry out 'O miserable and wretched body! How long will you torment me...Why do you delay me from seeing the face of Christ? When will you abandon me so that my soul can return freely to its Creator?' The answering accusation came from the same mouth, 'O miserable soul! Why are you tormenting me in this way? What is keeping you in me and what is it that you love in me? Why do you not allow me to return to the earth from whence I was taken...?' Then, before his eyes, a loving reconciliation took place; Christina seized her feet in both hands and kissed their soles fervently, saying 'O most beloved body! Why have I reviled you? O best and sweetest body, endure patiently...'"

Now I like that account very much and I do believe that in it, Miss Christina The Astonishing says something to us all in these most peculiar of 21st century days.

Despite the massive cult of Western body worship, there still exists a most uneasy coexistence of both body and soul in most people. Indeed, I would go so far as to say that if we look and if we truly see, most tortured souls still in some way or another, also torture their own bodies. I lie in bed tonight, feeling the scar tissue of an old vasectomy, tracing my fingers over another hair line scar of an umbilical hernia repair, whilst resting a once dislocated elbow on currently broken abdominal muscles which even now, yield themselves to another this time, massive ventral hernia repair, and a few other unmentionable surgical invasions, and thinking of the damage, my breathing becomes slightly labored as air fights its way through nostrils twice repaired by rhino-plasty and past the 'dog's breakfast' removal of an ancient tonsilectomy. I could list a lot more evidence of bodily decay due to age and the ravages of sin but most disturbingly of all, I could list evidence of definite and soulish, physical self abuse.

> *Over time, there has for all of us I am sure, been an uneasy co-existence between soul and body which for many of us, and especially you ladies, has grown into a repugnant, silent and stinky self-hatred of your own God-given body.*

Obesities, addictions, and a multitude of other bodily self-hatreds with all their attendant maladies and manifestations are here to be seen all around us and most especially in us. Over time, there has for all of us I am sure, been an uneasy co-existence between soul and body which for many of us, and especially you ladies, has grown into a repugnant, silent and stinky self-hatred of your own God-given body. To counteract the devastation of such a soulish self hatred, I believe the action of body and soulish reconciliation as observed by the hiding priest, yes, that very body and soul reconciliation which took place in Christina The Astonishing, in Christina, the patron saint of the mad and the mentally ill, needs to be adopted and put into practice by very many of us as well!

I wonder that if we gave voice to our bodies tonight, that they too would cry out to us in their need for more considerate care and more kindly concern? That they too would cry out to us tonight for a mightier mastery and a more helpful honour. That they too would cry out to us tonight for a truer love, for a more real respect and for right and righteous attention.

Methinks that some of you have some apologising to do to your bodies tonight. Some of you maybe have some cleaning to do in your physical house, some repairs and maybe even, much maintenance. I have no doubt that many of you have a great need of reconciliation within your most divided of houses. Yes, some of you need to weep over your own feet tonight, kiss them and embrace them to yourself. Yes, many of you have need of a righteous reconciliation with yourselves even this very night.

Those who have ears to hear, let them hear.

Listen: *"Do you not know that you are the temple of God and that the Spirit of God dwells in you? If anyone defiles the temple of God, God will destroy him. For the temple of God is holy, which temple you are." 1 Corinthians 3:16 NKJV*

Pray: Lord, help me make my body a partner in Your service and not a beaten slave to mad desire. Lord, forgive me please the abuse of this Your temple and the disdain I have put upon myself and the disaster I may have brought myself to. Lord, I pray tonight for a healing reconciliation into wholeness, that my body soul and spirit may be one, even as You are with the Father and the blessed Holy Spirit, one in purpose, one in desire and one in direction. In Your great name I ask it, amen!

Night-Whisper | **LONGING**

Rabboni

It was just yesterday that I was reading for the Nth time *My Utmost for His Highest* by Oswald Chambers. In his opening paragraph he says, "It is possible to know all about doctrine and still not know Jesus. A person's soul is in grave danger when the knowledge of doctrine surpasses Jesus, avoiding intimate touch with Him. Why was Mary weeping? Doctrine meant no more to her than the grass under her feet. In fact, any Pharisee could have made a fool of Mary doctrinally, but one thing they could never ridicule was the fact that Jesus had cast seven demons out of her; yet His blessings were nothing to her in comparison with knowing Jesus Himself. 'She turned around and saw Jesus standing there, and did not know that it was Jesus…Jesus said to her 'Mary!' Once He called Mary by name, she immediately knew that she had a personal history with the One who spoke, 'She turned and said to Him, 'Rabboni!'"

John 20:15

"Jesus said to her, 'Woman, why are you weeping? Whom are you seeking?' She, supposing Him to be the gardener, said to Him, 'Sir, if You have carried Him away, tell me where You have laid Him, and I will take Him away.'" NKJV

It is possible to know doctrine, thoroughly, absolutely, pinned down and buttoned up tight. It is possible to love doctrine, to defend and justify your particular pet position, to write volumes about it, debate with others concerning it, even, may God help us all, yes even to die for doctrine! All this can be done, indeed has been done, and indeed is being done without knowing Jesus, without having a personal relationship and history with Him.

With my own eyes, I have seen our institutional machines turn out young men in their thousands who know doctrine but do not know Jesus. My own shoulders have rubbed with those of seeming super magnificent success and I tell you right now, I have sensed a supreme absence of Jesus, His fragrance, His passion, His presence. I have seen pastors that need seven demons cast out of them! I have seen falls, oh my God, I have seen the falls of the doctrinal grand masters, of the powerful and politically placed pundits of professional Christianity, come crashing to the ground. I have seen the desolate shells of doctrinal death; lay like empty husks along fine paved yellow brick doctrinal roads, all from the land of Laodicea and all leading nowhere.

At some point you will realize that feelings are most important, feelings are very important, feelings are paramount.

Yesterday I prayed with a woman who was bemoaning a distance from Jesus that she felt had come upon her soul. In tender love, she told Him how much she missed His presence, how much she longed for Him. I tell you friend, I was greatly convicted. I must ask myself today and in doing so I must ask you, "How on earth do you cope and even continue in your walk, with the felt absence of His presence?"

If your answer to that question was a doctrinal one that says "According to the Scriptures, Jesus has said, "I will never, no never, no never, leave you nor forsake you," then may I say, I greatly worry for your Laodicean laxidasicalness. At some point you will realise that feelings are most important, feelings are very important, feelings are paramount. Call me a heretic if you will, but I have seen professors attempt suicide, great men, blood bought and distraught doctrinally correct disciples of Christ, destroyed in their very being because Jesus was not a felt manifestation of person with them along the hard road they travelled. In their distress, their beloved doctrine became to them not even as important as the worms in the grass under their heavy feet.

A personal relationship with Jesus so often taught and touted in the big and bombastically brandished multiplexed screens of our mega churches must, I say again, must be a living reality with us on a Monday morning. If it is not, then you must doubt your salvation. If doctrine is not translated into the felt and manifest known and loving presence of a living God within our lives then we must doubt our salvation! Better, we have the pain of this deceit and the felt pleasure of discovering Him this side of heaven, than to arrive before God's throne and hear him say, *"Depart from me...I never knew you."* I fear with all my heart that this most sad refrain shall be spoken to hundreds of thousands of dead but doctrinally correct folk that have taught and walked the aisles of our lovely Laodicean churches.

Chambers finished his thought yesterday by saying, *"Do I have a personal history with Jesus Christ? The one true sign of discipleship is intimate oneness with Him – a knowledge of Jesus that nothing can shake."* Well do you? O lover of Jesus, you will forgive me if the eight shot from my blunderbuss has peppered your heart tonight, but I have to ask even myself, "Oh my soul, Oh spirit of Robert Farrell, do you have that kind of a relationship?"

Listen: "By night on my bed I sought the one I love; I sought him, but I did not find him. 'I will rise now,' I said, 'And go about the city; In the streets and in the squares I will seek the one I love.'" Song of Solomon 3:1-2

Pray:

Jesus, lover of my soul, let me to Thy bosom fly,
While the nearer waters roll, while the tempest still is high.
Hide me, O my Savior, hide, till the storm of life is past;
Safe into the haven guide; O receive my soul at last.

Other refuge have I none, hangs my helpless soul on Thee;
Leave, ah! leave me not alone, still support and comfort me.
All my trust on Thee is stayed, all my help from Thee I bring;
Cover my defenseless head with the shadow of Thy wing.

Wilt Thou not regard my call? Wilt Thou not accept my prayer?
Lo! I sink, I faint, I fall—Lo! on Thee I cast my care;
Reach me out Thy gracious hand! While I of Thy strength receive,
Hoping against hope I stand, dying, and behold, I live.

Thou, O Christ, art all I want, more than all in Thee I find;
Raise the fallen, cheer the faint, heal the sick, and lead the blind.
Just and holy is Thy Name, I am all unrighteousness;
False and full of sin I am; Thou art full of truth and grace.

Plenteous grace with Thee is found, grace to cover all my sin;
Let the healing streams abound; make and keep me pure within.
Thou of life the fountain art, freely let me take of Thee;
Spring Thou up within my heart; rise to all eternity.

Charles Wesley

Night-Whisper | **RECLAIM**

A new anthem for the redemption of your Jerusalem

Concerning the nicely named "prophetic poet" William Blake, the poet Wordsworth wrote: *"There was no doubt that this poor man was mad, but there is something in the madness of this man which interests me more than the sanity of Lord Byron and Walter Scott."*

Numbers 12:6
"Hear now My words: If there is a prophet among you, I, the Lord, make Myself known to him in a vision; I speak to him in a dream." NKJV

It was this same William Blake who in his preface to his work entitled *"Milton"* wrote the following lines, *"Jerusalem"*.

*And did those feet in ancient time
walk upon England's mountains green?
And was the holy Lamb of God
on England's pleasant pastures seen?
And did the countenance divine
shine forth upon our clouded hills?
And was Jerusalem builded here
among these dark Satanic Mills?*

*Bring me my bow of burning gold!
Bring me my arrows of desire!
Bring me my spear! O clouds, unfold!
Bring me my chariot of fire!
I will not cease from mental fight,
nor shall my sword sleep in my hand,
till we have built Jerusalem
In England's green and pleasant Land.*

Over one hundred years after the first penning of this verse, during the ravages of the Great War and its enormous losses, that a search was made for some magnificent verse and music which would continue to instil patriotism and sacrifice into the masses. It was Blake's preface to his poem "Milton", that was utilised to continued and great effect. This same verse was later popularised by the music of Sir Edward Elgar and the stirring rendition which he produced has subsequently been widely adopted by various English institutions and even political bodies to be their very own anthem. Indeed, in 1922 in the city of Leeds, King George V himself said that he preferred replacing "God Save the King" with "Jerusalem" as the national anthem! Britain however, though it has never had an official national anthem, refuses to adopt this great and most popular of poems, mostly because it has four questions in the first verse, that must all I am afraid to say, be answered with a very literal no! Nevertheless, it is to those same four questions posed by Blake, which I want to turn our attention to tonight.

> *Glastonbury, with the fall of Christianity in England, has now become the centre for pagan mysticism in all its far-out and freaky forms.*

This poem by Blake is built upon an ancient legend, that Jesus whilst still a young man came and visited the ancient town of Glastonbury, accompanied by Joseph of Arimathea. This is not an unusual legend for Glastonbury Tor is reputed to lie on the centre of numerous lines of earth energy (lay lines) and has been a mystical and spiritual centre for thousands of years. There is no doubt that geographically, Glastonbury Tor could have once been the ancient and legendary island of Avalon. It is of no surprise then, that Glastonbury is also the focal point for most of the legends regarding King Arthur, Joseph of Arimathea and The Holy Grail. As I write this piece today, Glastonbury, with the fall of Christianity in England, has now become the centre for pagan mysticism in all its far-out and freaky forms. Yes, God help us! Even the spiritual world abhors a vacuum.

Blake's poem "Jerusalem", based upon on these same Glastonbury Christian legends, not only mourns the rise of the destructions concerning the dark satanic mills of the industrial revolution (or, if you like, the Church of England) but also seems to indicate two further things.

First of all, in the first stanza of the poem, Blake gives some acquiescence to his belief in the Glastonbury legends themselves. That is especially, that Jesus visited Glastonbury and established the first church in England right there. You see, in Blake's mind, I believe those first four questions are answered in the affirmative! Yes! Christ did arrive in England, and yes, Christ did plant Jerusalem, the metaphor for heaven, the metaphor for Zion, the metaphor for the city of the people of God, right here in England. It is total 'tosh' of course but I wonder if Blake believed it!

> *Jerusalem my friends, must be built again, in all our green and pleasant lands. He who has ears to hear, let him hear.*

Secondly and much more importantly, is the driving import of Blake's affirmation to these questions, which is found in the second stanza of the piece. Blake says in effect, *"As God himself has begun a good work in us, in our land, and that with a personal visitation, then as we now look around at the ruins of our Christian culture, of our Christian community, of our once magnificent Christian England, we must take up our spiritual weapons and fight to regain these lost lands of Jerusalem!"* Blake then goes on to invoke both powerful and prayerful pictures of a great and determined desire, when he calls for heavenly weaponry to help fight a spiritual war right here on earth. Would to God that the remnant of the church of the living God in our time would choose to do the same. Selfish spiritual masturbation is the order of the day rather than selfless exertion.

In all former Christian lands, now lost or losing out to false religions of every kind, these old words of Blake must become our new battle anthem. In all personal battles that are fought within our own heart, our own homes, our own relationships, indeed, in all the regaining of lost ground to that most murderous and thieving enemy of ours, these old words of Blake must become our new and powerful, our new and personal battle anthem.

Jerusalem my friends, must be built again, in all our green and pleasant lands. He who has ears to hear, let him hear.

Listen: *"Pray for the peace of Jerusalem: 'May they prosper who love you. Peace be within your walls, Prosperity within your palaces.' For the sake of my brethren and companions, I will now say, 'Peace be within you.' Because of the house of the Lord our God, I will seek your good." Psalms 122:6-9 NKJV*

Pray:

> *Be Thou my Vision, O Lord of my heart;*
> *Naught be all else to me, save that Thou art.*

Thou my best Thought, by day or by night,
Waking or sleeping, Thy presence my light.

Be Thou my Wisdom, and Thou my true Word;
I ever with Thee and Thou with me, Lord;
Thou my great Father, I Thy true son;
Thou in me dwelling, and I with Thee one.

Be Thou my battle Shield, Sword for the fight;
Be Thou my Dignity, Thou my Delight;
Thou my soul's Shelter, Thou my high Tower:
Raise Thou me heavenward, O Power of my power.

Riches I heed not, nor man's empty praise,
Thou mine Inheritance, now and always:
Thou and Thou only, first in my heart,
High King of Heaven, my Treasure Thou art.

High King of Heaven, my victory won,
May I reach Heaven's joys, O bright Heaven's Sun!
Heart of my own heart, whatever befall,
Still be my Vision, O Ruler of all.

Translated from an ancient Irish hymn.

Night-Whisper | CHANGE

Turning disaster into discovery

Operation Jubilee was put into action today.

The year of jubilee was a semi-centennial celebration of the Hebrews. Every fifty years, lost ground would be recovered, those in slavery would be released and all debts would be cancelled. Easton's Bible Dictionary wonderfully describes the benefit of such a system in that: "It would prevent the accumulation of land on the part of a few to the detriment of the community at large. It would render it impossible for anyone to be born to absolute poverty, since everyone had his hereditary land. It would preclude those inequalities which are produced by extremes of riches and poverty, and which make one man domineer over another. It would utterly do away with slavery. It would afford a fresh opportunity to those who were reduced by adverse circumstances to begin again their career of industry in the patrimony, which they had temporarily forfeited. It would periodically rectify the disorders which crept into the state in the course of time, preclude the division of the people into nobles and plebeians, and preserve the theocracy inviolate." Wonderful. Bring on the Jubilee that's what I say!

Today in 1942 the Allies put into action operation Jubilee, which was in fact a large raid on the well fortified and Nazi occupied French port of Dieppe. The purpose of the raid was to seize and hold a major port for a short period of

Lamentations 3:40-47

"Let us search out and examine our ways, And turn back to the Lord; Let us lift our hearts and hands To God in heaven. We have transgressed and rebelled; You have not pardoned. You have covered Yourself with anger And pursued us; You have slain and not pitied. You have covered Yourself with a cloud, That prayer should not pass through. You have made us an offscouring and refuse In the midst of the peoples. All our enemies Have opened their mouths against us. Fear and a snare have come upon us, Desolation and destruction." NKJV.

time, both to prove it was possible and also to gather intelligence from prisoners and captured materials, while assessing the enemy responses. The raid was also intended to use air power to draw the Luftwaffe into a large, planned encounter and glorious air victory for the allies!

The raid on Dieppe however, was nothing short of a disaster. No major object was achieved, the Royal Navy received a basting, the Royal Air Force a roasting and out of the 6,000 mostly brave Canadian soldiers involved in the raid, over 50% of them were either killed, wounded or captured. No land was recovered, no debts were paid and no slaves were released. In truth, Dieppe's Operation Jubilee meant disaster for the Allies.

> *Unless you take time to discover, examine and correct all the glaring failures of past attempts, no amount of courage, no amount of perseverance and no amount of faith is going to gain you success.*

It would be two years later when the massive Allied landings would take place in Normandy. This success of those later D-Day Landings was most definitely linked to the rectifying of the forms of failures that were discovered at the disaster of Dieppe.

Tell me tonight, how many Jubilee joys of yours have been turned in Dieppe disasters in your life? How many times has attempted deliverance just led to further captivity? How many times has this kept happening?

If disappointment and disaster dog your heels dear friend, then you need a full debrief with yourself and with your Lord, so as to thoroughly examine the forms of your failures and then implement courageous corrections, to make sure your next Operation Jubilee is not just another costly disaster. I tell you now that unless you take time to discover, examine and correct all the glaring failures of past attempts, no amount of courage, no amount of perseverance and no amount of faith is going to gain you success. You must take time to turn all your disasters into fields of discovery for future footholds, bridgeheads and battlefield victories ever to occur.

In the first week of September 1944, the 2nd Canadian Infantry Division liberated the same port of Dieppe where their previous disaster had occurred. The Nazi garrison fled before them as the division approached. The Allies had discovered all the problems of the Dieppe raid and rectified each and every one of one of them. There was no way that the enemy wanted to face Canadians intent on and certain of, a most definite and all-conquering victory in the field.

Friends, the fresh and better prepared and trained Canadian soldiers and all the Canadian Dieppe survivors, this time recovered the land, recovered the debt, released those in Nazi slavery and had a victory parade to boot!

> *It's time to start dreaming about and planning your victory parade tonight, but you can't do that until you have turned all of your disasters into fields of discovery.*

It's time to start dreaming about and planning your victory parade tonight, but you can't do that until you have turned all of your disasters into fields of discovery. So, I reckon them that it's time to get debriefed dear friends. It's time to pick over the wreckage and examine the bodies.

Listen: "My eyes overflow with rivers of water For the destruction of the daughter of my people. My eyes flow and do not cease, Without interruption, Till the Lord from heaven Looks down and sees. My eyes bring suffering to my soul Because of all the daughters of my city. My enemies without cause Hunted me down like a bird. They silenced my life in the pit And threw stones at me. The waters flowed over my head; I said, 'I am cut off!' I called on Your name, O Lord ,From the lowest pit. You have heard my voice: 'Do not hide Your ear From my sighing, from my cry for help.' You drew near on the day I called on You, And said, 'Do not fear!'" Lamentations 3:47-57 NKJV

Pray: O Lord, to us belongs shame of face, to our kings, our princes, and our fathers, because we have sinned against You. To You O Lord our God belong mercy and forgiveness, though we have rebelled against You. So Lord, come and rifle through our wreckage, heal us of our damage and so lighten us of our baggage, that we may be more than conquerors through Christ who loved us and gave Himself for us. Amen.

| Vol | 01 | Q3 | NW00233 | August 20ᵗʰ |

Night-Whisper | **TRAIN**

Of Butchers and Bolters

Yesterday evening I spoke about Operation Jubilee and the disastrous raid on Dieppe carried out in 1942. Though no major object was then achieved by the attacking allies, on Orange beach, No4 Commando had however, successfully landed in force and destroyed their targets thus providing the only success of the whole operation! It was Simon Fraser, the 17ᵗʰ Lord Lovat, who led this successful attack, providing the template for all future Commando operations. Indeed, Lord Lovat would later be promoted to Brigadier and head up all the D-Day Commando landings and most especially, the crossing and keeping of the American-held Pegasus Bridge. But that is another story for another day.

Judges 11:1-6 "Now Jephthah the Gileadite was a mighty man of valour, but he was the son of a harlot; and Gilead begot Jephthah. Gilead's wife bore sons; and when his wife's sons grew up, they drove Jephthah out, and said to him, "You shall have no inheritance in our father's house, for you are the son of another woman." Then Jephthah fled from his brothers and dwelt in the land of Tob; and worthless men banded together with Jephthah and went out raiding with him. It came to pass after a time that the people of Ammon made war against Israel. And so it was, when the people of Ammon made war against Israel, that the elders of Gilead went to get Jephthah from the land of Tob. Then they said to Jephthah, "Come and be our commander, that we may fight against the people of Ammon." *NKJV.*

It was after the disaster of the Normandy evacuations that Winston Churchill cried out for the creation of a small and highly skilled, well-trained raiding force, armed with all the latest weaponry, to attack the smug-faced enemy. Churchill wanted a force to attack, and then his own words, "butcher the enemy and then bolt!" As Churchill was the man of the moment to head up a wartime government, Simon Fraser was just the man, just the man of the moment, to head up all the "butcher and bolt" operations.

Many years ago, I remember sharing the firing range and the training ground of the regiment of Scots Guards. It was to this regiment, that Simon Fraser was initially inducted into his military training. Indeed, for centuries his Highland clan had been churning out fierce warriors ready for a fight. Simon's father had in his very own moment, formed the Lovat Scouts and deployed them during the second Boer war. Militarily speaking, Simon was already trained, ready and reared to think outside of the box. Simon was ready to "dare to do" what ordinary forces would never dream of!

> *Jepthah was a bastard. Jepthah was an outcast. Jepthah was jettisoned from the family and the land he loved.*

I love to hear the stories of people's lives. In doing so, I have concluded that most folks are prepared for special moments in time, and like it or not, God does breed some Christians for special moments of conflict, both within and without the church. Some folks are brought forth for war, both civil and otherwise and when outside of this destiny, I have observed these same folk, become depressed and distraught and sometimes even wither, dither and die!

Jepthah was a bastard. Jepthah was an outcast. Jepthah was jettisoned from the family and the land he loved. In his sovereignly prepared banishment, Jepthah became as Easton's Bible Dictionary so wonderfully describes him, *"A wild and daring, Gilead mountaineer, a sort of warrior Elijah."* Yes indeed, Jepthah was the man for this particular moment in the history of the people of God, and his beloved band of butchers and bolters, no doubt trained the Israelite wimps, to whoop the Amorite adversaries and deliver Israel once more. Jepthah was a man prepared for this moment in time. Jepthah was a man prepared for *his* moment in time. Do you see that?

If you are a leader in the church of the living God, I counsel you tonight to see if God may have peppered your fellowship, your congregation with a few Jepthahs-in-waiting. If so, then if all you are doing with them is trying to tame the beast and teach them to speak nice and to drink tea from China cups, then my dear friend, may God forgive your lady-like control and your terrible lack of Biblical vision! Learn war yourself and then learn how to put a weapon into the hands of your Jepthahs and release them to make war upon the enemy. God created them for this. I say again, God created them for this, so you make sure that you release them into it.

If you are a Jepthah, if you are a son of thunder or if you are a daughter of Deborah, please *stop* repenting of your warlike attitude and my friend, go and start looking for a fight! For I tell you, there are people in the church of the living God destined to die with their boots on and a time is coming, when we shall thank God for all these great hearts!

The motto of the Fraser clan is "All my hope is in God". The family motto of the Lovat family is "Je suis prest", or "I am ready!" How about you O warrior of God? Are you ready? Is all your hope in God?

This evening maybe you need to go to bed and get a good night's sleep, for tomorrow I am sure for many of you, that it is time to get back into training. Go get 'em tiger!

Listen: *"So Jephthah advanced toward the people of Ammon to fight against them, and the Lord delivered them into his hands. And he defeated them from Aroer as far as Minnith — twenty cities — and to Abel Keramim, with a very great slaughter. Thus the people of Ammon were subdued before the children of Israel." Judges 11:32-33 NKJV*

Pray: Lord, please forgive us for turning our tigers into fireside pussycats and for spiritually emasculating all those who dare to stand up and fight the wars of the Lord! Lord fill our churches with warriors so in love with You, that they would fight through enemy lines to bring You water from the well of Bethlehem. Oh for such warriors to now appear within Your church O God! Please Lord Jesus, do not let us be left without them, in the conflict so shortly to come upon us. Amen.

| Vol | 01 | Q3 | NW00234 | August 21st |

Night-Whisper | **SAVE**

The sweet sauce of God

At the time of writing this evening, I have been in the USA for over five years now. Unlike my home country of England, it is incredibly cheap to eat out over here at the moment. Indeed, due to this comparative cheapness of eating out, in my observation, compared to the home family food factories of Britain and Europe, most American home kitchens are virtually redundant!

1 Corinthians 10:13

"No temptation has overtaken you except such as is common to man; but God is faithful, who will not allow you to be tempted beyond what you are able, but with the temptation will also make the way of escape, that you may be able to bear it." NKJV.

However, on the whole and in my humble opinion, food though far more expensive, tastes so much better in the old country. I say this with two highly notable exceptions, and those are steaks of any kind and Omaha Steaks, Gourmet Steak and Chop Sauce in particular! This rich, brown, to-die-for delicacy is better than anything I have ever tasted and I tell you, if your were to pour it on dry cardboard, you would give thanks both before and after the sumptuous chewy delicacy you had just been enabled to most eagerly consume. I am thrilled to assure you tonight dear friends, that along with chocolate, British brewed beer, Cornish pasties and Heinz baked beans, Omaha Steaks, Specialty Gourmet Steak and Chop Sauce will indeed be on the menu in heaven. Thank you Jesus, for this most magnificent word of knowledge tonight! Mmm, Mmm!

There is no doubt that some of you tomorrow, may well have to do some cardboard crunching! Some of you tomorrow, may well have to consume some most distasteful of situations. Some of you tomorrow, may well have to sit down with heathens and eat monkey brain. In all your unwanted eating of the morrow, may I call to mind those prophetic words of Julie Andrews that proclaim most correctly to us that, *"A spoon full of sugar"* does indeed *"make the medicine go down, in the most delightful way!"*

In all seriousness, I do believe that some of the ways of escape spoken of in our text for this evening, can often manifest themselves when God makes our messes more than manageable, even edible, by applying His very own Omaha Steaks, Special Gourmet Steak and Chop Sauce to the most unpalatable of situations. And why not? For did you forget that God is in the business of making the bitter taste sweet? Remember then for tomorrow, that some ways of escape are made manifest most especially, when God makes sweet all the bitter tastes of life. May God grant all you cardboard crunchers some heavenly sweetening to your situations with is even tastier than Omaha Steaks, Gourmet Steak and Chop Sauce!

Some ways of escape are made manifest most especially, when God makes sweet all the bitter tastes of life.

Listen: "Oh, taste and see that the Lord is good; Blessed is the man who trusts in Him!" Psalms 34:8 NKJV

Pray: Father God, throw the sweet Jesus tree into all my bitter waters and then tomorrow make them sweet to me. In His sweet name I pray, Amen!

| Vol | 01 | Q3 | NW00235 | August 22nd |

Night-Whisper | **STICK**

Sticky situations demand a very sticky church

In Ridley Scott's epic movie, *Gladiator*, I am reminded of the scene where General Maximus with his small band of gladiators are placed in the Coliseum before some huge gates. Death, in dread but unseen shape, lies ready behind those gates to come out and not so speedily devour them from the earth. In face of such a growing fear among his men, in double quick time, Maximus speaks to his men saying:

"Whatever comes out of these gates...we've got a better chance of survival if we work together. Do you understand? If we stay together, we survive. Stay close! Come together! Lock your shields! Stay as one!"

And all the while their enemy is speaking to them, shouting in their ears:

"Kill! Kill! Kill! - Soon all your men will be slain.- You don't have a chance!"

If there ever was a more better picture for absolute necessity of the unity of the local church as it comes against the gates of hell and of the terrible fear and discouragement, that our enemy pours into our hearts through our alert and open ears, then it is this! We survive when we stick close together.

Hebrews 10:23-25

"Let us hold fast the confession of our hope without wavering, for He who promised is faithful. And let us consider one another in order to stir up love and good works, not forsaking the assembling of ourselves together, as is the manner of some, but exhorting one another, and so much the more as you see the Day approaching." NKJV.

My thoughts for your consideration tonight then are very simple. You must lock your shields with your brethren, stay close and stay as one. You see, a sticky church is not one that applies assimilation principles to keep the back exit as small as possible, no, a sticky church is a church that is storming the gates of hell and where its blood bought soldiers have been taught how to fight. Did you get that, they have been taught how to fight and not throw tea parties and they also know, that if they do not stick close together in that fight against the enemy, lock shields, hold the line and stay as one, that they will be isolated and killed. Amidst all the managerial hype in the Christian marketplace, please remember that a sticky church is a fighting church. Don't forget that. Don't lose sight of that! For if you do, it just might cost you your life. Stick together in the fight.

Listen: "I do not pray for these alone, but also for those who will believe in Me through their word; that they all may be one, as You, Father, are in Me, and I in You; that they also may be one in Us, that the world may believe that You sent Me. And the glory which You gave Me I have given them, that they may be one just as We are one: I in them, and You in Me; that they may be made perfect in one, and that the world may know that You have sent Me, and have loved them as You have loved Me." (John 17:20-23 NKJV)

Pray: Deliver is from that prowling lion that great red dragon waiting to eat us up. Give us O Lord, sticky fear, sticky wisdom and good shepherds, to glue us all together in Jesus name I pray amen.

Night-Whisper | **THINK**

Of men and mind control – 'What me, worry?'

In a large amount of charismatic Christendom, we seem to live in an age where thinking is paramount to heresy. Indeed, any verbalised thought, any questionable comment regarding the content, style and direction of another man's ministry, movement or even their maniacal machinations, is often branded by enraptured onlookers, as a direct rebellion against a move of God and such a questioning rebellion, may according to the enraptured, even emanate from the pit of hell itself! That strange condemnation of those rightly questioning folk is course a load of old hoohah. In addition to that, the manifestations and actions which people with just a little common sense are questioning is also more than likely a load of old hoohah!

2 Timothy 2:14-16

"Of these things put them in remembrance, charging them before the Lord that they strive not about words to no profit, but to the subverting of the hearers.15 Study to shew thyself approved unto God, a workman that needeth not to be ashamed, rightly dividing the word of truth. But shun profane and vain babblings: for they will increase unto more ungodliness." KJV.

It was New York Jew, Harvey Kurtzman, (who by the way, *The New York Times* refers to as one of the most important figures in post-war America) who introduced the term hoohah into the vocabulary genre of those most famous of *Mad Magazine* characters which he created. No one really knows the origin of the word hoohah, but it may be come from the Hungarian word for "wow"! Or more likely, it is simply a mix of Yiddish and European languages placed into the mouths of *Mad Magazine* characters in what was always an insane and sometimes very funny satire of American life. Hoohah, then, was brought into the vernacular being by the *Mad Magazine* editors and has come to mean a big commotion, a "to do", or a large amount of nonsense!

Clear moves of God fulfil the Scriptures and in no way whatsoever are contrary to them. Clear moves of God, both honour and lift Jesus high. Clear moves of God are unstoppable. Anything else is simply a big commotion, a to-do, and a large amount of nonsense. Hoohah! Let's have the courage and the Scriptural rootedness to call it like it is, for I tell you this for nothing, as we speed toward the time of the end, the incidence of old hoohah shall be dramatically on the increase and it's deception shall be shockingly powerful.

Learn to shout load with me please then, are you ready? "Hoohah!"

Listen: "Then if anyone says to you, 'Look, here is the Christ!' or 'There!' do not believe it. For false christs and false prophets will rise and show great signs and wonders to deceive, if possible, even the elect. See, I have told you beforehand." (Matthew 24:23-25 NKJV)

Pray: Lord, I have a simple and two fold prayer tonight, that first we might not be those that mock mysteries and second that the word hoohah would turn our very breath into the deadly and devastating, destruction of all deception, in Jesus name I ask it, amen.

Night-Whisper | **OBEY**

The unequivocal affirmation of the heart – hooah!

"Hooah" is of course completely different in meaning to "hoohah", the latter referring to a large amount of pointless commotion and the former to a certain and most definite doing, or if you will, an unequivocal affirmation of the heart.

Matthew 21:28-31

"But what do you think? A man had two sons, and he came to the first and said, 'Son, go, work today in my vineyard.' He answered and said, 'I will not,' but afterward he regretted it and went. Then he came to the second and said likewise. And he answered and said, 'I go, sir,' but he did not go." NKJV

The word "hooah" is commonly associated with the United States Army, the actor Al Pacino in the film *Scent of a Woman* most thoroughly exemplifying its most affirmative use. Investigation into the etymology of the word hooah and its derivatives in the other branches of the US armed forces are all quite interesting, indeed, the word is also associated with the armed forces of other nations as well. Even in deepest history, yes, from Mongol armies to British Redcoats, "hooah" is rooted in the cry of "huzza" and "hurray". Yes, the word hooah is a word found to be in use throughout history, even from the secular to even sacred!

However, one of my favourite linkages, is that the word hooah could refer to a three-letter abbreviation, that being, HUA, which of course means someone who has their Head Up their, well, we'll call it their rear end! In other words, HUA, or hooah is a negative affirmation, a comical and military acceptance of any order! Which in effect says: "HUA! You've got to be kidding me sir, I think you have your head up your rear end, but I'll do it anyway".

In summary then, the response of hooah to any given order by a superior, is that no matter how seemingly ludicrous the command, or outrageously costly the carrying out of it, "Hooah! It shall be done." I like that.

Indeed, our text for tonight could be summarized under that one single word, hooah! Jesus commends to us two things here. Up to Matthew 21:32, Jesus first of all commends and makes note of the immediate received forgiveness of what might be considered the worst of sinners, who, in their desperation and joy are seemingly taking the Kingdom of God by storm! In turn, their lives and communities, families and relationships are all being redeemed and being changed. This living redemption was impacting society in the most visible of ways; indeed, the veracity of this repentance as seen in the outworking of such redemption, was absolutely undeniable! Even so and most condemningly so, despite such certain signs of the power of the Gospel among their own communities, there was still no hooah from the religiously reluctant; yes, there was still no turning redemption in the religious far right of the day. In this parable then, secondly, Jesus is once again calling the religious to repentance, trying to get them to say, *"Hooah! We might not have obeyed you at first but based on all that we see, we shall at the last now obey thee ------ Hooah!"*

> *Some of you who have publicly had "yes" on your lips but have lived out a "no" in your hearts and lives.*

Some of you who have publicly had "yes" on your lips but have lived out a "no" in your hearts and lives, need to most thoroughly repent of this cowardly and deceitful sin. Yes, some of you disobedient children need to begin to say "hooah" tonight. Get to it now! HOOAH!

Listen: "'Which of the two did the will of his father?' They said to Him, 'The first.' Jesus said to them, 'Assuredly, I say to you that tax collectors and harlots enter the kingdom of God before you. For John came to you in the way of righteousness, and you did not believe him; but tax collectors and harlots believed him; and when you saw it, you did not afterward relent and believe him.'" (Matthew 21:31-32 NKJV)

Pray: O great heart seer, O overseer of our souls, have mercy on the denials of our outworked lives and come encourage and promote, come praise and reward all those affirmations of our hearts, so that in the end, we ourselves with all Your help will put to shame all the initial offences of our most disobedient of lips and legs. In Jesus name we ask it, amen.

Night-Whisper | **PURSUE**

Nothing great is easy

"As we stood face to face I compared the fine handsome sailor I had first met with the broken-spirited and terribly altered appearance of the man who now courted death in the whirlpool rapids. His object was not suicide but money and imperishable fame." So was the comment of Mr. Robert Watson regarding his long time friend, Captain Matthew Webb, who was soon to die in the Whirlpool below Niagara Falls, as he pursued his $24,000 swimming attempt at fame and fortune.

1 Timothy 6:10

"For the love of money is a root of all kinds of evil, for which some have strayed from the faith in their greediness, and pierced themselves through with many sorrows." NKJV

It was today in 1875 that Captain Webb became the first person to swim the English Channel. Covered in porpoise oil, beginning at Dover he appeared out of the waves some 21 hours and 45 minutes later, wading ashore at Calais. From this point on Webb became a legend in his own lifetime. The winning of other worldwide professional swimming races, coupled with extensive foreign lecture tours, brought in both the kudos and the cash this other Shropshire lad so evidently craved.

No doubt, being almost assuredly aware of this grim attempt of his at Niagara Falls, he was heard to say to himself, *"If I die, they will take care of my wife."* Die he did and they found Webb's body way downstream, some four days after the start of his ill-fated swim. His head had been smashed by the raging whirlpool current into the jagged rocks below the surface. Webb had pierced himself and his family through with many sorrows.

Captain Webb's personal motto was "Nothing Great is Easy." How true, yet this legend's focus was in fact rooted in the passing greatness of worldly fame and fortune and when these two seas come together in any man's heart friend, they will rip his hull in two. Our text for this evening says that the love of money and all its associated fortunes and fame is like impaling yourself on a roasting spit and torturing your own soul in all its attending, like licking flames. So we glean from our text tonight, that such a double death pursuance, is indicative of a shooting star grossly off its course and destined for adverse grief, for severe and piercing, pounding and penetrating sorrow! Interestingly enough this same Greek word for "piercing" is translated as "falling" in *Acts 27:41,* where we read. "And 'falling' into a place where two seas met, they ran the ship aground; and the forepart stuck fast, and remained unmovable, but the hinder part was broken with the violence of the waves." What a picture for tonight, regarding the pursuit of fortune and fame, regarding the pursuit and love of money. "Doing this," says the Scriptures, "is like swimming through a whirlpool of pounding seas, it is like impaling yourself upon jagged destruction, it is an eventual drowning in grief, it is the imploding of your life, leaving it like broken and washed up wreckage on the shores of your epitaph."

> *The possibility of deserting Christ and His call, of seeking my financial security rather than His Kingdom grows stronger in me with each passing day.*

Now the Bible could not be any clearer on the destructive and deathly results of the final outcome of this love of money and this pursuit of all the confidence and comfort of this world's goods. Nevertheless, I tell you friends, the older I get and the less I have of money and of worldly security, the stronger becomes the desperate pull of this mad pursuance. The more I see my contemporaries seemingly settled and safe, then the more this measuring madness rises up within me. The possibility of deserting Christ and His call, of seeking my financial security rather than His Kingdom grows stronger in me with each passing day.

It is easier as a young man to be sold out to Christ, when the seeming safety of time yet to pass, allows the possibility of there to be yet some gathering in. Ah, but when time passes and all the planting seasons with it, when others' crops are gathered in before your watching eyes, it is hard then not to sell out Christ and it is easy to bear the sad and now pale and poxy face, of a once strong faith now gone. "As we stood face to face I compared the fine handsome sailor I had first met with the broken-spirited and terribly altered appearance of the man who now courted death in the whirlpool rapids. His object was not suicide but money and imperishable fame."

As we get older the call of Christ must get louder. As we get older the pull of His kingdom must get stronger, as we get older the focus of our eyes must get more laser-like and then, like old war horses, we must be blinkered in the slips so that no distraction should take our feet from the sure path we have been walking on for so long.

Where is your focus tonight, young person? Where is your focus tonight old man? Do you hear the rush of water and the pounding of waves, are you in the thrashing middle of the crush of two seas clapping their salty hands around your ears? Remember, "Nothing Great is Easy", but consider and consider well, just what it is, that is God's considered greatness!

Listen: "But you, O man of God, flee these things and pursue righteousness, godliness, faith, love, patience, gentleness. Fight the good fight of faith, lay hold on eternal life, to which you were also called and have confessed the good confession in the presence of many witnesses. I urge you in the sight of God who gives life to all things, and before Christ Jesus who witnessed the good confession before Pontius Pilate, that you keep this commandment without spot, blameless until our Lord Jesus Christ's appearing, which He will manifest in His own time, He who is the blessed and only Potentate, the King of kings and Lord of lords, who alone has immortality, dwelling in unapproachable light, whom no man has seen or can see, to whom be honour and everlasting power. Amen." 1 Timothy 6:11-16

Pray: Lord, some of us tonight are desperate enough to throw ourselves under Niagara Falls. Lord some of us tonight have thoroughly lost our focus. Would You please once again throw into our lives that ever buoyant promise, of seeking first Your kingdom and with it, the promise of the addition of all things necessary for this life and this calling of Yours on ours. Help us tonight Lord to get that ring of rescue around our waist and underneath our armpits, then will You lift us safely from these raging torrents and deliver us safe to Your most settled shores of goodness, we pray this in Jesus name, amen!

| Vol | 01 | Q3 | NW00239 | August 26th |

Night-Whisper | **REVEAL**

The man whom Jesus let die

Joseph referred to by the angel Gabriel as the son of David, gave to Jesus the Son of God, all the adoptive rights that a father could legally give. This same Jesus, then became the son of David through the adoptive declarations of Joseph. This primary declaration of Joseph is clearly seen in the enormous action of faith, when he took the divinely pregnant and virgin Mary to be his wife. Colin Kerr in the *International Standard Bible Encyclopedia*, writes concerning Joseph that, *"If a type is to be sought in the character of Joseph, it is that of a simple, honest, hard-working, God-fearing man, who was possessed of large sympathies and a warm heart."*

Matthew 1:18-21

"Now the birth of Jesus Christ was as follows: After His mother Mary was betrothed to Joseph, before they came together, she was found with child of the Holy Spirit. Then Joseph her husband, being a just man, and not wanting to make her a public example, was minded to put her away secretly. But while he thought about these things, behold, an angel of the Lord appeared to him in a dream, saying, 'Joseph, son of David, do not be afraid to take to you Mary your wife, for that which is conceived in her is of the Holy Spirit. And she will bring forth a Son, and you shall call His name Jesus, for He will save His people from their sins.'" NKJV

"Joseph the Just" was so honoured by heaven that he is the three-time recipient of direct revelation from God. Yes indeed, Joseph the Just was an honourable and magnificent man of faith to marry Mary in the midst of all the then and no doubt continued gossip regarding the origins of Jesus. The Holy family lived their lives under a cloud of suspicion regarding the faithfulness of Mary and the probable illegitimacy of Jesus. Origen suggests that this was to purposely throw the Devil off the trail of the incarnation of the promised Redeemer, for who would imagine the Word made flesh living and being brought up under such a cloud of suspicion? Yet He was, and Joseph the Just bore the brunt of all the under-the-breath suspicions. Make no mistake about it, Joseph the Just was an enormous man of faith, a pious man, a providing man, a precious man to Mary and to all the other children later born to them through her.

The best of men may follow the greatest of Divine purposes in faithfulness, quietness, piety and pain.

No doubt Joseph was also an older man and therefore in the scheme of this fallen world, was destined to depart its shores before the younger Mary. We know for a fact that Joseph was around as a faithful provider and practicing Jew when Jesus was aged twelve but it is evident that Joseph is no longer around when Jesus begins His public ministry when then aged thirty. Sometime then, in those intervening eighteen years, Joseph the Just died in the arms of Mary and no doubt in both the face and the presence of Jesus. Think about that. Why did "Jesus the Good" let this bad thing happen to Joseph the Just in His family, in His Holy family?

My very strong suggestion is that because a time was coming when Jesus would publicly begin revealing but one Father, His true Father, His heavenly Father to the world. Then there could be no doubt whatsoever, that this revealing and proclamation made no reference whatsoever to an earthly father. At this point, not only would the mystery and all the gossip regarding the conception of Jesus add to the veracity of His heavenly claim but the long absence of Joseph from his earthly life, would remove all possible pointers to an earthly father and so clearly indicate our Lord's proclamation to be but of His one, true and heavenly genealogy. This was the plan, this was the purpose and in light of that, despite the grief and despite the pain, despite the loss to other loving children and to the loving arms of Mary, Joseph the Just just had to go.

The best of men may follow the greatest of Divine purposes in faithfulness, quietness, piety and pain. Yet for whatever reason, should their continuance eclipse the revelation of the Father from heaven, then they shall be removed from the earthly scene. To that end, Jesus let this just man die.

I am sure that I am wrong but I wonder if in heaven there shall be special gated communities, where adjacent to the fields of gold in the private gardens of God Himself, quiet, unheard of and quickly forgotten folk, magnificent men like Joseph, shall reside in such an honoured and well loved bliss, that we well blustered and noisy disciples, could never enter in? I am sure I am wrong concerning this but I am sure you also get my point.

Tonight, this will come as a shock too many of you I know but your life, disciple of Christ, is not about you! The purpose of your life is to reveal the Son and so in turn, to reveal the Father. If you need to die to do this better, then friend, you simply need to die.

He who has ears to hear, let him hear!

Listen: "All things have been delivered to Me by My Father, and no one knows who the Son is except the Father, and who the Father is except the Son, and the one to whom the Son wills to reveal Him." Luke 10:22 NKJV

Pray: Father by Your grace You have separated me from my mother's womb and brought me into this world of Yours. Now Father, reveal Your Son in me, that I might preach Him amongst the Gentiles and amongst the Jews. I pray that in me, both He and You would increase and that I might decrease. I know this is a hard thing I ask O Lord, yet Father, make it so. Yes, amen, and make it so.

Night-Whisper | **PERSEVERE**

UB40

I was watching TV last night and saw them again and wondered if they shall indeed go down in history as one of the great white reggae bands? UB40 was formed in 1979 out of $8000 dollars damages which the lead singer received from an under-aged bar fight he was involved in. The band advertised their presence in the city of Birmingham before they ever had or could play any instruments! Interesting eh! Oh and by the way, at the time of their formation they were all claiming unemployment benefit.

Actually, UB40 was the number and name of an unemployment benefit claim form. (Unemployment Benefit Form 40) Whenever you signed on as being unemployed but available for work, you would fill in a UB40 and then of course, you would be entitled to unemployment benefit, job seekers allowance, indeed, whatever the financial support was then called, together with all the other personal and family social security benefits.

For those who cannot work, either through lack of fitness, lack of training, or simply lack of work availability, this quite frankly phenomenal national provision of finances for food and clothing formed in the United Kingdom after the Second World War, has been the physical salvation of many folk. For those who will not work through laziness through

2 Thessalonians 3:6-11

"But we command you, brethren, in the name of our Lord Jesus Christ, that you withdraw from every brother who walks disorderly and not according to the tradition which he received from us. For you yourselves know how you ought to follow us, for we were not disorderly among you; nor did we eat anyone's bread free of charge, but worked with labour and toil night and day, that we might not be a burden to any of you, not because we do not have authority, but to make ourselves an example of how you should follow us. For even when we were with you, we commanded you this: If anyone will not work, neither shall he eat."
NKJV

indolence, or through theft, it has proven to be a curse to them and a burden to the nation as a whole. For there is a *great* difference between those who cannot work and those who will not work and it is to that difference that our text speaks this evening. There are three things I need to say here.

The first is for those folk who are immediately grieved on their heart on reading these words. You may have been unemployed for some time and you may feel yourself hopelessly unemployable. The morning brings for you nothing but dark clouds, for you daily see others rise from their beds and get off to their profitable labour while you drag yourself from yours to try and make it through another day of disappointment and rejection. The words in our text for today are not for you. I can only speak from what I am and what I am is a man, and I tell you tonight, there is no greater weight on the spirit of a man than for him not to be able to earn his own bread. Real men when jobless, especially over long periods of time, become sick at heart and sick in the head. There is only one answer for such men and that is that they are afforded the opportunity of profitable labour! Until then, if this is you, you must on the morrow count your search for work as a full time job in itself and one of the hardest jobs you shall ever undertake. I say again tonight, looking for a job is a full time job and one of the hardest on the planet. In this you are to be most commended. Keep at it friend, keep at it my brother, my sister. No, this text is not for you tonight.

> *If you have every intention of not using the system to assist you in finding employment, but rather abusing the system of your nation's provision with all intention of taking and no intention of making an effort to gain employment, then you are a thief.*

The second thing that needs to be said is that if you have every intention of not using the system to assist you in finding employment, but rather abusing the system of your nation's provision with all intention of taking and no intention of making an effort to gain employment, then you are a thief. You should be allowed to go hungry and your hunger should force you to change your lackadaisical ways. This is tough, but it is tough love, for I tell you that a nation of skivers have no honour in themselves and brings no honour to their community or their nation. Such a people brings nothing to the table, such people bring nothing to any table! Such a people leave others hungry but really should themselves be left to go hungry. These are very hard but very necessary words.

The third and most important thing I must say is addressed in particular to the religious worker and those disorderly religious workers in particular, those religious workers who are in fact, out of order! Before I continue, let me say right now that my experience of religious workers, those labouring in preaching teaching and planting, has been to see them and their families mostly over worked! Indeed, my experience has been that most religious workers over exert themselves in their calling to the detriment of their own body soul and spirit. On the whole, I have seen them work like mad monkeys and get paid in just the same kind of monkey currency, *peanuts*! However, there are those religious workers who quite frankly are fleecing the people of God in both their laziness and their trickiness. They are soldiers out of rank, exhibiting such slackness in their marching, that they have become disrupters of the rest of the rank and file. These people are clearly seen, in that they are nothing short of meddlers, busybodies, bustlers and hustlers, always sticking their spoon in someone else's cup, always telling others how to buy and sell, what to do and where to go and how to do it when they get there! They are to be seen always busying themselves in trifling and in the end, useless matters. Avoid such "religious workers" and make sure you do not support their financially philandering lifestyles.

> *To the religious worker the Word of God is especially clear, be orderly in your work, and may I say that means, be accountable!*

In closing may I suggest that religious workers need three levels of accountability. First of all to God, secondly to themselves and thirdly and probably most importantly, to points of reference, points of accountability, points of safety, points outside of themselves. To the religious worker the Word of God is especially clear, be orderly in your work, and may I say that means, be accountable!

Listen: "For we hear that there are some who walk among you in a disorderly manner, not working at all, but are busybodies. Now those who are such we command and exhort through our Lord Jesus Christ that they work in quietness and eat their own bread. But as for you, brethren, do not grow weary in doing good. And if anyone does not obey our word in this epistle, note that person and do not keep company with him, that he may be ashamed. Yet do not count him as an enemy, but admonish him as a brother." 2 Thessalonians 3:11-15

Pray: Lord, bless your workers. Lord bless those folk who are robbing other churches to do the work You have directed them to do in the hard places of the world. Lord please provide for all Your workers, remove the muzzle from the Oxen and give them their daily bread. Lord, bless those without profitable labor tonight and grant them hope in the morning, grant them a mighty perseverance and with that, a real prosperity that follows hard on its heels. Lord please provide for and reward, both all your workers and all those that seek to work, in Jesus name we pray this together, Amen!

| Vol | 01 | Q3 | NW00241 | August 28ᵗʰ |

Night-Whisper | **COURAGE**

Bight me!

A long, long time ago, one of my first torturous petty officers in the Royal Navy, was proud to have served on an old Leander Class Frigate called HMS Naiad. We knew he was proud of this because he wouldn't shut up speaking about, prefixing each dreadful diatribe of his with, *"When I was on the Naiad...yadi yadi yada."* Good grief, I can still hear him now, droning on and ever on.

1 Samuel 14:6 & 12-14
"Then Jonathan said to the young man who bore his armour, 'Come, let us go over to the garrison of these uncircumcised; it may be that the Lord will work for us. For nothing restrains the Lord from saving by many or by few.'---------Jonathan said to his armourbearer, 'Come up after me, for the Lord has delivered them into the hand of Israel.' And Jonathan climbed up on his hands and knees with his armorbearer after him; and they fell before Jonathan. And as he came after him, his armourbearer killed them. That first slaughter which Jonathan and his armourbearer made was about twenty men within about half an acre of land."
NKJV

In those seeming golden olden days, all of the naming of ships within Her Majesty's Navy, must have been done by someone with an Oxbridge classical education for Leander of course, was the name of a man rooted in Greek mythology, who himself drowned in the sea whilst swimming across deep waters to make love to his beloved Hero. It was this same Hero who that particular and very stormy night, had allowed the wailing wind to blow her guiding night light out. You have to watch those Greek women, that's for sure, for they are most unreliable, especially those chaste virgin nymphs, of which the Naiads of course, were nymphs associated with water. One such water nymph was called Arethusa!

You need to hear Richard Burton reading Dylan Thomas's "Under Milk Wood" to appreciate the smooth sound and subtle silkiness of a Welsh man pronouncing the name of a ship called the Arethusa, rolling those heavy Rrrrs, like the waves of the salty sea, riding high upon a sandy, crescent mooned shoreline. Such a crescent shaped shoreline is referred to as a Bight and today in 1914, the first naval battle of the Great War was fought off the German coastline along the Heligoland Bight.

It was Commodore Reginald Tyrwhill on HMS Arethusa, who led the small formation of warships that struck into the heart of the German Navy, who also later in the battle, with the arrival of larger cruisers, inflicted one hundred times as many dead upon the enemy as themselves and sank several ships.

The First Sea Lord of the admiralty at that time, a one Mr Winston Churchill, later observed regarding the daring attack that, "All the Germans saw was that the British did not hesitate to hazard their greatest vessels as well as their light craft in the most daring offensive action and had escaped apparently unscathed. They felt as we should have felt had German destroyers broken into the Solent and their battle cruisers penetrated as far as the Nab. The results of this action were far-reaching. Henceforward, the weight of British Naval prestige lay heavy across all German sea enterprise. The German Navy was indeed 'muzzled.' Except for furtive movements by individual submarines and minelayers, not a dog stirred from August till November that year."

> *God demands of all Jonathans, of all lovers and best friends of Jesus, that in the face of overwhelming odds, they nevertheless have the faith and courage to strike into the very heart of enemy territory, knowing that their blow is indeed backed by all the forces of the First Sea Lord of heaven and earth, The Great God Almighty Himself!*

In our Bible text for this evening, there is no doubt that Jonathan, so lightly armed and in the face of such overwhelming Philistine forces, sailed like the Arethusa right into the heart of enemy territory, and like the Arethusa, Jonathan and his armour bearer were not alone in their endeavour but very heavily supported, by the weight of unseen sailing forces, speedily steaming to their rescue and the real cause of Jonathan and his armour bearer's most astonishing victory!

God demands of all Jonathans, of all lovers and best friends of Jesus, that in the face of overwhelming odds, they nevertheless have the faith and courage to strike into the very heart of enemy territory, knowing that their blow is indeed backed by all the forces of the First Sea Lord of heaven and earth, The Great God Almighty Himself!

So I say to you tonight O Jonathan of God, *"Love Jesus! Give him your all, fight for Him and in the face of seeming overwhelming odds, dare to do great things for Him, for no other King is worth hazarding your very life for. Give your life for Him! For He gave His life for you."*

Listen: "And there was trembling in the camp, in the field, and among all the people. The garrison and the raiders also trembled; and the earth quaked, so that it was a very great trembling. Now the watchmen of Saul in Gibeah of Benjamin looked, and there was the multitude, melting away; and they went here and there." 1 Samuel 14:15-17 NKJV

Pray: Lord, help me be like Jonathan of old; a man who out of great love, is willing to hazard his life for the land he is from, the people he has been joined to and the good God he now serves, in Jesus name I pray, Amen!

Night-Whisper | **NEW**

Driven by the demonic

I remember listening to two missionaries who had worked for many years amongst tribal people, recount their experiences of occult and paranormal practices amongst those same poor people. The missionary of a more practical character and nature, pooh-poohed both the occult ideas and experiences of the tribal people he worked amongst and the other, more poetical and mystical in his character and experience, validated the presence, practice and product of occult magic amongst tribal people. Some ignorant and nasty stuff is a-carried on amongst ignorant tribal people you know!

Now for tonight, it does not matter witch side of the fence you come down on (no that's not a spelling mistake) for I would like to focus not so much on the validity or otherwise of the observations of these two missionaries but rather, how we as fallen human beings respond to the practice and seeming evidence of occult paranormal activity amongst us. This is important, for in the 21st century, it is now reported that Papua New Guinean tribal folk are in fact burying alive people who are HIV infected AIDS victims! Why is this happening and does it have any bearing on us civilised and not

Revelation 18:2-6

"And he cried mightily with a loud voice, saying, 'Babylon the great is fallen, is fallen, and has become a dwelling place of demons, a prison for every foul spirit, and a cage for every unclean and hated bird! 3 For all the nations have drunk of the wine of the wrath of her fornication, the kings of the earth have committed fornication with her, and the merchants of the earth have become rich through the abundance of her luxury.' And I heard another voice from heaven saying, 'Come out of her, my people, lest you share in her sins, and lest you receive of her plagues. For her sins have reached to heaven, and God has remembered her iniquities.'" NKJV

demonised by occult practice, people of the West!?

May I suggest three reasons why we these poor and ignorant demonised folk are burying their problems?

The first is that occult practices always flourish in ignorance. Ignorance of the facts, ignorance of science and ignorance of God's Fatherly goodness. Don't be a dummy in avoiding the facts of any matter. Don't be a stupid witch. Don't be a silly shaman. Don't be ignorant of the facts! If you are burying people alive then you are obviously under the sway of a terrible darkness. In the West of course we would never do that, we are far more civilised and wise and this is clearly seen in the way we treat our young; cutting out the backs of their live little necks and sucking the brains out of all those small and unwanted little babies, or soaking them in salt, or vacuuming them alive out of their mummies womb in tiny little pieces, then incinerating them or…well, you get the picture. Thank goodness that it is only those crazy Papua New Guinean tribal folk that are under the sway of dark occult like practices!

> *Occult practices always flourish in ignorance. Ignorance of the facts, ignorance of science and ignorance of God's Fatherly goodness.*

The second reason we bury our problems alive, is that the human heart needs help, even those hearts ignited in the fiery compassion of God, need help. For without blowing provision on the flickering of goodness, any hope that flourishes like a flame amongst humans can be so easily extinguished. Humans need help! The help of education, the help of administration, the help of provision, the help of rest, the help of finances, the help of comfort, even the help of chastisement and correction, for without help, hope so easily dies in the human heart and the icy cold hopelessness that death leaves behind, then makes room for a dreadful occult darkness to arise. Thank goodness we have hope in the West! Where no mentally ill person sleeps under a bridge, where no child is left behind, where cities sunk beneath the waves are not abandoned, where the suicide rate is virtually non-existent in all our young men, who all have the certain hope of good futures with excellent jobs and no access to mind numbing life devouring all addictive drugs! Thank goodness we have hope in the West and are not under the influence of any occult like practice of deception.

The third and most terrible reason we bury our problems alive is that we are essentially, the most evil of creatures. When hopelessness stalks the land, when all the faces of the goodness of God are eclipsed, then we humans crawl like rancid head lice amongst the matted darkness. We refuse to see how evil we truly are. Left to ourselves, I say again, left to ourselves, we would utterly consume one another, for the profound propensity of the human heart to propel itself towards the icy depths of a deep darkness is absolutely shocking! Yes, when left to ourselves, occultism rises and our response is mostly cannibalistic.

However, thank goodness! That is not us in the West! Thank goodness that we do not need guns in America and thousands of rounds of ammunition to keep us safe at night! Thank goodness our children can play out in the street and be mentored and guided, cared for and cuddled, by all the wiser and watchful older folk. Thank goodness we can trust our elected officials, thank goodness we don't need medical insurance and that our doctors don't need malpractice insurance. Thank goodness we only put the best of nutrition into our bodies and the most wholesome of information into our minds. Thank goodness I say, that here in the West, when left to ourselves, only the very best is made manifest! Good grief, the crown jewel of the New Orleans sky line, the Louisiana superdome itself, is testimony to that one sure fact that in the West the best is made most manifest. Thank goodness we are not under the influence of any dark occult practice.

> *The terrible truth is that ignorance, lack of help to fan the flame of any hope into practical goodness and our terrible, evil hearts, sitting like self serving kings at the centre of our own universe, are all manifestations of occult like influences and practices.*

The terrible truth is that ignorance, lack of help to fan the flame of any hope into practical goodness and our terrible, evil hearts, sitting like self serving kings at the centre of our own universe, are all manifestations of occult like influences and practices. Under such occult like sway, the outworking of sin, which is the preservation of self at any cost and at any price, is evidently manifest among us all and clearly seen when we bury all our problems and devour our young alive!

The truth is, we are all being consumed by occult like influence and devilish practices. God help us all, for without Him, without Him implanting new hearts within us and those same new hearts, sucking in the air of His hope and breathing out the practicalities of His goodness, we as humanity are well and truly finished!

This new heart transplant is the essence of the good news about Jesus Christ and this is the message that we purveyors of salt and light, should be preaching to those willing to hear. I say willing to hear, for many do not want to listen. We twice blinded, imbecilic barefaced baboon like bombastic self congratulating deceivers of our own true selves, are not willing to hear, not willing to consider our own evil, for we are under the influence of such occult like manipulation that even in the face of such barbed and brutal evidence, we still believe that humans are essentially, good!

In Papua New Guinea it is reported that ignorant people consumed by darkness are burying their problems alive. Thank goodness that's not me. Thank goodness that's not you. Thank goodness, that's not us!

Listen: *"Finally, my brethren, be strong in the Lord and in the power of His might. Put on the whole armor of God, that you may be able to stand against the wiles of the devil. For we do not wrestle against flesh and blood, but against principalities, against powers, against the rulers of the darkness of this age, against spiritual hosts of wickedness in the heavenly places. Therefore take up the whole armor of God, that you may be able to withstand in the evil day, and having done all, to stand." Ephesians 6:10-13 NKJV*

Pray: Our Father in heaven, hallowed be Your name. Your kingdom come. Your will be done on earth as it is in heaven. Give us this day our daily bread and forgive us our debts, as we forgive our debtors. And do not lead us into temptation, but deliver us from the evil one. For Yours is the kingdom and the power and the glory forever. Amen. (Matthew 6:9-13 NKJV)

| Vol | 01 | Q3 | NW00243 | August 30th |

Night-Whisper | **RETURN**

Let's face the music and dance

These past few years of my sojourn here, I have walked the road with not a few long-time Christians who have lately proclaimed that, *"I don't know if I have ever truly believed?"* or, *"I don't know anymore about the reality and truth of Christianity,"* and often, *"You know Robert, I have lost God and so much so, I wonder if I ever had Him."* It's quite a concern don't you think?

Deuteronomy 6:5

"You shall love the Lord your God with all your heart, with all your soul, and with all your strength." NKJV

Whenever this is said out loud, it is usually by people who have an overwhelming tiredness about them. Whenever this is said out loud, it is usually by folks who have an overwhelming sense of a disappointment in God and especially a disappointment in His people, the church. More frighteningly though, is the fact that this is felt by so many people, who have never previously had neither the desperation nor the courage, to vocalise out loud their most definite and inward experience! Let's face it, these proclamations dear friends, are increasingly common.

Let me tell you right now, that whenever I hear that long-time Christians have "stopped believing in God", I do not believe it! In fact their extreme tiredness and disappointment in God, is usually indicative of their continued belief, rather than a contradiction of it, for you do not get disappointed and distraught, you do not get desperate and disillusioned, about someone you had no real investment or value in, or experience of! What's happening here then? Why are so many long standing Christians now seemingly disowning God altogether?

I believe the first reason for disowning God, is that there has often been a low value put on personal experience. There has been a low value put on the emotional content of their faith. I tell you now though, that how you feel about God and how you experience your walk with Him, is so very important! Your experiential relationship with God is absolutely vital to your continued spiritual health! If the Words of the Bible are not received as Spirit words into your experiential soul, then your following unfulfilled and ravening hunger for the experience of God will eat you up! Your unquenched and rapacious thirst for an experiential encounter with God, will leave you as parched and dry as an empty old seed husk, left broken and cavernously open beneath the greenest of trees. To stop this happening, you *must* cultivate an experiential walk with God! The Bible itself will not suffice, for it is only the Bible declared and Bible promised accompanying the manifest presence of God, that is sufficient for life, that is sufficient for love and that is sufficient for the pursuit of happiness.

> *The third reason for the disowning of God, is that the product we are selling will not do the job we are telling!*

The second reason for the disowning of God, has been a failure to maintain our own vineyard. Most of these folks that have uttered these words to me, have been former faithful servants of the most High God. However, they have been sucked dry in the service of God, bashed about, chewed up and spat out like green snot sputum on the grey and gravely ground. No, it's not nice, no, it's not nice at all. It is so easy to become dehydrated in the service of God. It is so easy to compare and to compete with one another in such a fashion, that we just cannot keep up the race, we cannot keep up the pace. These folks are simply and most profoundly burnt out

The third reason for the disowning of God, is that the product we are selling will not do the job we are telling! Yes, we ministers of Christ are sales people. We invite people to come and buy, to taste and see, to turn and learn, to open and invite, to have God make things better for them, better for their health, better for their finances, better for their family, better for their future! However, when the product does not perform in this "better way" in the way in which we have said it would, then the buyers reject it and we the sellers, eventually, get very disappointed in the veracity of the product itself.

The fourth reason for people disowning God, is quite simply sin. I have observed that unrequited love, desperate thirst and harbouring hunger, if not fulfilled righteously, will be fulfilled unrighteously. When people get desperately disappointed dear friends in close relationships that promised so much but gave so little, they feel betrayed, they feel robbed, they feel they have lost out in their righteous restraint, and often their response to these strong feelings, is to break all previous boundaries in trying to have that hunger filled, to have that thirst quenched, to have that sense of so severe a loss, somehow now satisfied. Of course, these my lovely brethren, have simply taken poison to themselves and often locked the door behind them as they left the building of God to die quietly alone. Now, they are more hungrier than they ever imagined, but now they have nowhere to go.

Tonight then, I leave you with five antidotes to a possible future disowning of God. Oh, and don't be arrogant in thinking these things might not happen to you, for I have seen it happen to better men than either me or thee!

> *Is your Gospel working? Check it out and if it is not working, then chuck it out for you've undoubtedly not got the real deal.*

FIRST then, be sure to experience God! You must *feel* your relationship with your Father. The pump of desire must be primed and the circle of satisfaction must be complete. Make sure your emotional life is satisfied in God, is satisfied *with* God. If it isn't, then there may be trouble ahead!

Secondly, take care of yourself, for no one else will! You had better get that brother, no one else will! Take time to rest, take time to recharge, take time to rejuvenate, take time to court Jesus in the courts of the Most High God. Make the most of the moonlight and the music, of the love and the romance. Take time to dance! You need to do this friend, before the fiddlers flee thee.

Thirdly, if the product you are selling is not working, then maybe you've not read the instructions correctly or, you've got the wrong product! Is your Gospel working? Check it out and if it is not working, then chuck it out for you've undoubtedly not got the real deal. Get the real deal! You need to do this before the bill needs paying.

Fourthly, you need to rejoice in the wife of your youth and let her breasts satisfy you at all times. Can the Scripture be any more clearer than this? Make sure you have a passionate relationship with God and that your satisfaction is found fully in Him. This has to happen! If it doesn't, then there maybe teardrops to shed.

Fifthly, recognise that you have the key to your heart and therefore the key to unlock the door of this your heart and to return to God your maker, return to Christ your lover. Dear friend, you have the possibility to re-open the door of your heart to desire! Tell me, if you are desirous of the reality and the fullness of the Father at no matter what the cost, indeed at any cost, do you think that He would be interested in such a proposition?

I tell you, God is always interested in the propositions of your heart! Always!

Listen: "'Remember these, O Jacob, And Israel, for you are My servant; I have formed you, you are My servant; O Israel, you will not be forgotten by Me! I have blotted out, like a thick cloud, your transgressions, And like a cloud, your sins. Return to Me, for I have redeemed you.' Sing, O heavens, for the Lord has done it! Shout, you lower parts of the earth; Break forth into singing, you mountains, O forest, and every tree in it! For the Lord has redeemed Jacob, And glorified Himself in Israel." Isaiah 44:21-23NKJV

Pray: Jesus, when You have fallen in my heart and Your flavour and the scent of Your presence and power have become to me but a rumour on the wind, have mercy upon me and please come knocking upon my doors once more. Jesus, lover of my soul, come and throw stones at my window, get me up from my death bed and ask me to marry You once more. Amen and Amen and Amen.

Night-Whisper | **POWER**

Deep speaking

I remember speaking to another minister whose longstanding friend from high school years was demonised to such an extreme and possessive extent, that you would have called him possessed! In his more lucid moments this same possessed man reported that he knew when other people he met were demonised because that which possessed him, communicated with that which possessed them. In other words, he was aware of the darkness in him communicating with the darkness in them.

John 6:63,64

"It is the Spirit who gives life; the flesh profits nothing. The words that I speak to you are spirit, and they are life." NKJV

Believe it or not, there is a spiritual principle here us children of Light to really get hold of. We as sons and daughters of The Light can and should communicate with all the other children of light. I am not talking about social communication, or what we so glibly refer to as "fellowshipping" with one another! I am talking about three of the most underutilised but powerful modes of communication you could ever use top side of this earth and underside of heaven! I need to tell you as well that there are three levels of life giving power associated with these three modes of life giving communication. Let me start with the latter.

First, the three levels of communication are as follows.

Level one communication is cerebral. It is from one mouth to one ear landing one brain. You might share something from the Word of God, a verse, a text, an insight and it's good, it's powerful and it's right but it's only been fired from the mind through the mouth, into an ear and lodged itself in another person's mind. It easy to deliver at this cerebral level and relatively easy to receive and consider. It's level one communication.

Level two communication is deeper in its source for it is a soulish communication, it is emotional in content and context, it is from one heart to another. The delivery of such communication demands openness on the part of the communicator and some transparency, some authenticity and some vulnerability but its content is received at a felt level and therefore a truly known level and an understood level! This is powerful level two communication level.

Level three communication is the deepest of levels it is guttural in both its delivery and reception, it is spiritual, it is commanding, it is declarative, it is life-changing. It is exceptionally powerful. It is communication at a completely different dimensional level, it is spirit communication, it is deep calling to deep.

Just what level of communication have you been mostly communicating in today? How just how deep can you go?

Level three communication is the deepest of levels it is guttural in both its delivery and reception, it is spiritual, it is commanding, it is declarative, it is life-changing. It is exceptionally powerful. It is communication at a completely different dimensional level, it is spirit communication, it is deep calling to deep.

Now if these are the three levels of communication for the children of light let me now share with you the three modes of communication.

Mode one communication is affirmation. It is right and proper, it is necessary and vital that we all participate in this mode of affirmative communication. This takes the form of acknowledge of who the other person is, their existence, their calling, their gifting, their anointing, their good choices, their right directions. We need to at a guttural level, a deep spiritual level, acknowledge and honour the very being, position, personhood and standing of one another in Christ. Imagine the power of this, imagine the affirmation of personhood and position to other members of the body.

Mode two communication is impartation. It is right and proper, it is necessary and vital that we all participate in this mode of impartative communication. This takes the form of speaking words of power, words of direction changing encouragement, words of wisdom, words of knowledge, words of strength, comfort, love, words that will swallow loneliness and breed a family that stands like an army on which the gates of hell will fall and break in two. Imagine the power of this, imagine the ability to impart all that is necessary to one another to stand victoriously.

Mode three communication is declaration. Not only is it right and proper, is it necessary and vital that we all participate in this mode of declarative communication but Oh God! This is something which is so sorely missing in the church of the modern day. Oh how we need to put into practice the ability to call forth life from the dead, the ability to in faith declare the things that are yet to be seen and experienced in another person's life! Now I am not talking about a God like activity of calling into being the things that are not but rather, calling into the open the things that are hidden, calling into vision those things which have been lost, calling to attention those things which have been ignored, left alone, underutilised, calling onto the field of battle the manifold, life changing, life giving, blessings of the Father toward us in Christ Jesus our Lord, that they might be made manifest and actioned right onto the hearts and into the very spirits of the sons of His love.

> *Now is the time to communicate effectively*

So tell me. How have your communication skills been today dear friend? Tomorrow, I want to challenge you to move into a mode three and level three communication with the other saints. *Now* is the time to let our words change each other, change the world, shape each other, shape the world. Now is the time to communicate effectively.

Listen: "These things we also speak, not in words which man's wisdom teaches but which the Holy Spirit teaches, comparing spiritual things with spiritual. But the natural man does not receive the things of the Spirit of God, for they are foolishness to him; nor can he know them, because they are spiritually discerned. But he who is spiritual judges all things, yet he himself is rightly judged by no one. For 'who has known the mind of the Lord that he may instruct Him?' But we have the mind of Christ." 1 Corinthians 2:13-16 NKJV

Pray: Lord, give me words of power. Lord, give me words of life. Lord, give me words of formation and change, words of resurrection and life, Lord anoint my lips with living words and dancing light, anoint my lips with the sound of many voices, the rush and crash of waterfalls, the solid certainties of Your deep calling unto deep, in Jesus name I pray, Amen!

IT'S TIME TO ORDER YOUR NEXT QUARTER OF....

Night Whispers

& maybe order one for a friend as well!

Check us out at

www.NightWhispers.com

Order at | WWW.TheologyShop.com

------------------------O------------------------

Night-Whispers is authored by Victor Robert Farrell, produced by WhisperingWord Ltd and licensed for the sole use of:

The 66 Books Ministry

A modern day,
Back to the whole Bible,
Boots on The Ground,
Proclamation Movement.

www.66Books.tv

| Vol | 01 | Q3 | NW00245 | September 01ˢᵗ

Night-Whisper | **CONTROL**

Wearing the sheath

"*But Jesus said to him, 'Put your sword in its place...'*" *Matthew 26:52*. Topos! That's the Greek word that is used in this verse from the Gospel according to Matthew, topos! It is a very versatile word, which is translated in many places simply as "place"! The context is quite obvious here in Matthew though and therefore as it refers directly to the place you would store your sword, the obvious inference is that of a "sheath".

Ephesians 4:26-28

"'Be angry, and do not sin': do not let the sun go down on your wrath, nor give place to the devil." NKJV

Over the centuries the body has been referred to by many writers as the "sheath of the soul" or the "sheath of the spirit". The body is but the outward storage space of that which is the truly important. The sheath may be plain or it may be bejeweled, it may be leather, wood or brass or some other substance either of greater or lesser value, the point is that whatever it is made of and however it is outwardly adorned, it is simply irrelevant because it is but the sheath, the protective house of that which is truly important.

Now beginning at our text for tonight, allow me to connect some dots that I think are there! You see, our text for tonight says "do not give place to the devil," "do not give topos to the devil," "do not give 'your sheath' to the devil," "do not give your body, no part of your body, to the devil!" Now I would like to link this use of the word place directly to mean specifically the sheath for the sword, or rather, the body for the soul and spirit. I kind of think that this is a great way for us to view our bodies, as sheaths for our very own double-edged eternal sword of soul and spirit! Are you with me so far? Good!

Now unfortunately we view our sheath as that much more important than our weapon! Yes indeed, in fact we wield the sheath as the weapon, no more than that, we allow the sheath to wield the weapon! Are you getting this? We have it the wrong way around. We should be using the body as our protective servant of the soul and spirit. We should be in control of our sheaths. Indeed I think the Scriptures as a whole clearly say, "Make sure it is only your sword that rests in your sheath. Do not give the devil a foothold, a short-term lease, access, uses, utilization of your sheath or any part of it in any way, for any period of time!"

Tell me, what have you been doing with your sheath today? Who has been using it?

Maybe if we began to view our bodies as simply sheaths for that which is most important, it might help us to take more control of the temporary and apply more honor to the permanent? Your body, your sheath and every and any manifestation of constituent parts, must not be inhabited or polluted by any part of the devil.

Tell me, what have you been doing with your sheath today? Who has been using it?

Listen: "Do you not know that to whom you present yourselves slaves to obey, you are that one's slaves whom you obey, whether of sin leading to death, or of obedience leading to righteousness? But God be thanked that though you were slaves of sin, yet you obeyed from the heart that form of doctrine to which you were delivered. And having been set free from sin, you became slaves of righteousness. I speak in human terms because of the weakness of your flesh. For just as you presented your members as slaves of uncleanness, and of lawlessness leading to more lawlessness, so now present your members as slaves of righteousness for holiness." Romans 6:16-19 NKJV

Pray: Lord, I yield to You my all, O my God come and take full possession of your blood bought purchase. Lord I give you my all, every part of my being, every room and corner of my spiritual house and my sheath like abode. Amen!

| Vol | 01 | Q3 | NW00246 | September 02nd |

Night-Whisper | **CLEAN**

Sun down

Leaping from last night's meditation, allow me take the out-of-context springboard tonight and jump right into Lake Extrapolation will you? Remember in the Gospel according to Matthew it says, "But Jesus said to him, 'Put your sword in its place…'" Matthew 26:52. Yes? Well here we go then, you see Jesus says, very simply, put *your* sword in its sheath. Make sure that it is you that that have your sword in your sheath. Make sure that you are in control of your body. In this rather large lake of Extrapolation, just kick back and swim with me here will you?

Ephesians 4:26-28

"'Be angry, and do not sin': do not let the sun go down on your wrath, nor give place to the devil." NKJV

The problem we all have is at times some of the parts of our sheath get occupied and used by the enemy. The text for tonight is very honest in saying that it's OK to be angry but it's dangerous and especially dangerous to remain so after sundown! Anger is an emotion that rises within us and is often connected to righteous indignation. Indignation in the spirit will cause a rising of anger in the soul. That's OK, but when this happens the sheath is open more than it is safe to be so. Anger that remains in the soul manifests itself in the body. Anger than remains in the soul can and often does turn poisonous even toxic. Anger if not dealt with, if left in the soul causes and occupation of sorts in the body for toxic poison and the eventual presence of darkness. So I believe this verse is saying to us, "Come sundown, deal with anger! Vent it, bleed it, vomit it away! Make peace with the person and or the problem even if this peace between person or problem can only be constructed in the spiritual realm, do it! Empty your sheath, because if you do not, then you will give your sheath to the devil!"

God gives us days to live by. Sufficient for the day is the evil that comes against us and the strength we are given to combat it. God gives us days to live by and twilights of dealing time, and blazing sunsets to incinerate our septic toxins in. God gives us sundowns to do the business of emptying the sheath of all the poisons and possessions of the day.

Most healthy people at the end of the day defecate their waste away. In the same way, we too must emotionally defecate our spiritual waste away. If not, then unhealthiness and all the manifest possessions of darkness will make themselves known in our bodies.

> *Most healthy people at the end of the day defecate their waste away. In the same way, we too must emotionally defecate our spiritual waste away.*

That's something worth considering tonight, and practicing at every future sundown. Let wholeness and light fill our temples. Let our soul and spirit fully fill our sheaths lest we have some squatters move in.

Listen: "When an unclean spirit goes out of a man, he goes through dry places, seeking rest, and finds none. Then he says, 'I will return to my house from which I came.' And when he comes, he finds it empty, swept, and put in order. Then he goes and takes with him seven other spirits more wicked than himself, and they enter and dwell there; and the last state of that man is worse than the first. So shall it also be with this wicked generation." Matthew 12:43-45 NKJV

Pray: Lord tonight with every exhaled breath, I let go of all the hurts of the day. Lord with every exhaled breath, I breath forgiveness on those who have wronged me. Lord, with every inhaled breath I take in your comfort and Your great forgiveness. Thank You Lord! Amen.

| Vol | 01 | Q3 | NW00247 | September 03ʳᵈ |

Night-Whisper | **FOUND**

How far will you go?

T he city of Fargo is situated in Cass county of South Dakota. In 1996, *Fargo* became the title of a Coen brothers film which was in fact filmed totally in Minnesota around their fictional version of the small town of Brainerd, which like a multitude of other small towns in the mid west, also claim to be the birth place or lodging place of the fictional lumberjack of legendary fame, Paul Bunyan and his famous blue Ox, called Babe. That however, is a whole other story, "Yah, you betcha!"

Psalm 119:174-176a

"I long for Your salvation, O Lord, And Your law is my delight. Let my soul live, and it shall praise You; And let Your judgments help me. I have gone astray like a lost sheep; Seek Your servant..." NKJV

Winning the Oscar for best actress in the film *Fargo*, it is the actress Frances McDormand who stars as Marge Gunderson, a seven months pregnant police chief whose affable, folksy demeanour and fantastically dippy dialect, hide an exceptionally smart investigative mind. The film, set in a landscape, like "Siberia with family restaurants" is so strange that that it just has to be fiction! However, *Fargo*, this particular Coen brothers film, backed by a haunting Norwegian fiddle playing a folk number called "The Lost Sheep", does in fact begin its black comedic story line, with these printed words on the screen: "THIS IS A TRUE STORY. The events depicted in this film took place in Minnesota in 1987. At the request of the survivors, the names have been changed. Out of respect for the dead the rest has been told exactly as it occurred."

Of course, none of it is true. I mean none of it! The place, the characters, the events, the kidnappings, the killings, the snow and of course the ransom money, hid and buried in that same white flat, never ending snowy landscape. Yet, five years after the release of the film, Ms Takako Konishi, a young Japanese woman, arrived in the Fargo area and just a few days later , was found dead in the snow.

The inquest declared that a combination of various drugs but predominantly the biting cold, was in all likelihood and most probably, the final cause of her death. Prior to Ms Takako's sad demise, exceptionally poor communication with many people of the area and even the police, led them all to believe that this sad, mad little Japanese woman, was in fact looking for the fictional lost ransom money from the very fictional film, which was left buried in the then, "brought in and even made overnight, just for the film" equally fictional snow! It was three weeks after her death however, that the arrival of her suicide note at her parents house in Takako's home country of Japan, that the real story of a broken-hearted and jilted young woman, arriving in America in search of her married American lover, would also reveal a double intent to either reunite with him or kill herself in the process. Ms Takako came to Fargo with the intent to kill herself.

> *Beware of isolation. Lost sheep, are sheep that have wandered away from the safety of the fold and are open to every cold-hearted and self-destructive lie that the enemy will most definitely throw at them.*

This poor lost little Japanese sheep was culturally, emotionally, psychologically and in every way most exceptionally isolated. Beware of that. Beware of isolation. Lost sheep, are sheep that have wandered away from the safety of the fold and are open to every cold-hearted and self-destructive lie that the enemy will most definitely throw at them. I am of the mind, that all suicide is demonic in its source. The devil methinks, takes great delight in sheep doing away with themselves in front of his gleeful gaze.

Now tonight, if you are plagued with thoughts of worthlessness, feelings of abject loneliness, of utter and stark, snowy landscape covered set Siberian cold, chilled to the very bone hopelessness and thoroughly believe, that it best that you remove yourself from the sad and sorry scene of your own life, then I want to tell you right now, that of a certainty, all you will accomplish, is the giving of pleasure to the macabre and dark vulture-like voyeurism, of the mad monster from hell, the devil himself

No! This shall not happen! For I say to you tonight, in the mighty name of Jesus, that He is the Good Shepherd and He has been out looking for you, Oh lost sheep of His, and as you read these words, *he has found you*! Now, right now, *he has found you*! Now He places your sorry carcass over his broad shoulders and lifts you from your cliff ledge. Now He carries you from your pit. Now He is taking you home and if you listen, you can hear Him singing! You're not singing I know that! You're not supposed to be singing just yet! You will though, yes you will but not yet. Even so, listen to Him! He is singing and He is rejoicing because He is taking you home to be with Him, right where you belong. I am not talking about heaven here, no not yet, I am talking about back home to the fold, back home to the place of His greener pasture, back home to still waters, back home to sunshine vales of love, back home to protection, back home to provision, back home to a the place called Found. You have been *found* tonight not might how far you've gone, not matter how far you go and He is rejoicing over you with singing! Get ready for comforts I say, get ready for caring, get ready for wine and for oil and plenty, plenty party times, for they are coming I tell you, they are coming!

You have been found tonight not might how far you've gone, not matter how far you go and He is rejoicing over you with singing!

To the rest of us, wondering at how sad a person can get to want to take their own life, I say this tonight to you, "Do you know of any lost sheep out there? Out there in the snow, looking for treasure that does not exist? Do you know of any lost sheep out there, out there in the heartbroken wastelands, empty cold and lost? I know you do, I just know you do. So, tomorrow then, you had better go and get them."

Listen: "What man of you, having a hundred sheep, if he loses one of them, does not leave the ninety-nine in the wilderness, and go after the one which is lost until he finds it? And when he has found it, he lays it on his shoulders, rejoicing. And when he comes home, he calls together his friends and neighbours, saying to them, 'Rejoice with me, for I have found my sheep which was lost!' I say to you that likewise there will be more joy in heaven over one sinner who repents than over ninety-nine just persons who need no repentance." Luke 15:4-7 NKJV

Pray: Find it Lord! Find Your lost sheep. Find it Lord, search the cold and lonely wilderness, search behind every rock and search under every sorry, scraggy tree. Find it Lord, ransack the dark ravines, climb the cliffs and trudge the night long dale. Find it Lord, find Your lost sheep and then place it on your shoulders and bring it home rejoicing! Amen.

Night-Whisper | **POMEGRANATE**

Of pictures in a pomegranate

I could lose weight by eating pomegranates. The one I ate today took me a full twenty minutes to get through and in the end, my paper plate looked like some flattened road kill I had just pulled from under the wheel of my car and my red stained and sticky fingers, branded me a murderer whilst my bloody lips and chin proclaimed me to be a cannibal of unquenchable proportions! There were bits of blood and flesh just all over me and all over the table! The opened pomegranate looked good though and my oh my, it tasted even better!

Exodus 39:24-26

"They made on the hem of the robe pomegranates of blue, purple, and scarlet, and of fine woven linen. And they made bells of pure gold, and put the bells between the pomegranates on the hem of the robe all around between the pomegranates: a bell and a pomegranate, a bell and a pomegranate, all around the hem of the robe to minister in, as the Lord had commanded Moses." NKJV

The pomegranate is the fruit of a particular seed-bearing shrub which grows anywhere from five to eight metres tall. The apple-size fruit it produces, contains an abundance of edible pearl white seeds, surrounded by a pellucid blood red juicy pulp. The religious symbolism of this fruit has for centuries been rooted in art, history, medicine, mythology, music and of course the Bible! Tonight, I want to get just a few of its seeds rooted in us!

The Jews say the 613 laws of the Torah are represented by 613 seeds in the pomegranate. Now depending on your variety and size, it could be plus or minus 200 but I like the sound of the symbolism! The twelve seed sacks within the pomegranate, says the Jews, represent the twelve tribes of Israel, the abundance of seeds represent the overwhelming fruitfulness of the promised land, its crown represents the Royal line of King David and so we could go on. My point is that this pomegranate fruit is so exotic and wonderful, so life-giving and delicious, so propitious and effective that it has rightly been utilised as the picture of passion, resurrection, hope, and life giving fruitfulness.

Some say that it was this seeded apple that was in fact the fruit of the tree of life. Some say that it is wine made from the Pomegranate mixed with spices that was used at the last supper and shall be used again at the marriage supper of the lamb. Some say that it is the saints that prepare the wine for the bridegroom and that we shall set the table of the lamb with this gift of marriage wine. I wonder…

You should have learnt by now that in life, nothing good is cheap.

Tomorrow, get yourself a bib and some wet wipes and then go and buy yourself a pomegranate. It will be expensive but it will be worth it. You should have learnt by now that in life, nothing good is cheap. Then turn the TV off and sit down and take some time to undress this most alluring of fruit. Look at it, taste it, then drink it in with faithfulness and some far-sighted vision. See within this one and only, Royal and rich coloured robe of purpled crowned and Kingly fruit, all the pearl bought children of God, set neatly in their place. See them washed pure in His own blood bought red. See the torn flesh, ripped open and removed from the bent barked thorny trees. Yes, "taste and see that the Lord is good."

Tomorrow, may you have pomegranate for your evening meal and may it become to you the antipasto of heaven, a sweet foretaste of what is to come and is even, both fast and fragrant on the midnight breeze.

Listen: *"Oh, that you were like my brother, Who nursed at my mother's breasts! If I should find you outside, I would kiss you; I would not be despised. I would lead you and bring you Into the house of my mother, She who used to instruct me. I would cause you to drink of spiced wine, Of the juice of my pomegranate." Song of Solomon 8:1-2 NKJV*

Pray: Lord, Your priests of old were robed in golden bells and Pomegranates of purple, blue and scarlet. Lord may the sound of my walking before Your Holy throne, be a life proclaiming jingle of joy! Lord may my pillars of firmness and strength before Your Holy face, be crowned with all the colours and shades of purity and fruitfulness and the sweet smell of prepared and expectant love, in Jesus name I pray, Amen.

| Vol | 01 | Q3 | NW00249 | September 05ᵗʰ |

Night-Whisper | **TIME**

The real time Lord

I started this year of writing behind schedule. Many items in my to-do list had begun the year in alarmed and flashing red. It's September now and I have spent the last nine months playing catch up. However, I have failed to catch up. Oh most miserable of men!

You see my friends there are just not enough hours in the day. There is just not enough time to accomplish all that I want to. Motorcycling back to my study this morning from a visit to my chiropractor, I found myself once again musing on the demands of the rest of the day and my lack of time to service those same demands. I wonder if this same seeming lack of time, has left important things undone in your life and the lack of time you know you will encounter tomorrow, is already tying a knot in your tired little bowels tonight? If so, then I pray the next few paragraphs of musings will provide you with some timeless comfort to help you rest a little easier in the arms of the Lord of time.

The longest running science fiction series in the world was created and first aired by the BBC in 1963. *Dr Who* is the story of an eccentric alien from the now destroyed planet of Gallifrey. Dr Who, an on the run Time Lord, wandering through the cosmos fighting injustice wherever he finds it, in a broken time machine which is shaped like a 1950s police telephone box! Suffice to say, that as a child of the 1960s I too joined the many millions who hid behind the sofa during the scary bits of the TV series. A Time Lord in popular folk lore, has been understood then as, "a being who has

Galatians 4:1-5

"Now I say that the heir, as long as he is a child, does not differ at all from a slave, though he is master of all, but is under guardians and stewards until the time appointed by the father. Even so we, when we were children, were in bondage under the elements of the world. But when the fullness of the time had come, God sent forth His Son, born of a woman, born under the law, to redeem those who were under the law, that we might receive the adoption as sons." NKJV

time as his slave". Imagine that. Imagine time being your slave. Of course, this is not the case. On the whole, we all are slaves to the manipulation of time. We are slaves to time! Let me give you a few examples for there are in fact five kinds of time that I exist in and I would describe them to you as follows:

> *We observe from the Scriptures then, that God is the creator of time. Time is under His personal direction and control.*

Scheduled time. This is time I am slave to. Either my boss, or my diary, my wife or my children, my dentist or my doctor, my congregation and all the demands of my days have required of me to be at a certain place, dressed in a certain way, to complete certain tasks. I am a most certain slave to this kind of time. Not obeying the demands of this time will have serious consequences on the enjoyment of other times. Guaranteed!

Intended time. This is the time I intended to arrive at an event. The time I intended to give to preparing that sermon. The time I intended to dedicate to that person. Intended time for me is mostly unrealised time. It is fictitious time.

Apologetic time. This is the time I take saying sorry for not delivering on my intended time. Apologetic time is for me real time because it is the time I am there at the event, in the groove, with the person actually doing what I intended to do, even if it's not at the time I intended to do it! It's better than nothing.

Fighting time. This is the time I spend waiting for other people and other entities to win the battles and make the ways for me to place my feet. This is the time that I spend either butting my head against doors which God has closed, or kicking doors that the devil is trying to keep closed. This is fighting time and to someone like me who is shall we say, not the most patient of individuals, it is bowel knotting time, it is wasted time, it is frustrated time!

Fullness time. God does in fact deal only in this kind of time. It is a mystery for me that all of God's creation function and fluster in the other four kinds on time, yet God, as the only real Time Lord can breathe easily in our four experiences of time because He is the Lord of Time. This is a mystery and mysteries can only be observed and experienced, they can never be explained. God deals only in fullness time. All time to Him, the Great Time Lord, is fullness time.

We observe from the Scriptures then, that God is the creator of time. Time is under His personal direction and control. God is the transcendent Lord of Time! He is over it, in it but not subject to what we might deem to be, both the capricious and unrelenting nature of time. God is the bookend at both ends of time! God is the first and the last of time. God is the ether of time in that, He always is and in this present "I am" in which we live and move and have our being!

> *So, for our sanities' sake, somehow we must begin to see time as His time, we must begin to see time from God's perspective.*

These facts alone reveal time to be God's created sphere in which His plans and purposes are actualised and realised. All time then is His time.

We slaves of time and its unrelenting onward march, whether it is with us or without us, we subjects of time, live our lives out in the daily and nightly experience of scheduled, intended, apologetic or fighting time. All of this we shall daily affirm in our late evenings, to be frustrating time, foggy time and even life sucking time. As we fall ever rapidly from the top of our three score years and ten, ground zero and its six feet of wet earth, await open mouthed for all our forthcoming impacts. Yes, to live in these four experiences of time alone, is indeed and quite simply for humankind, an ever-tiring exercise in seeming futility. Somehow, we must begin to see time as His time, we must begin to see time from God's perspective. We need to see time as the fullness time of the Great Time Lord for at the moment, for too many of us, time has us as its slave.

You see, the eternal framework of time, was allowed by God to hernia-like, burst into and become the boundary for space, for time to become even the very habitation of space and all the material reference points of which we are part of in space. The pollution of sin however, within this space time framework, has fogged and dogged, clogged and bogged our comprehension of time, our apprehension of time, our appreciation of time, leaving us like lost children, and like well demented men, who have forgotten the whereabouts of their car in the vast parking lot of life, we are troubled, we are confused. When approached and then asked to describe the transport of our desire, we fail miserably to adequately describe the vehicle we are looking for and even if we at some point believe we have discovered it, then the frantic search for keys in every hung out trouser pocket will only leave us in further heart despair. For we are truly lost in time and greatly troubled by its slavish and troubling presence. So, for our sanities' sake, somehow we must begin to see time as His time, we must begin to see time from God's perspective. We need to see time as the fullness time of the Great Time Lord for at the moment, did I tell you this? Time has us as its slave.

> *We must understand God's Fullness Time and we must see it punctuate our days with goodness.*

Time passes. Listen outside your window tonight, time passes. Unless we can hook our souls on the eternal God and Lord of Time, we shall remain so very troubled. Unless we can have faith in His Fullness Time, then we shall remain so very troubled. Unless we can embrace and testify to the mystery of such Fullness Time, such goodness time, such jubilee marked marching of time, such weeping through the night but joy cometh in the morning kind of time, then we shall remain slaves for all of our time in this body and in this world. We must understand God's Fullness Time and we must see it punctuate our days with goodness.

On your lips tonight and on your tongue in the tingling morning, let this medicinal refrain be heard dancing upon your lips...

Listen: "But as for me, I trust in You, O Lord; I say, 'You are my God.' My times are in Your hand." Psalms 31:14-15NKJV

Pray: Lord, in the fullness of time You sent forth You Son, Jesus Christ our Saviour into the world. Lord of time, You moved an empire to ensure Your Son was birthed in the prophesied place of Bethlehem. Lord of Time, You moved stars, You moved kings, You moved angel forces and a multitude of other magnificent and mundane things, butterfly and angel wings all to fulfil Your most unstoppable will. Lord of time, tomorrow, deliver me from the bondages and mummified bandages of time. In Jesus name I pray, Amen!

| Vol | 01 | Q3 | NW00250 | September 06th |

Night-Whisper | **HONOUR**

She devils, sponging males and the Jerry Springer Show

Linophryne Lucifer! What a name for a fish. It is however, these "Leftvents", these small deep sea angler type fish, occupying the sea depth some three to four thousand metres below the waves that I would like to consider this evening. I am telling you friends, these triangular headed, elongated, scale-less but gelatinous bodied creatures, are the most ugliest looking pieces of work I have ever seen. Indeed, if I ever took the view that Satan attempted to create beings in the material world, then I would most certainly say that this was one of his freaky Frankensteinian experiments gone wrong and is rightly kept hidden in the darkest depths of the deepest seas. The female of the species are the ugliest of the sexes and are often four times the size of the males, having dagger like teeth surrounding their ever open mouths and are able to swallow prey at least twice their size. These females rarely move, but wait, fat and motionless for both their mate and their prey to arrive.

Amos 4:1,2

"Hear this word, you cows of Bashan, who are on the mountain of Samaria, Who oppress the poor, Who crush the needy, Who say to your husbands, 'Bring wine, let us drink!' The Lord God has sworn by His holiness: 'Behold, the days shall come upon you When He will take you away with fishhooks, And your posterity with fishhooks.'" NKJV

Now here's the interesting bit regarding these monstrosities and Wikipedia puts it like this: *"Once a female is located, the male latches onto her with his otherwise useless teeth. Through enzymatic processes, the tissues of the male gradually begin to coalesce with the tissues of the female, resulting in a permanent attachment and a shared circulatory system, forming a hermaphroditic chimera. The development of the male's large testicles, which were delayed prior to this point begins, and all other organs in the male's body degenerate. Several males may thus attach to the same female with no apparent ill effects befalling her."*

Before I continue, I want to tell you that I have nothing against fat females or small, underdeveloped men. I am one of them myself! However, there is something spiritual for us to get hold of here. Unfortunately, to see the spiritual, I also have to point out its manifestation in the material world. Bear with me now, for you will agree with me no doubt, that in this strange world of ours, there are a large number of fat devil women lounging about, with a well hidden ability to lure little men to them and absorb them into themselves. This is very strange but very true and I have seen it for myself, many, many times. In addition to my own personal experience, if you have ever had the peculiar punishment of being witness to that modern day freak show hosted by Jerry Springer, you will see that these fat devil fish and the very, very little men that attach to them, are together with their freaky offspring, the bread and butter of that outrage we have come to regard as entertaining television.

Like it or not, these fat and open-mouthed devil women abound and the simple little men whose testicles only grow when they attach to them seem to abound yet more and more!

> *Like it or not, these fat and open-mouthed devil women abound and the simple little men whose testicles only grow when they attach to them seem to abound yet more and more!*

It is also of note that amongst these little men, as their virility increases their other organs do indeed diminish and chiefly that organ in between their ears!

Surely, God has created these devil fish for us to observe and wonder at. Surely, these Lucifer fish, waddle in the dark depths with a living message in their mad and massive mouths? I think so and to add to your nightmares tonight may I make the following three observations.

First, that society is crumbling beneath our very feet. When I have to counsel so many young men to get a court action to ensure that the offspring from the large woman they have attached themselves to is theirs, (and it rarely is) then society is crumbling beneath our very feet. Unless we take action now, then it is only a matter of time before it all comes crashing down.

Secondly, that there is a problem with masculinity in our land. When a man cannot become a man without being attached to a woman, then he has nothing to give, but everything to have taken from him. Men must learn to become men in and of their own right. Men must become strong of stature, stout of heart and steady in purpose and provision before they ever allow themselves the consideration of approaching a female. Yes I mean it! Strong men, stout hearted men, men of substance would never go near a fat devil fish. Many of our men need a good swift kick in the pants to get them off the road to hell and the temporal dissolution of themselves.

> *Our text for tonight refers to the well off, well healed Samarian women of power. God calls them fat cows!*

Thirdly, there is a problem with femininity in our land. Let me say first, that if you are a wife and a mother, then you have the most important job in the world! It's not very politically correct for me to say that, but it is Biblical and it is true. However, you should not be a mother before you become a wife, and may I say, you should not be a wife before you get yourself a life! Get an education! Get a job! Get some money behind you! Buy some land! You can set your sights high and still make a plan to get a man you know, and yes, it is a man you need, it is a man who already has got his masculinity developed, got his manhood in full sail, pulled tight against the wind and steaming ahead into his destiny. Get yourself a man woman! Someone who already has his testicles fully developed, and not an underdeveloped boy!

Our text for tonight refers to the well off, well healed Samarian women of power. God calls them fat cows! Rich or poor it doesn't matter because it's the same fat cow disease and produces the same sickness at every level of society. There is a sickness in our land, silently rotting the foundations of our society. The Linophryne Lucifer have come up from the depths and are flapping around on our shores. It's got to stop friends and we haven't got long to stop it before the fat cow fishhooks are cast towards us once again.

Listen: *"'I sent among you a plague after the manner of Egypt; Your young men I killed with a sword, Along with your captive horses; I made the stench of your camps come up into your nostrils; Yet you have not returned to Me,' says the Lord. 'I overthrew some of you, As God overthrew Sodom and Gomorrah, And you were like a firebrand plucked from the burning; Yet you have not returned to Me,' says the Lord. 'Therefore thus will I do to you, O Israel; Because I will do this to you, Prepare to meet your God, O Israel!'" Amos 4:10-12 NKJV*

Pray: Lord, to us belongs shame of face, for we have failed to teach our young boys to be men and our young girls to be women. Can this be redeemed O Lord? Help us all tonight Lord to be better examples tomorrow of what it means to be a man and a woman before Your face O Lord. Amen.

Night-Whisper | **COST**

Of Hell and Texas

In my kitchen cupboard I keep one of the largest mugs you have ever seen! Its bulbous proportions means it can hold at least twelve ounces of hot steamy tea and I tell you that on cold winter mornings it comes in very useful indeed! Another unusual feature about this mug is that it has a quote emblazoned on the front of it that reads, "You may all go to hell and I shall go to Texas!"

2 Samuel 23:20,23

"Benaiah was the son of Jehoiada, the son of a valiant man from Kabzeel, who had done many deeds. He had killed two lion-like heroes of Moab. He also had gone down and killed a lion in the midst of a pit on a snowy day. And he killed an Egyptian, a spectacular man. The Egyptian had a spear in his hand; so he went down to him with a staff, wrested the spear out of the Egyptian's hand, and killed him with his own spear. These things Benaiah the son of Jehoiada did, and won a name among three mighty men. He was more honoured than the thirty, but he did not attain to the first three. And David appointed him over his guard." NKJV

It is said that when he was but twelve years of age after beating the tar out of a bully at his new school, that he ran away from home to avoid having the same tar beaten out of him by his father! It would be seven years later, after stopping for refreshment at a New Tavern now owned by his father and run by his family, that one of his sisters would recognise this now six foot tall, statue of frontier manhood. Davy Crockett, "King of the Wild Frontier" was welcomed home at last by all of his family.

Descended from fleeing French Huguenots, protestant believers of Roman Catholic France, it seemed Crockett's whole recent family line had been frontier people. Davy Crockett had inherited all of that frontier spirit and need for adventure but on arriving home after some no doubt very daunting adolescent years, it was now time to settle down and settle down he did.

Jilted by Miss Margaret Elder of his first engagement, Crockett would later marry twice, the second marriage after the death of his first wife and father in total some six children. Living in Tennessee in the early 1800s meant that he was involved in the Indian Wars. Some of his relatives had been previously killed, maimed and scalped alive by Indians so Colonel Crockett had no problems with being involved in such wars, such land wars at that!

> *"I told the people of my district that I would serve them as faithfully as I had done; but if not then you may all go to hell, and I will go to Texas."*

Davy ran four times to serve as a Congressman in the House of Representatives and won twice but it was just prior to his last election defeat, that he was remarked as saying, "I told the people of my district that I would serve them as faithfully as I had done; but if not then you may all go to hell, and I will go to Texas." Following his defeat, he did just that. Why?

Well for one reason Texas, that vast and ever inviting frontier region, was beginning to break away from Mexico and in 1836 Crockett and 65 other men signed an oath before judge Forbes to serve the provisional government of Texas for just six months. His pay for that service would be 4,600 acres of land. "Sign me up!" I say, "Sign me up!" Land and lot's of it! Could there be any better reason to go to Texas?

However, it would be just a couple of months late that the King of The Wild Frontier would arrive with James Bowie to aid William Barret "line in the sand" Travis, the commander in charge at the siege of the Alamo and on March 6th of that same year, Davy Crockett and the other 180-230 Alamo soldiers would be massacred by an overwhelming Mexican force. There are three lessons for us here tonight.

First, remember that certain folk are frontier folk. Like it or not, they will not die on their beds but in likelihood will perish far away from home, seeking a fortune of one kind or another. If you are a frontier person, make sure you hazard your life for that eternal land of liberty. No other land is a fruitful, is as pleasant, is as safe and is as guaranteed as God's good land.

Second, understand that folk are known by the company they keep. It is no accident that Crockett would be found dead along with that other adventurer, Bowie and his famous knife. When people often ask me what they should do with their lives I tell them to see who they naturally gravitate towards, who do they desire to be with and in some way emulate. Your peers, both real and desired, are usually a good indicator of the similar stuff that flows through your veins. What company do you keep? Look, for therein lies a picture of your destiny.

> *What company do you keep? Look, for therein lies a picture of your destiny.*

Thirdly, despite the facts and the folklore, people are not perfect. Bowie was an angry knife fighter who made his money in the slave trade and his name in bar brawls and gunfights. Crockett, the bear butcher hunter of Tennessee had utilised his story telling abilities so well, that it got him into successful politics, and further utilised this story telling abilities by marrying it with such affability and humour,(It ain't braggin if it's true!) that he was largely able *by himself,* to ensure he became a legend in his own lifetime and beyond!

These were all extraordinary people but people nevertheless and imperfect people at that. Legends are made out of imperfect people. God uses imperfect people, He can do no other. Never forget that.

If you are looking for eternal treasure, if you have an adventure that will be rewarded with land on the other side of Jordan, then call me up will you, sign me up will you please, for I am a frontier person and I shall not die with boots under my bed. How about you?

Listen: *"The bows of the mighty men are broken, And those who stumbled are girded with strength. Those who were full have hired themselves out for bread, And the hungry have ceased to hunger. Even the barren has borne seven, And she who has many children has become feeble. 'The Lord kills and makes alive; He brings down to the grave and brings up. The Lord makes poor and makes rich; He brings low and lifts up. He raises the poor from the dust And lifts the beggar from the ash heap, To set them among princes And make them inherit the throne of glory.'"* 1 Samuel 2:4-8 NKJV

Pray: Lord, please give us all a frontier like spirit, that we might spread your Gospel to the ends of the earth. Lord, grant us land in Your Kingdom! Lord if the rest of the world shall go to hell, then we shall choose to go to Texas even if should become our very own Alamo. So give us this spirit, so revive Your church. In Jesus name we pray, Amen!

| Vol | 01 | Q3 | NW00252 | September 08th |

Night-Whisper | **PREPARE**

"I can hear your strong winds blowing"

For me, one of the most powerful country songs ever written and sung was by Hank Williams Junior and it was entitled, "Country Boy Can Survive." This song is really a celebration of the frontier spirit and in particular that spirit once found in the honest, hard working, tough living, self-supporting and self-reliant Southern folk of the United States of America. The opening lyrics of *"I live back in the woods, you see, a woman and the kids, and the dogs and me. I got a shotgun rifle and a 4-wheel drive, and a country boy can survive..."* describes very typically some of the people in my life that I have been privileged to get to know. At that time of writing these thoughts, I have lived somewhat in the backwoods myself, surrounded by these folk for nearly eighteen months. My front door has remained physically open for all of that time to allow our hunter killer cats free roaming access, for my wife you see, is a softy.

When we first moved into our place back in the woods, tired from the long trek from Miami, I asked the owner for the key to the front door and he just scratched his head and said that he, "Wasn't quite sure if he had a key?" Having just moved up from South Florida where we wouldn't put the garbage out without locking the door behind us, I asked, "Well, what do you do if someone breaks in?" His response was quick and simple: "We shoot 'em." And they would! And so yes indeed, a country boy can survive. Yet I do wonder about the next

Matthew 24:4-8

And Jesus answered and said to them: "Take heed that no one deceives you. For many will come in My name, saying, 'I am the Christ,' and will deceive many. And you will hear of wars and rumors of wars. See that you are not troubled; for all these things must come to pass, but the end is not yet. For nation will rise against nation, and kingdom against kingdom. And there will be famines, pestilences, and earthquakes in various places. All these are the beginning of sorrows. NKJV generation of country folk, who even now exhibit that same bruised fruit syndrome of the younger generations of this world, in that the world owes them a living and drugs is better than work. I am not sure if the next generation of Southern country folk could survive. No sir, I am not sure at all.

Along with Davy Crockett of yesterday evening's Night Whisper, I want to go to Texas again tonight and to Galveston, along the Texan Gulf Coast in particular, for today in the year 1900, Galveston was hit by an unnamed hurricane, which wreaked such havoc upon that once fair Southern city, that it has become the deadliest natural disaster the United States has so far faced.

> *"Galveston, oh Galveston, I still hear your sea winds blowin."*

Investigation of archives showing still photographs of the devastation and some old footage shot with the only four cameras available in the United States at that time, (imagine that!) show this once jewel in the crown of Texas, to have been brutally stamped from the face of the earth! With anywhere between 8,000 to 12,000 dead, simply dumping the bodies at sea was not enough to water bury the dead, as the returning tide simply brought the terror and the decomposing corpses back into land. So, makeshift funeral pyres burnt for days, and survivors involved in the mass burnings were given whiskey as they threw their own family members on to the fires, mothers, brothers, wives, daughters and sons, all burning in a heap around the wind blitzkrieg wreckage of a once abounding and beautiful city. All gone in just one storm. I can hear Glen Campbell singing right now, "Galveston, oh Galveston, I still hear your sea winds blowin."

Interestingly enough, the inhabitants of Galveston had not some little sensibility towards the possibility of a disaster, but it was another meteorological false prophet by the name of Isaac Cline, who in 1891 wrote an article in the *Galveston Daily News* in which he gave his official meteorological opinion, that the thought of a hurricane ever doing any serious harm to Galveston was, *"An absurd delusion!"* You see, many residents had called for a seawall to protect the city but Cline's statement helped to prevent its construction. The residents of Galveston, though fully aware of the impending possibility of disaster, failed to protect themselves. They utterly failed to prepare.

Forecasting the weather is probably one of the most difficult jobs in the world. It's like keeping a lion for a pet. You can love it, lead it and lay your hands lovingly along it's lovely main but it's still a lion and don't

you ever forget it, because the day you do, it will turn around, leap on you and rip your throat out and eat you alive.
No, weather forecasting is not for me.

Tonight though, I want to talk to you all too briefly about preparedness and in particular, preparing for disaster.

> *Disasters have occurred. Disasters will occur. Disasters are occurring.*

Disasters have occurred. Disasters will occur. Disasters are occurring. Statistically speaking as well, it is of note that in these days, we are in fact experiencing increasing disasters of greater and greater intensity. The Bible and indeed the Lord himself, warns us not to be dummies about these things, but to expect them and therefore to prepare for them! In these very uncertain times, as we ever speed toward 'the time of the end,' we Christians must assume much more of a war footing when it comes to preparing for the very near future. I am not a survivalist, I am not an end times freakoid who is hooked on wild, wild novels but I do read the Word and I do look at the signs of the times and everything in my spirit does cry warning! Warning! So, tonight then, I really do want to talk to you all, far too briefly, about preparedness and in particular preparing for disaster.

The priority of course is not to listen to false prophets, whoever they are and especially if they work for the government! Get the facts and then trust your gut. Get a plan friend and make sure that plan encompasses the following:

Evacuation
Nutrition
Medication
Communication
Transportation
Immediate Protection
Future Provision
and for us Christians, an ongoing, Declaration!

The preacher man might still be singing, *"It's the end of time and the Mississippi River she's a goin' dry. The interest is up and the Stock Markets down and you only get mugged if you go downtown,"* but make no mistake about it, disasters are coming.

Tonight, in your bed, thinking of when these hard times shall surely come upon us, maybe you could think through what you need to gather and accomplish, to make the survival of you and your family and maybe even the survival of others that you know, much more of a reality. Do I sound extreme? Think about that tonight. Do I sound extreme? Maybe, but a may I ask you, *"Hey country boy, can you survive?"*

Listen: "Proclaim this among the nations: 'Prepare for war! Wake up the mighty men, Let all the men of war draw near, Let them come up. Beat your plowshares into swords And your pruning hooks into spears; Let the weak say, "I am strong." Assemble and come, all you nations, And gather together all around. Cause Your mighty ones to go down there, O Lord. 'Let the nations be wakened, and come up to the Valley of Jehoshaphat; For there I will sit to judge all the surrounding nations. Put in the sickle, for the harvest is ripe. Come, go down; For the winepress is full, The vats overflow — For their wickedness is great.' Multitudes, multitudes in the valley of decision! For the day of the Lord is near in the valley of decision. The sun and moon will grow dark, And the stars will diminish their brightness. The Lord also will roar from Zion, And utter His voice from Jerusalem; The heavens and earth will shake; But the Lord will be a shelter for His people, And the strength of the children of Israel. 'So you shall know that I am the Lord your God, Dwelling in Zion My holy mountain. Then Jerusalem shall be holy, And no aliens shall ever pass through her again.'" Joel 3:9-17 NKJV

Pray: Lord, give us oil in our lamps and keep us burning, for we watch and wait for You O Bridegroom. Give me wisdom and teach me how to prepare. In Your great name I ask it, amen.

| Vol | 01 | Q3 | NW00253 | September 09th |

Night-Whisper | **BUZZ**

God! On a vespa?

In the Bible of course, we see God riding a white horse, riding a donkey and even riding on the back of one the most fantastical of angelic creatures called a cherub! However, as I sat astride my own motorcycle today, speeding nicely down the road in hot, humid weather, baking and basking in the afternoon sun, the question did occur to me as to what kind of a motorcycle the Lord Jesus Himself might choose to ride if He were to join today me on a road trip?

M Joshua 24:12,13

"I sent the hornet before you which drove them out from before you, also the two kings of the Amorites, but not with your sword or with your bow. I have given you a land for which you did not labour, and cities which you did not build, and you dwell in them; you eat of the vineyards and olive groves which you did not plant."
NKJV

Most American men would imagine Jesus riding on a black over chromed Harley, as tough as Arnold Schwarzenegger, wearing cool dark glasses and sporting a black leather jacket, with a large red Heaven's Angels logo emblazoned across the back. Arriving at stop lights He would be shouting warnings of a coming judgment day, and reaching out His hands to passersby and saying, *"Come with me if you want to live!"* Ha! Most Englishmen know that the Lord would not be riding a Harley, but like us would be sat astride his proud and perfect Triumph! What do I think? Well I actually think God would not ride either of those two mighty motorcycles, but He might just ride a scooter and a Vespa scooter at that!

In Nebraska, it was the Cushman motor company, founded in 1903, who began diversifying from the production of engines for just farm equipment. Yes, diversification was around and was a driving necessity even at the beginning of the 20th century! So in 1936, this same company also produced the first motor scooter, even selling them as a product line in Sears! Cushman were so successful and their manufactured product so sturdy and reliable, that during the Second World War, not only were thousands of Cushman scooters furnished for the US Army in general but many were produced solely for use by the airborne regiments! These robust airborne scooters were then dropped by parachute along with those flying soldiers, those screaming eagles, right into enemy territory, right into the heart of Europe.

Toward the end of the war, the fall of Italy and the destruction of its road and rail infrastructure, meant that the need for adequate post war transport was a severely pressing one for the nation. Renaldo Piaggio, his once booming fighter aircraft factory now destroyed, crippled by the severity of a post war economy and the severe restrictions placed on a defeated nation, had to take his manufacturing skills elsewhere. Piaggio then, turned his eyes on the obvious transportation needs of his post war country. He looked around and asked himself, "Just what was it that he could produce cheaply and in vast quantities, that would meet the needs of the day?"

"Sembra una vespa!" or, "It reminds me of a wasp!"

At that time, the olive green machines of the Nebraskan, Cushman scooter company, were buzzing around post war Europe and no doubt, became the obvious stimulus for the design style of the new, and cheap, stylish Italian vehicle for the masses. It was Enrico Piaggio, who beholding the brand new mass-produced Italian scooter design with both his eyes and ears for the first time who said with delightful surprise, "Sembra una vespa!" or, "It reminds me of a wasp!"

Actually, the Italian Word for wasp, Vespa, is in fact the genus name of all true hornets! Yes, the same hornets mentioned in our text for tonight. Fierce and voracious, with a far more deadly sting than a wasp, hornets are only mentioned in but three places in the Bible and each place singularly references all of God's miraculous interventions in fighting for His people. Each three references refer to His use of hornets in making sure of their possession of the Promised Land!

As there are no Biblical accounts of hornets actually being used on the field of battle, some commentators take these three references and therefore our text for tonight along with them, to be metaphorical, in that God would send amongst the enemies of Israel, not actual hornets but nevertheless a real consternation and fleeing madness of the mind, as if literal hornets were viciously attacking them! Frankly, I do not know which sounds worse, the reality or the metaphor! As for me, I take both points of view. I believe there was both the reality of utter panic, pain, fear and confusions, sown by God amongst the minds and hearts of the enemies of Israel and that God also, on occasion, sat sternly astride His very own Vespas and rode them out and into battle.

My points for your consideration this evening are but two fold.

First, note that although Reuters has long since reported that modern-day Israel has produced a Bionic Hornet, small enough to by stealth, photograph and even assassinate its enemies and also, that the rise of all our militaries use of nano-technology is far more complex and advanced than we ever realised, nevertheless, God was already using insect armies thousands of years ago! Get that, God is at the head of insect nations and uses them in the lives and destinies of His people!

On this first point of tonight then ponder this. God will use anything to accomplish His will for you. God will manoeuvre stars and planets, wind and waves, animals and insects, horses and even hornets, to accomplish His will for you. There is nothing He will not whistle for, to come running to your aid. Nothing!

On this first point of tonight then ponder this. God will use anything to accomplish His will for you. God will manoeuvre stars and planets, wind and waves, animals and insects, horses and even hornets, to accomplish His will for you. There is nothing He will not whistle for, to come running to your aid. Nothing!

Secondly, that in your rescue and in your aid, God will also miraculously give to you, things that you do not deserve, items and goods which you have not worked for, planted or prepared for. God will give these things to you.

Be assured tonight dear friend, that God is out riding His Vespa and will always send the hornet to the apple of his eye. Always.

Listen: "Moreover the Lord your God will send the hornet among them until those who are left, who hide themselves from you, are destroyed. You shall not be terrified of them; for the Lord your God, the great and awesome God, is among you." Deuteronomy 7:20-22 NKJV

Pray:- Great and awesome God, may I hear You buzzing by my side as I travel tomorrow up the road to glory. In Jesus name I pray, Amen.

| Vol | 01 | Q3 | NW00254 | September 10ᵗʰ |

Night-Whisper | **POWER**

Big bang day and the Word of the Big Book

This morning in 2008, 300 feet below the town of Crozet in France, the 27km circular tunnels of the Large Hadron Collider, powered up and began to collide particles at just below the speed of light, smashing them together in an attempt to reproduce the residual energy present at what many consider to be the fact of the big bang, or, when all of this mass of this present cosmos was produced from an infinitely small amount of matter, which in effect, had no dimensions at all. Indeed, with respect to the space-time somethings in which we exist, was in fact, nothing! It's an interesting theory.

Acts 17:23-29

"Therefore, the One whom you worship without knowing, Him I proclaim to you: God, who made the world and everything in it, since He is Lord of heaven and earth, does not dwell in temples made with hands. Nor is He worshiped with men's hands, as though He needed anything, since He gives to all life, breath, and all things. And He has made from one blood every nation of men to dwell on all the face of the earth, and has determined their preappointed times and the boundaries of their dwellings, so that they should seek the Lord, in the hope that they might grope for Him and find Him, though He is not far from each one of us; for in Him we live and move and have our being, as also some of your own poets have said, 'For we are also His offspring.'"
NKJV

Joel Achenbach, writing for *National Geographic* produced a most amazing article on this same subject. Commenting on the billions of dollars in money both spent and continuing to be spent on the project, he remarked, *"The exact number (in dollars spent) is elusive, the science will be precise, but the accounting apparently follows the Uncertainty Principle."* So just why has humanity spent such vast amounts on this project? For sure, it is because we have a need to understand our environs. Unlike the animal, insect and plant kingdoms of our world, we humans have real need to arrive at a complete cosmological prioperception of our universe. In other words, we need to know just why and where we are in space and time and to know that, we must first know what space and time is. The questions of *"just what is this place in which we live and why am I here?"* are the ever-haunting questions of the human heart, which presently now ever rush to find an answer from the great doctor wizards who practice in the dark arts of particle physics. No, we humans are not just searching for technological advantage in military and commercial terms, not just searching for commercial prosperity in a new wave of advanced consumer goods, no, we are searching for answers to the meaning of life!

The 2008 almost metaphysical search in the CERN, (The European Organisation of Nuclear Research) is not in the mud, but rather, is *for* the mud! Theoretical physicist John Ellis, gives a picture of their field of search when he remarks that different fundamental particles, *"Are like a crowd of people running through mud. Some particles, like quarks, have big boots that get covered with lots of mud; others, like electrons, have little shoes that barely gather any mud at all. Photons don't wear shoes—they just glide over the top of the mud without picking any up. And the Higgs Field is the mud."* Yes, that is what they are looking for, The Higgs Field, which can be observed by the presence of the Higgs Boson, or The Higgs Particle, whose propositional existence was put forward by Peter Higgs more than 40 years ago! Again, Joel Achenbach elucidates with such clarity about this field of mud when he comments that: *"Most physicists believe that there must be a Higgs Field that pervades all space and that the Higgs Particle, would be the carrier of the field and would interact with other particles, sort of the way a Jedi knight in Star Wars is the carrier of the 'force.' The Higgs is a crucial part of the standard model of particle physics—but no one's ever found it."* It was Nobel Prize in Physics winner, Leon Lederman who dubbed this particular particle, *The God Particle!* The mud that holds everything together.

> *Theoretical physicists are searching in a vast library of lexicons or better still, in an enormous dictionary of words, and are in particular searching for that one key word, that single word which holds everything together, gives cohesiveness, symmetry, meaning and magnificence to the very Cosmos in which we live.*

May I suggest tonight that theoretical physicists are searching in a vast library of lexicons or better still, in an enormous dictionary of words, and are in particular searching for that one key word, that single word which holds everything together, gives cohesiveness, symmetry, meaning and magnificence to the very Cosmos in which we live. May I say that the power of that same spoken word is so connected with the word itself and so connected with the speaker, that that the expressive power, the word and the speaker, are in effect all one. These physicists, on their own religious terms are searching for what is to them an unknown God, but who is to us Christians, the known and most revealed, Christ the Lord, maker of heaven and earth.

Listen: "who being the brightness of His glory and the express image of His person, and upholding all things by the word of His power—" (Hebrews :3)

Pray:- JESUS!

Night-Whisper | **REMEMBER**

Two Twins

Matthew 24:37-44

"But as the days of Noah were, so also will the coming of the Son of Man be. For as in the days before the flood, they were eating and drinking, marrying and giving in marriage, until the day that Noah entered the ark, and did not know until the flood came and took them all away, so also will the coming of the Son of Man be. Then two men will be in the field: one will be taken and the other left. Two women will be grinding at the mill: one will be taken and the other left. Watch therefore, for you do not know what hour your Lord is coming. But know this, that if the master of the house had known what hour the thief would come, he would have watched and not allowed his house to be broken into. Therefore you also be ready, for the Son of Man is coming at an hour you do not expect." NKJV?

In England for me
It was a cold country cottage front room
Warmed by the monotone mid afternoon mourning news, and

One of the fingered towers from the fine
Fun financial district
Was smoking like a gun

Chatter

There was chatter
Didn't matter
Didn't matter
Didn't stop the racing plunge of a
Second scythe fuel filled tube full of franticly
Waving and screaming souls slamming into tower two…

Two...
Two...
Two twins
Tottering and swaying like a boxer
Felled but not yet fallen and the world was calling
Calling
Calling
As some distressed
Distraught
Burned and
Death bought
Tuesday morning coffee
Just another day at the
Bloody glue factory gals
Held hands
My God!
Held hands and
Chose the sky and
The quick rising earth to die in and
Together
Leapt into eternity

Two twins squeezing the life blood out of each
Fused gripped finger

Like a self peeling banana
They fell to their knees and closed their lids
Crumpling their once solid shoulders to the grey canvas floor
The death of giants is
Never pretty
The death of giants is
Never pure

The shimmering light
Like a tired Tinkerbell
Left their eyes and
Darkness filled
The plane pecked flesh of
Open sockets
And already
In the space between the weeping
I could hear the bombs fast falling
Falling and thumping like a fist

Across the white house desk

Listen: "There were present at that season some who told Him about the Galileans whose blood Pilate had mingled with their sacrifices. And Jesus answered and said to them, "Do you suppose that these Galileans were worse sinners than all other Galileans, because they suffered such things? I tell you, no; but unless you repent you will all likewise perish. Or those eighteen on whom the tower in Siloam fell and killed them, do you think that they were worse sinners than all other men who dwelt in Jerusalem? I tell you, no; but unless you repent you will all likewise perish." KJV

Pray: Lord, help us to always prepared either for our departure or for Your imminent arrival. Amen.

| Vol | 01 | Q3 | NW00256 | September 12th |

Night-Whisper | **SAFE**

Seeking Mark Twain and more

From our texts this evening, allow me to somewhat imitate the great Mr Clemens tonight, in proving a point by maybe overly exaggerating a few metaphors. In any event, I do believe old sailors have the license to swing the lights, dust the salt off their shoulders and do so anyways!

Ezekiel 47:5,6

"Again he measured one thousand, and it was a river that I could not cross; for the water was too deep, water in which one must swim, a river that could not be crossed. He said to me, 'Son of man, have you seen this?' Then he brought me and returned me to the bank of the river." NKJV

Samuel Clemens chose his writing name from the phrase that Mississippi riverboat leadsmen would shout out when sounding the depths of the river beneath the Captains keel. *"Mark one"*, for example, meant the river bottom was just six feet below the keel.

In 1883, Samuel Clemens writes as follows in an excerpt from *Life on the Mississippi*.

'The cries of the leadsmen began to rise out of the distance, and were gruffly repeated by the word-passers on the hurricane deck.
'M-a-r-k three!.... M-a-r-k three!.... Quarter-less three! .... Half twain! .... Quarter twain! .... M-a-r-k twain! .... Quarter-less--'

The cry of "Mark twain" is where Samuel Clemens got his world-famous writing pseudonym. "Mark Twain" of course, to a river boat captain meant safe water, or two fathoms or for us land lubbers, that is, twelve feet, of safe sailing and sure steaming water.

A river pilot is someone who has expert and intimate knowledge of the course of water you are trying to navigate. God the Holy Spirit is our Pilot on this river of our lives. He has intimate knowledge of just the kind of water, with its currents and eddies, its moving sandbars, fluctuating depths, seasonal changes and ever changing daily challenges, its dangerous sunken objects, ragged rocks and other unseen and lurking menaces, all hidden just below the surface of all our ever moving waters.

You need to listen to this God the Holy Spirit Pilot speaking. You need to listen to Him navigating. Indeed, if we are attentive to His presence we shall be open to His practice and invited to learn, for as the Pilot navigates His way round the river, even with His vast and intimate knowledge of the water, He still makes use of sentinels of various kinds which come and stand on our own decks and swing ropes with leaden ends.

A river pilot is someone who has expert and intimate knowledge of the course of water you are trying to navigate. God the Holy Spirit is our Pilot on this river of our lives.

On our boat then, on our ship, we have four main and useful leadsmen, four Holy Spirit sent sentinels, which it would do well for us to listen to that much more intently.

The first is on the bow side of ship and his name is Conscience. Now, depending on how sober he is of course, he will be a fast talking, loud shouting indicator of the depth of water we are sailing into. Listen to your Conscience for Conscience likes attention, *"After all,"* he thinks, *"I am at the very front of this vessel and really should be respected."* And I tell you friends, if he doesn't get that respect of attention, then he tends to begin to drop his voice, little by little, even to a whisper, and has in extreme cases, been known to become sullen, even seared into silence. As you can imagine, not a few, inattentive captains have run their vessel aground and even had them sink beneath them, whilst conscience has sat there with his arms folded and his lower lip stuck out. Listen Captain! Give conscience some attention, give him some acknowledgement, give him some respect.

The second is on our port bow. He is a little guy but has big lungs! Unfortunately, his stature amongst the other leadsmen means he isn't often taken as seriously as he should be. Indeed, many a mature ship's captain has ignored this little guy called Common Sense. However, when he is listened to, he is surprisingly accurate and exceptionally effective in giving you the true depth of the water beneath you. Make sure you fully utilise this powerful little guy called Common Sense.

The third is on the starboard side of ship and his name is Intelligence. This leadsman may have had to work hard to get where he is, but he knows a lot more than he is given credit for I can tell you! Captains, can sometimes be so stupid in that they forget, that on their right hand they have this remarkable guy called Intelligence who, with all his learning and experience, can really give them a good understanding of the running water passing beneath their feet. I am afraid that Intelligence is also far too often underrated.

The fourth and final leadsman, at the stern of the ship is called Memory. He gets a little jittery sometimes, as all us captains are well aware! Especially if he senses anything of past hurts and disasters looming up from beneath and because of this, maybe he is not always as accurate as the other leadsman but nevertheless, as all captains know, it's good to have a jittery voice behind you, just so as you don't get too cocky!

The Holy Spirit Pilot, invites us on the morrow then, to better listen to these leadsmen, and to make sure in all our sailing, that we hear the cry of safety, that we hear the cry of security, that we hear the cry of clearance and the cry of full steam ahead! "Mark - twain!"

The Holy Spirit Pilot, invites us on the morrow then, to better listen to these leadsmen, and to make sure in all our sailing, that we hear the cry of safety, that we hear the cry of security, that we hear the cry of clearance and the cry of full steam ahead! "Mark - twain!"

Listen: "Then he said to me: 'This water flows toward the eastern region, goes down into the valley, and enters the sea. When it reaches the sea, its waters are healed. And it shall be that every living thing that moves, wherever the rivers go, will live. There will be a very great multitude of fish, because these waters go there; for they will be healed, and everything will live wherever the river goes.'" Ezekiel 47:8-10 NKJV

Pray: Lord, You have said that out of our bellies shall flow rivers of living waters and further, that this flowing shall move to one great river of wellness whose trees shall produce leaves which shall be used for the healing of the nations. As I sail this river of my life, this river of Your life, this river of our life, help me to heed The Pilot and learn from Him, in Jesus name I pray, amen.

| Vol | 01 | Q3 | NW00257 | September 13th |

Night-Whisper | **PUKE**

An old Anacreontic song for some new poet prophets

What good is poetry? What good is a poet and an amateur one at that? In an age where words multiply like maggots on a corpse, you can be sure that these are two valid questions.

2 Kings 3:14,15

"And Elisha said, 'As the Lord of hosts lives, before whom I stand, surely were it not that I regard the presence of Jehoshaphat king of Judah, I would not look at you, nor see you. But now bring me a musician.'" NKJV

I remember the first time I started writing poetry. I was not angry when I picked up the pen, I was fuming! I was furious, I was a festering foulness ready to explode. On previous occasions when this sick and angry madness had overtaken me I had broken things. No, I had smashed things, obliterated them, crushed them, indeed our refrigerator at the time still had a large dent in the door that fit the shape of my boot. I remember the first time I started writing poetry, it was emotional vomiting, spewing black words on white paper. It was a wise money saving adventure and sure beat the heck out of breaking things! The writing of poetry began for me then, as an emotional outlet, giving me a chance to pick through the written emotional debris on the page and see what was going on.

This puke-picking practice revealed patterns in the writing. Rhythmical expressions which when pursued led to disclosure, led to sometimes even closure but always led to light! Poetry then became for me a discovery tool, an internal and external communication tool, a looking glass both for me and for anyone who chose to ride with me on the rhythm of the words, weaving in out of the complexities of life.

But really, what good is poetry? What good is a poet, and an amateur one at that? In an age where words multiply like maggots on a corpse, you can be sure that these are two valid questions.

James McHenry, a Scots Irish immigrant to the Americas, functioning as a surgeon soldier, became secretary of war under Washington and became so famous, that the fort that was built to defend the Port of Baltimore was named after him. Tonight in 1814, that same fort would both see action for the first and last time as the British Navy would begin a 25-hour bombardment in the Naval part of the Battle of Baltimore. During the attack on Fort McHenry, four Americans were killed and twenty-four wounded. Frankly, though more people are sacrificed on a single one of our highways, each week of the year, this fort and this night, looms large in American History and may I say world history at that. The reason for this is that an amateur poet, negotiating the exchange of prisoners on board the British Flagship, would be detained until the morning whilst the British action began, and then continued through the night.

Oh say can you see?

"Star Spangled Banner." Was put to a well known British drinking song tune, published and popularised.

On the morrow, Francis Scott Key, this lawyer and amateur poet negotiating the release of prisoners, would pen a poem commemorating the "The Defense of Fort Henry" and call it just that! It was Key's brother in law, Judge Joseph H Nicholson, who would take the poem, put it to a well known British drinking song tune, publish it and popularise it. Over the next hundred years the poem, tune and the popular song it now encapsulated, would slowly rise to such national fame, that in 1931 the opening lines of *"Oh say can you see.."* would be enshrined forever in the American National anthem, the *"Star Spangled Banner"*.

I first call upon my American friends tonight, to be gracious to me as I handle some of their most precious words. Taking the last stanza of this moving poem I would like to draw your attention and all of our attention to the last eight lines

Oh! thus be it ever, when freemen shall stand
Between their loved homes and the war's desolation,
Blest with vict'ry and peace, may the Heav'n-rescued land
Praise the Power that hath made and preserved us a nation!
Then conquer we must, when our cause it is just,
And this be our motto: "In God is our Trust"
And the star-spangled banner in triumph doth wave

O'er the land of the free and the home of the brave.

As I write these words, in this year of our Lord, 2007, all Christians must read those ancient words from an amateur poet and weep. The *"Heav'n rescued lands, praising The Power that preserved them and brought them to plenteous both freedom and pleasant pastures because their trust was in God,"* are on both sides of the pond and all sides, of this world, being over-run and decimated with a darkness that seems to come on ever stronger.

We need some new music, that the prophets of old may speak once more.

No earthly banners may long lick the wind of freedom's breezes unless they reflect the glories of heaven and the glories of the Man from Heaven in particular. Our nations are being stolen out from under God before our very eyes and I tell you tonight, that the unless the indifference of God toward us, can be turned to a passionate hotness once more by our own sincere repentance and a hot and holy ardour *for Him*, and honour *of Him*, our flags of freedom are coming down! Unless our love for Him, begins to glow red hot again in our hearts, in our houses, in our churches, in our schools and in our legislators, I tell you my freedom loving friends, it is Christ Himself who shall puke us out of His mouth and should this happen, then there shall be little left to pick through.

We need some new music, that the prophets of old may speak once more.

Listen: "You shall therefore keep My statutes and My judgments, and shall not commit any of these abominations, either any of your own nation or any stranger who dwells among you (for all these abominations the men of the land have done, who were before you, and thus the land is defiled), lest the land vomit you out also when you defile it, as it vomited out the nations that were before you." NKJV

Pray:

Holy words long preserved
For our walk in this world,
They resound with god's own heart
Oh, let the ancient words impart.

Words of life, words of hope
Give us strength, help us cope

In this world, where e'er we roam
Ancient words will guide us home.

Ancient words ever true
Changing me, and changing you.
We have come with open hearts
Oh let the ancient words impart.

Holy words of our faith
Handed down to this age.
Came to us through sacrifice
Oh heed the faithful words of christ.

Holy words long preserved
For our walk in this world.
They resound with god's own heart
Oh let the ancient words impart.

Ancient words ever true
Changing me, and changing you.
We have come with open hearts
Oh let the ancient words impart.

(Michael W. Smith - Ancient Words Lyrics)

Night-Whisper | **WARDROBE**

Forgotten days

In 1752, today, September the 14th really appeared out of nowhere! For it was today that the United Kingdom of Great Britain and its Empire (including that troublesome colony across the pond) left the old Julian calendar (OS-Old Style) and adopted the Gregorian Calendar (NS-New Style.) The only problem was that to do this, you had to lose eleven days. So, yes sir, yesterday in 1752 it was the 3rd of September!

Jeremiah 2:32

"Can a virgin forget her ornaments, Or a bride her attire? Yet My people have forgotten Me days without number." NKJV

The old Julian Calendar (OS) was slowly but increasingly getting misaligned with the seasons. That, coupled with the Roman Catholic church wanting to implement the 325AD Ecumenical Council of Nicea's idea to celebrate Easter at the time of its own suggested calculation, (almost like getting a pope-driven atomic clock for the whole church) meant that the Gregorian Calendar (NS) was eventually adopted by one and all. At last, I can find some justification for me at times not even knowing what day of the week it is!

There is encouragement here in this re-ordering of calendars for sometimes, there are days and even weeks of time that must be laid aside, must even be forgotten, so that we can enter into a more realistic and rightly rhythmical way of walking, way of living, way of moving on into our future, into our destinies. Yes indeed, there are some days that need to be consigned to the garbage heap. Maybe you had one of those days today? If so, then let it go, delete it, consign it to the waste bin.

We do however have an increasing number of other forgotten days. Days we have forgotten about God. Days we have had no conscious awareness of His presence, of His providence and of His protection. Frankly, this has not bothered us one bit either as we have had these forgetful days, well and truly junked up with a whole bunch of other stuff. It is not good to forget God.

Tonight, I have to tell you that it is far too easy for us to lose days with God, even days without number! I wonder then, if it would be good for us tomorrow if as we put on our clothes we also prayerfully put on our armour and in the so doing, remembered God? I wonder if it would be good for us all that that in the same way you ladies put on your makeup and your Jewellery in the morning, that we also adorn ourselves with the graces of God for the coming day and in the so doing, so adorn ourselves with the remembrance of Him. Yes, tomorrow friends, let us dress ourselves with God and let us have no more forgotten days of fellowship with our Father. Let us begin to actively remember God!

> *Yes, tomorrow friends, let us dress ourselves with God and let us have no more forgotten days of fellowship with our Father.*

Listen: "Who is she who looks forth as the morning, Fair as the moon, Clear as the sun, Awesome as an army with banners?" Song of Solomon 6:10 NKJV

Pray: Lord on the morrow help me to adorn myself with You and this night O Lord, in my thoughts and in my dreams, help me to pick out the right clothes to wear for the coming day. In Jesus name I pray, amen.

| Vol | 01 | Q3 | NW00259 | September 15th |

Night-Whisper | **HOPE**

Searching for grovel hogs

When people told themselves their pasts with stories, explained their present with stories, foretold their future with stories, the best place by the fire was kept for, The Story Teller!

These are the opening lines of Jim Henson's television series called *The Story Teller*, which was first produced in 1987. This remake of some ancient European fairy tales, was brought to life by integrating excellent animation, Jim Henson's puppets from his creature shop, brilliant acting and some of the best writing you will ever come across.

Mark 12:37b

Numbers 30,10-14

"If she vowed in her husband's house, or bound herself by an agreement with an oath, and her husband heard it, and made no response to her and did not overrule her, then all her vows shall stand, and every agreement by which she bound herself shall stand. But if her husband truly made them void on the day he heard them, then whatever proceeded from her lips concerning her vows or concerning the agreement binding her, it shall not stand; her husband has made them void, and the Lord will release her. Every vow and every binding oath to afflict her soul, her husband may confirm it, or her husband may make it void." NKJV.

The magnificent screenplay for *The Story Teller* was written by Anthony Mingella, however, for this series of nine stories, it was John Hurt who, playing the part of the Story Teller, stole the whole series with his even more magnificent performance! I kid ye not, it is so good that if I had my way I would make the watching and study of this whole series, mandatory in every homiletic class, in every Bible college and seminary throughout the world! For when it comes to learning how to fish for hearts with words of wonder and communicating those same wriggling and wondrous words in an enticing and enthralling way, John Hurt as the Story Teller is the most heaven sent homiletics professor I have ever heard.

The first story of the series is called *Hans my Hedgehog*. It is the ancient tale of an enchanted boy called a grovel hog, who returns a lost king to his kingdom, and his reward for so doing, is "the first thing that comes out to greet the king upon his return". Of course, the first thing to greet the king is not his dog as he expected but rather, his most beautiful and precious daughter, the Princess of Sweetness and Cherry Pie! How very Jepthah-esque.

> *"Looking without hope of finding and holding on for dear life." Really, is there any better phrase for describing pursuing love?*

Now, this same Princess, in marrying the grovel hog discovers on their hog like honeymoon that the horrible grovel hog actually turns into a handsome Prince after midnight and if she but keeps the secret of his midnight metamorphism, then on the third night of their wedding, her faithfulness and true love will break the spell forever! Of course the Princess of Sweetness and Cherry Pie spills the beans of the grovel hog's enchantment, breaking her promise and causing him to seemingly disappear from both her life and the face of the earth forever.

For years, The Princes of Sweetness and Cherry Pie walks and walks until she wears out the soles of three pairs of iron shoes, always looking for her husband until she eventually finds him, *"catching him up in her arms, snoodling him and hugging him to bits"*. Her once red hair which had turned white in her relentless and unremitting pursuance, now runs with red life once more, as her now expressed love for the grovel hog finally finds him, holds him fast and breaks the enchantment forever.

The story finishes with this wonderful redemptive statement:

"And so the princess who could not keep her promise, won back her husband through looking without hope of finding and holding on for dear life. And in time, her hair grew red again and there was another wedding all over."

"Looking without hope of finding and holding on for dear life." Really, is there any better phrase for describing pursuing love, for describing the mad faithful praying and the deep soul longing for a lost loved one, daily expressed in both prayerful pleadings and active pursuance. I think not.

I am sure that some of you tonight are the breakers of promises and of maybe one precious promise in particular and I wonder if because of this, you might also hold someone in your heart, with sadness and with tender regret, that is for now, lost to you.

If you have any desperate strength left within you, I want you to continue to look without hope of finding, and continue to hold on for dear life. For who knows, maybe tomorrow you too will come upon your lost grovel hog, catch them up in your arms, snoodling and hugging them to bits until the dreadful enchantment, made stronger by the broken promise, will be removed forever and the redness of a life renewed, will flow into your holy hair once more.

> *If you have any desperate strength left within you, I want you to continue to look without hope of finding, and continue to hold on for dear life.*

I need to say to someone tonight, *"Keep looking, keep hoping, and keep holding on,"* for who knows, the rejoicing and the renewal of another wedding, may still be in the offing.

Listen: "Praise is awaiting You, O God, in Zion; And to You the vow shall be performed. O You who hear prayer, To You all flesh will come." Psalms 65:1-2 NKJV

Pray: O God our husband, thank You for making null and void the hasty and impetuous vows we have made in Your house. But Lord, forgive our broken promises, especially those that have brought curses upon ourselves and upon others. Please forgive us O Lord. Now my Great Pursuer, I bring to You my lost loved one. Hopeless, I come to You! Helpless, I come to You! Help me to find them and love them despite their anger, that all curses may be broken and life, rich and red, would flow down once more upon all our tired heads. In Jesus name I pray, amen.

| Vol | 01 | Q3 | NW00260| September 16th |

Night-Whisper | **CHARACTER**

Equations on character and capacities

I was thinking tonight, musing if you will, about the old adage that "choices determine our destiny and character determines our choices", and therefore as Laurel said to Hardy "Ipso Fatso, character determines destiny."

Mark 12:37b

1 Chronicles 21:14

"So the Lord sent a plague upon Israel, and seventy thousand men of Israel fell. And God sent an angel to Jerusalem to destroy it. As he was destroying, the Lord looked and relented of the disaster, and said to the angel who was destroying, 'It is enough; now restrain your hand.' And the angel of the Lord stood by the threshing floor of Ornan the Jebusite. Then David lifted his eyes and saw the angel of the Lord standing between earth and heaven, having in his hand a drawn sword stretched out over Jerusalem. So David and the elders, clothed in sackcloth, fell on their faces. And David said to God, 'Was it not I who commanded the people to be numbered? I am the one who has sinned and done evil indeed; but these sheep, what have they done? Let Your hand, I pray, O Lord my God, be against me and my father's house, but not against Your people that they should be plagued.'" NKJV

I must say that I have always found this saying of 'character determining destiny' somewhat lacking in truth. After all, it was David, the man after God's own heart, who made many good and an awful lot of bad choices in his life, even to choosing national deceit, murder and adultery. These three were but a few of his bad choices! For some of his other bad choices would result in thousands upon thousands of his fellow countrymen being killed by God Almighty Himself. King David may have been a man after God's own heart but some of David's choices were not good ones and our text for tonight clearly shows that. Yes indeed, the Devil might have made him do it but do it he did! Maybe the Devil stirred but David chose and his destiny was greatly tarnished in the so doing. Even the best of men sometimes choose wrongly and that with disastrous consequences for themselves and others. Tell me then, has their destiny now been destroyed?

I have come to the conclusion that although character does shape choices and choices do determine earthly destiny, that this is only part of the equation. You see we consider our destiny, as our destination this side of heaven. However, I do not believe our present destination is God's ultimate destination for us, it is not God's destiny for us if you will! God has an eternal and infinite destination for us, and it's much more than position, power and place, and so because of this, this side of heaven, I believe His destination, His destiny for us, is always in the profound forging of character. There is a reason for this and I believe it is because character = capacity. The forging of our character is our destiny this side of heaven.

> *Character does shape choices and choices do determine earthly destiny, that this is only part of the equation.*

That however, is not enough for us, no, destiny for us this side of heaven, is a determined destination of position, power or place. Yes, it is for us a destination of goals accomplished, of feats achieved, of races that are run and fights that are won. Whatever it is, we want to stand atop our own Everest and say, "I have done it, I have finished the task given to me." Now there is nothing wrong with that, nothing wrong at all. However, I wonder if that declaration is in the end, a simple statement of our own felt perspective. Yes, unless God definitely confirms to us otherwise, I think it often most probably is. God's destiny for us you see, is bigger than any Everest of position place or power this side of heaven, for it is Godly character, built for ever rest. This side of heaven, all our own climbed Everest's prove to be so very tiring and unfulfilling.

Our earth side equation for the fulfilment of power, place and position can be split into ten parts. Let's take a look at the developement of our destiny equation. Here we go then:

Meta-Genetics (building material provided by The Creator God) + Simple Genetics (building material provided by earthly parents) = Temperament. (That is, the beginnings of quality of heart, our natural constitution if you will, our mouldable and innate tendencies.)

Temperament + Social Station and Social Situation + Pressures and Pleasures = Character (The provings, of heart quality, the expression of acquired features, whether good or bad.)

Character + Hungry Temperament (or Desire) (that is, our innate tendencies made hungry by want, by need, by anointing maybe or even by gifting) = Pressure of Expression.

Pressure of Expression = Persistent Pursuance.

Persistent Pursuance = Made Opportunity.

Realised Opportunity = Expression of Self.

Expression of Self =Fulfilment.

Fulfilment = The feeling of acquired destiny and therefore the fact of acquired destiny.

Acquired Destiny = Satisfaction.

Satisfaction = Rest/Peace.

It's all very complicated isn't it and as many millions attest, when you get to the top of your Everest, this seeming satisfaction of completion and possession rarely results in rest for the soul. Yes, our earth side equations of destiny all fail miserably when we arrive at top of all our not so "ever rests".

Our destiny this side of heaven is simple. It is to sacrifice ourselves in serving the Lord Jesus Christ. When we serve Christ, He will mould our innate tendencies and then shall, in our pursuance of such sacrificial service, add to them great embellishments of shimmering golden traits of God like characteristics. It is this Almighty moulding of the self, it this holy addition of golden wonders, that make character our destiny this side of heaven. Make no mistake about it, the formation of Christ-like character this side of heaven is God's desired destination for us all. Why?

Make no mistake about it, the formation of Christ-like character this side of heaven is God's desired destination for us all.

Before I answer that question, may I say that I do not believe this formation of character, this sanctification, halts when we are transformed from earth to heaven and that once there, what is here, is sealed there forever and can never be improved upon. No, not at all! If that were the case then frankly, what a very large and sorry bunch of individuals would walk the streets of Gold. Maybe the rewards and therefore the capacities of the enjoyments of God, are sealed in us at the judgment seat of Christ, but sealed only in their capacities for exponential growth. In other words, sealed in growth that is proportional to the starting size. I think so, maybe.

> *Christ like character results in the rewards of capacity, which in heaven allows an exponential growth in enjoyment, pleasure, fulfilment, glory in relationship, glory in construction, glory in creation, glory in discovery, glory in conquest and glory To God!*

Why do I believe that this side of heaven, the building of Christ-like character is our destiny? Because this Christ like character results in the rewards of capacity, which in heaven allows an exponential growth in enjoyment, pleasure, fulfilment, glory in relationship, glory in construction, glory in creation, glory in discovery, glory in conquest and glory To God!

Know this tomorrow then, that God is interested in your character because therein lies the key to all future eternal capacities. Yes sir, in this context then, the answer to my opening equation is correct. Character does indeed, determine *eternal* Destiny.

Listen: "Grace and peace be multiplied to you in the knowledge of God and of Jesus our Lord, as His divine power has given to us all things that pertain to life and godliness, through the knowledge of Him who called us by glory and virtue, by which have been given to us exceedingly great and precious promises, that through these you may be partakers of the divine nature, having escaped the corruption that is in the world through lust. But also for this very reason, giving all diligence, add to your faith virtue, to virtue knowledge, to knowledge self-control, to self-control perseverance, to perseverance godliness, to godliness brotherly kindness, and to brotherly kindness love. For if these things are yours and abound, you will be neither barren nor unfruitful in the knowledge of our Lord Jesus Christ." 2 Peter 1:2-9 NKJV

Pray: Lord, add to my faith and increase my eternal capacity to enjoy You and glorify You forever. Amen.

Night-Whisper | **SERVE**

"We the people…"

Today in 1787, the Supreme Law of the United States of America was adopted in its original form. This now most famous of documents begins with a most stirring pre-amble: "We the People of the United States, in Order to form a more perfect Union, establish Justice, insure domestic Tranquility, provide for the common defence, promote the general Welfare, and secure the Blessings of Liberty to ourselves and our Posterity, do ordain and establish this Constitution for the United States of America.…" Thus indicating that this writing came not from any king, emperor, potentate, or any other authority, but from "we the people". How wonderful.

Matthew 6:24

"No one can serve two masters; for either he will hate the one and love the other, or else he will be loyal to the one and despise the other. You cannot serve God and mammon." NKJV

This original constitution was both later and amended. One of these amendments, amendment thirteen, though appearing in some earlier transcripts of the constitution appears to be "missing" in the constitution of the present. The so-called missing thirteenth amendment, or Titles of Nobility Amendment (TONA), which was proposed by the 11th Congress on May 1, 1810, would have ended the citizenship of any American who accepted "any Title of Nobility or Honour" from any foreign power. Without going into the whys and the wherefores and the usual American conspiratorial ménage of why it was never ratified, may I say that I like the idea! Indeed, I think this amendment should be ratified for it shows that no cleaving can occur without a leaving. Did you get that? Whatever might take away your stickiness, your glue-likeness, get rid of it. Do not let anything come between that which you pledged an allegiance to. Why? Well the answer is easy, you cannot serve two masters.

Mammon is simply a Greek transliteration of an Aramaic word referring to "riches in general". So our text tonight holds within it, the seeds of the Christian TONA amendment. Jesus says, "You cannot serve two masters." If money has put any title of Nobility or Honour upon you, (Jesus is brutal about this next bit) then *get rid of it.*

Luke 14:33 So likewise, whoever of you does not forsake all that he has cannot be My disciple. NKJV

What can we do in light of these intransigent statements from the lips of Jesus? Well, how about: *"We the People of God, in Order to form a more perfect Union with Him, establish Justice, insure domestic Tranquility, provide for the common defence, promote the general Welfare, and secure the Blessings of Liberty which is in Christ Jesus to ourselves and our Posterity, do ordain and establish this Constitution for the Serving of our Master."*

Article 1- *Jesus has the power to comamnd whatever He wills in our life.*

Article 2- *He can do this because He has complete and undisputed Executive power and authority in HIS kingdom of which we are part.*

Article 3– *He is the judge of all things and of His church in particular.*

Article 4– *There is no limit to His power, neithers is their limit in execution of His power.*

Article 5–*There are no amendments to His consititution because everything in Him is ratified as both yes and let it be done.*

Article 6– *Aall power is His. All glory is His. All monies are His. All money not used in His service, whether rightly or wrongly gained, is tainted money. For His followers, it is tainted with the intent of both theft and misuse.*

Article 7- Like it or not, this constitution is in effect. It has already been ratified. Get on with it.

Maybe we need that TONA amendment though. How about you tonight, do you need it?

Listen: ***"So when Jesus heard these things, He said to him, 'You still lack one thing. Sell all that you have and distribute to the poor, and you will have treasure in heaven; and come, follow Me.' But when he heard this, he became very sorrowful, for he was very rich. With God All Things Are Possible And when Jesus saw that he became very sorrowful, He said,***

'How hard it is for those who have riches to enter the kingdom of God! For it is easier for a camel to go through the eye of a needle than for a rich man to enter the kingdom of God.' And those who heard it said, 'Who then can be saved?' But He said, 'The things which are impossible with men are possible with God.'" Luke 18:22-27 NKJV

Pray: Lord, I yield to You, both my wallet and my bank account. I hereby this day, deny all honours and all titles that Mammon has laid upon me and pledge allegiance to Your bloody flag this day and to the constitution of Your eternal kingdom. Amen.

| Vol | 01 | Q3 | NW00262 | September 18th |

Night-Whisper | **CONSIDER**

Making the moon stand still

Last night, yes I remember, last night my dreams were plagued with pictures of emptiness. Empty pockets, an empty head with no new ideas, an empty mouth with nothing to say, emptiness, emptiness, all was embarrassing emptiness, for you cannot bless others if you have nothing to give! My dream life last night was full of the sense of running out of resources of every kind.

Zechariah 14:7c

"But at evening time it shall happen that it will be light."

The previous day had set the scene for my troubling night-time, unconscious introspection. Finances were drying up, bills were howling to be paid and the yard sale money I had made that day, was quickly spent. I will not tell you what I bought with the yard sale money but my wife had remarked that, "We didn't sell our stuff for you to frivol it away." She was right, I had frivoled away my resources. Last night, yes I remember, last night in my dreams I came up empty, worried and embarrassed.

My male midlife crisis has been going on for seventeen years now. It started when I reached the age of thirty. What I wouldn't give to be thirty years of age right now! I look down the coming years and in another seventeen years from this point of my journey I shall be sixty-four and nearing retirement age. Like many men my age now, I feel that I have accomplished little of my goals, little of my dreams and the felt destiny of my youth has ended in the so far, pale disappointment of the present. Last night, yes I remember, last night in my dreams I came up empty, worried and embarrassed. Yes it's all very depressing. Maybe I have indeed, frivoled away my life resources. Do you ever feel like that?

However, in the providence and mercy of God, the clouds of my recent days have dispersed and tonight, the moon in my sky is high and bright causing me to remember that in a moment, Jesus turned water into wine. I like that. With a simple word from the Lord, all of life's embarrassments and emptiness can be changed for the better and that real quickly. When the water was turned to wine, then that which was natural, plain and tasteless, became full and fruity, rich and robust, abundant in blessing, pleasing in taste, amazing in quality and all, in all of that happened just in a single a moment of time.

We have our days and they pass too quickly. Yet, God has His days as well and they last a thousand years! I believe that God can cram one of His days into one of ours! Do you? Yes, God can cram a thousand years of age into a single day. I believe that God can cram a thousand years of accomplishment into a day, a thousand years of blessing into a day, a thousand years of fruit into a single day! I believe that God can make us quantum leap into higher orbits of energy, activity, influence and light. More than this, I believe tonight in His moonlight fair, that He will do it for me. Yes, I believe tonight that He will do it for you, if you ask Him.

> *I have often thought that God sheds old people like an oily old snake skin and of necessity, is always taken up with youth, always focusing on the next generation for His plans, always flirting with the younger models………*

I have often thought that God sheds old people like an oily old snake skin and of necessity, is always taken up with youth, always focusing on the next generation for His plans, always flirting with the younger models, yes, that God, like some lecherous old man, always has His eyes lusting on the possibilities bound up in the emerging generations. As I age, I have felt increasingly betrayed by God in this. I was wrong of course, for it is only this present world, this ever-changing culture, this machinery of convenience and consumption that looks so lecherously on the young and so disdainfully on the old. God is not disappointed with age, au contraire, He values it and calls us older folks to look at the promised land from far greater heights than any pimply youth could possibly do, than any big busted beauty would ever dare or even want to do. Yes, God values age, He takes note of our callous feet, our scars, our wounds and our greater gasps for breath, especially if it is His breath we are gasping for. God gives hope to aged pilgrims, especially those who have not given up the fight. Where there is life, there is always hope.

Me thinks as well, that God disdains the seeming disappointments of our both our younger and our older days and therefore, so should we! For God looks at the years the locust has eaten and says restore! Yes, God looks at the coming evening of our lives and says to us before we sleep tonight, "But at evening time it shall happen, that it will be light." NKJV Oh, please Lord, let it be so. It's never too late for the goodness of God to fall upon us.

May your dreams this moonlit night, be full of hope, be full of expectancy, be full of fruit, be full of light, be full of possibilities, be full of strength, be full of might! May your dreams tonight be full of Jesus.

Listen: "Now both Jesus and His disciples were invited to the wedding. And when they ran out of wine, the mother of Jesus said to Him, 'They have no wine.' Jesus said to her, 'Woman, what does your concern have to do with Me? My hour has not yet come.' His mother said to the servants, 'Whatever He says to you, do it.' Now there were set there six water pots of stone, according to the manner of purification of the Jews, containing twenty or thirty gallons apiece. Jesus said to them, 'Fill the water pots with water.' And they filled them up to the brim. And He said to them,'"Draw some out now, and take it to the master of the feast.' And they took it. When the master of the feast had tasted the water that was made wine, and did not know where it came from (but the servants who had drawn the water knew), the master of the feast called the bridegroom. And he said to him, 'Every man at the beginning sets out the good wine, and when the guests have well drunk, then the inferior. You have kept the good wine until now!' This beginning of signs Jesus did in Cana of Galilee, and manifested His glory; and His disciples believed in Him." John 2:2-11 NKJV

Pray: Lord, I believe, Lord I have to believe, Lord I do believe that You have kept the good wine until now. As the coming day is long O Lord, so let my strength be. As the coming day is long O Lord, so let Your light shine. As the coming day is long O Lord, lengthen it still further until I see all my dreams stand upright before me. O Lord of the whispering night, this night I command the moon to stand still in my valley of Aijalon until I have revenge upon all the enemies of my purpose, and victory over all my robbing darkness. Tomorrow, I will awake with a sword in my right hand and a trowel in my left and on my lips shall be the shout of victory. Lord I believe, Amen!

Night-Whisper | **HUMILITY**

How to behead yourself

Michelangelo Merisi da Caravaggio, jumped and mugged coming out of a bar in Sicily, is so savagely beaten that he is reported in Rome as being dead! When the report came that he was alive, it was also reported that he was nevertheless, severely disfigured, having had his head seemingly attempted to have been removed from his body. Many artist historians say that this was Caravaggio's darkest hour, and during his recovery, whilst trying to gain pardon for a murder he had committed during a duel in Rome, in 1606 Caravaggio painted *David With The Head of Goliath*. Caravaggio, a fleeing murderer, had a reward on his own head. Literally if anyone brought in his head, they would get a reward.

Ezekiel 30:6

"Thus says the Lord: 'Those who uphold Egypt shall fall, And the pride of her power shall come down. From Migdol to Syene Those within her shall fall by the sword,' Says the Lord God."

The painting, *David With The Head of Goliath* is in fact a Caravaggio self-portrait. The young David is Caravaggio as a younger man and the miserable dead head of Goliath in the painting's sad hands of David, is Caravaggio in the here and now. Charlie White, American artistic photographer in his series *Everything is American* and the photograph called "Champion" uses the same David and Goliath theme and artistic trick in substituting his features for the younger David and the severed head of Goliath. No, the difference in the two works of art is substantial. The photographic art of White shows the self-portrait trick but Caravaggio most certainly shows the event itself, the slaying of the giant, and in particular his deep involvement in the same. What most separates these two pieces of artwork, is neither material nor method, neither background nor distance in time, but rather the presence of David's sword. In Caravaggio's work, David still holds his sword and on it is inscribed "H-AS OS", that is, "humilitas occidit superbiam", or "humility conquers pride"!

Tragedies of life can many times move us out onto the field of battle to meet our own personal giants. Giant pride is one which we shall meet again and again. Whilst most of the time we are content to deal with the disposal of cobwebs, personal tragedy invites us to deal with the spider and that spider often is called Pride. Carravagio had a multitude of personal problems, emotional and most definitely psychological. What would we expect? For what else is giant pride but pure, blind madness. It needs dealing with friends so tell me, what tragedies have come upon you, come upon you continually? Tell me, what truth, what bad, sad, malevolent and self-murdering truth have you been running from within your soul? Tell me, within you, has David got Goliath's head, or Has Goliath got David's head?

> *The power of truth, not least about ourselves, for if we are ever to have a chance of redemption it must begin with an act of recognition that in all of us, the Goliath competes with the David."*

Produced by the BBC, Simon **Schama's eight-part serial on the Power of Art so wonderfully** tells the story of Carravagio. *"For me,"* he says, *"The power of his art is the power of truth, not least about ourselves, for if we are ever to have a chance of redemption it must begin with an act of recognition that in all of us, the Goliath competes with the David."* How very honest!

In finally summing up the story of the maniacal genius of Caravaggio, Schama, visibly moved by this particular portrait, wonderfully deciphers the sullen art work as being painted in colourful brail, shadows, light and half light, remarking that it tells of the artists plea to the Roman authorities. *"'Here I am,' says this dead face which seems still alive, 'They said whoever delivers my head will get a reward, well, I am turning myself in, will that do, can I have my reward, can I have my pardon?'"* Sinner, you must Turn yourself in to God. Confess your head right off and turn yourself in to God.

Listen: "Pride goes before destruction, And a haughty spirit before a fall." Proverbs 16:18.NKJV

Pray: Lord, here is my head. Please forgive me my sin and this spider in Your court. Lord, please renew me into my right mind, in Jesus name I pray, Amen.

Atonemints

I am writing today from the Starbucks of Louisville's International airport in Kentucky. Louisville is a weird place; indeed, it tries too hard to be weird! It's like a freshman student who isn't really comfortable and at home in their own body and therefore being out of place, being out of their comfort zone, being out of sorts, they are always trying to too hard to be a student. "Hey look at me!" they say, "Goofy bag, Bud-beer, piercings, tattoos, ripped jeans and T's with an offensive but cool print! Yeah, look at me! Look at me! I'm a student!" Louisville tries too hard to be weird. It needn't try that hard, for the spiritual tectonic plates of the South and North of the USA meet right underneath the deep bed of the Ohio river and the constant rubbing and a grating of the old South's past, always gripping like a spastic bowel on the North's imposing present during the warm cricket creaking night, forces a noxious flatulence to break forth and bubble up across the whole Ohio river valley, the green bogeyman gas, filling people with an insane need to be different and be different in a very different but very weird kind of way! No, it's not just the inbreeding that causes a weirdness in Louisville, it's the titanic and continuing clash of two spiritual fronts, which in the end always sucks and blows people out to the West, even as far as Seattle. Kentucky has always been a jump off point for those heading West. Strange but true.

It is of no surprise then that such a place should produce a number of weird individuals, one of whom is regarded as the founder of Gonzo journalism, Mr Hunter Stockton Thompson. One of my favourite quotes of his is regarding the music industry where he says, "The music business is a cruel and shallow money trench, a long plastic hallway where thieves

Matthew 21:12,13

"Then Jesus went into the temple of God and drove out all those who bought and sold in the temple, and overturned the tables of the money changers and the seats of those who sold doves. And He said to them, 'It is written, "My house shall be called a house of prayer," but you have made it a "den of thieves."'" NKJV?

and pimps run free, and good men die like dogs. There's also a negative side." Ha! I like this quote because it belongs to any successful business, which whilst utilising the talents of artists and tradesmen, is in the end after profits rather than excellence. You can have both. If you have faith to believe I suppose you can have both! However, I often find that in reality, there is always a trade off between profits and excellence. Good grief, go into any Christian bookstore and the presence of yards and yards of shelving full of published and well publicised drivel is quite a testimony to that truth.

> *God's Kingdom is not of this world, though it would be nice to see an occasional manifestation of it in the Christian publishing industry, in the Christian clergy industry, in the Christian theological training industry, in the Christian local church industry.....*

Which brings me tonight to a reality check for those involved in the Christian marketplace and God help us, in this consumer-driven Laodicean church age which we presently inhabit, we are all involved in the business of Christianity at some level. Unfortunately, those of us actually working in it, trying to make a living from it, know that it is more cut-throat, merciless, more forgetful, more rude and loveless, than the secular arena could even try to be and would be allowed by law to be. You know it's true! How many of you would rather do business with Christians or non-Christians? How many of you have been well and truly burned by the religious industry? Give me a dollar for everyone I know who has the singe of the religious machine upon them and the smell of burning compost about them and I shall retire to Tenerife and live handsomely for the rest of my days.

God's Kingdom is not of this world, though it would be nice to see an occasional manifestation of it in the Christian publishing industry, in the Christian clergy industry, in the Christian theological training industry, in the Christian local church industry, indeed, in all the many and varied Christian industries that we have created. However, in the money driven weirdness of it all, it's rare friends, the Kingdom is so very rare to see.

I have made my piece with the religious Christian industry in recognising it for what it is. It's like a freshman student who isn't really comfortable and at home in his own body, out of place, out of his comfort zone, out of sorts, you know, trying to too hard to be a student. *"Hey look at me!"* It says to the watching world and the shallow masses that fill our pews *"Look at me! Tungsten carbide laser etched personalised Bible, excessively long rat haired goatee, punctured piercings' with nails of the cross, 'Oh the wonderful cross' keeping the holes open. Celtic, Klingon-style tattooed Scripture verses in Hebrew and in Greek, ripped jeans and Ts with a thorny black Chez Guevara style Jesus, dripping blood on my Nike trainers, iPod ear buds filling my ears with the latest Christian bands! Yeah, look at me! Look at me! I'm a Christian and I'm armed to the teeth by the religious industry to meet the demands of the present age. Come and get it whilst it's hot!"*

Frankly, the religious Christian industry is all a little weird and if you don't watch out, it will bite your hand off and I have observed that the infections from Christian industry religious bites are particularly nasty ones.

I'm not ranting tonight, honest, just using a little Gonzo, just mixing some fact and some fiction to prove a point and if you do not get the point yet, then let me speak quite clearly. All that we Christians buy and most of what we see, hear and build, has absolutely nothing to do with the Kingdom of God whatsoever but rather, has everything to do with business, with profits and with money.

Most of what we see, hear and build in Christianity, has absolutely nothing to do with the Kingdom of God whatsoever but rather, has everything to do with business, with profits and with money.

Ride the beast if you will but do be careful you never fall beneath its pounding hooves. I wonder tonight just what Hunter Thompson would have said about the religious Christian industry? What do you think?

Listen: *"No one can serve two masters; for either he will hate the one and love the other, or else he will be loyal to the one and despise the other. You cannot serve God and mammon." Matthew 6:24 NKJV*

Pray: Lord, help us. Lord help me to touch and to taste, to hear and to see, to feel and to enjoy, the reality of Your Kingdom. Lord, may Your Kingdom come and Your will be done in my life, in our lives, at every conceivable level. Amen.

| Vol | 01 | Q3 | NW00265 | September 21ˢᵗ |

Night-Whisper | **MUSIC**

Bring me a musician

At the beginning of the 21st century the key personnel components to a numerically growing church is a good communicator in the pulpit and a good musician on the stage. If it's a choice between just one of these components, then choose the good musician every time because good music brings in the punters and when the punters open their pockets, well, you can then buy yourself a good pulpit monkey who purchases in his sermons off the internet, anytime you please. Ah, bring me a musician. Having made that observation however, what I am about to talk about tonight has unfortunately nothing to do with the postmodern church, or that mutton dressed as lamb, the mega-modern church. No, this is not surface stuff I am talking about but a deep and intrinsic connection, between the soul and the prophetic spirit. Yes, bring me a musician.

2 Kings 3:14

"And Elisha said, 'As the Lord of hosts lives, before whom I stand, surely were it not that I regard the presence of Jehoshaphat king of Judah, I would not look at you, nor see you. But now bring me a musician.'" NKJV?

I was performing some poetry one night and had the opportunity once again to perform a piece with the accompaniment of a professional musician. It was a public exercise in answering the question of the possibility of ‚eta-physical synchronisation. Could the heart and ears of the speaker and the heart and ears of the player, synchronise the voice and words, with the fret gripping, finger plucking sounds of the musician? Always to the audience's surprise, this works well and something different and beautiful is produced every time and it is always something that is in step, that is in rhythm, and friends, anything that is in step and in rhythm, will release a beauteous truth. Yes, bring me a musician.

Now Elisha is no pussy anyways, but it is obvious that the arrival of these three kings and especially the wicked King of Israel, had put him in an especially angry mood, had got his hackles up, had put him first on the defence and then on the verbal attack! One man against thousands, telling the King of Israel where to get off! I imagine his heart was pumping in fiery indignation against those who had rebelled against the Lord. It was only the presence of King Jehoshaphat that day that saved the situation, and with mounting disdain for the Kin and King of Israel Elisha says, **"As the Lord of hosts lives, before whom I stand, surely were it not that I regard the presence of Jehoshaphat king of Judah, I would not look at you, nor see you. But now bring me a musician."** Now in the middle of such a tirade, why on earth did Elisha demand a musician?

His emotions were not eliminated here but rather they were brought into a receptive play.

Well, I believe that Elisha needed calming down and he knew it! For when the musician played, Elisha was then eased into a ready frame of mind, yes that's it, Elisha's soul, was so calmed by the music, that his spirit could rise up above the boisterous emotional waves and speak in prophetical and practical terms. Of course this was most important, this was most necessary for it was his spirit that was the conduit for God's voice. Now don't think that the seat of his emotions were an emotional blockage that needed removing, no, but rather by the music, the rhythm of his emotional soul was syncopated with his spirit to release the testimony, yes, his soul was brought into a revelation rhythm of disclosure. His emotions were not eliminated here but rather they were brought into a receptive play. Ah yes, bring me a musician.

It was Luther who taught that "darkness abhors sweet sounds" and certainly the antipathy of this is seen in our days, in that darkness, always attach itself to shall we say, some not so very sweet sounds! Certainly, the soul needs a mood to make heaven speak. I say again, certainly the soul needs a mood to make heaven speak and that mood is a rhythm and it is a rhythm which is in rhyme with heaven, a soul and a spirit both in syncopation with each other and with the Holy Ghost. Ah yes, bring me a musician.

Now you will notice that the text makes no mention of either the style of music or the instrument it was played on. Was it calming music? Was it stirring music? Was it pleasant in tone, or provocative in tune? We don't know. All that we can say is that this music was an ordering of his soul and a release to his spirit in a very trying situation. Ah yes, in all our trying situations, bring me a musician.

I do not want you to think that your emotional soul is a hindrance to communication, no indeed it is an integral part of communication. However when the soul is out of rhythm with the spirit, listening for the message from God is like looking for a drowning man in a raging sea. That sea needs controlling. The rhythm of the waves needs reining in. Ah, bring me a musician.

You do know that what you listen to, will indeed influence your soul and in turn then will either bound or release your spirit.

You do know that what you listen to, will indeed influence your soul and in turn then will either bound or release your spirit and remember, it is your spirit that inhabits the spiritual realm and it is your spirit that has communicative content. I wonder then, that if you are not hearing from God, it is because you are in fact out of His rhythm and nothing, I mean nothing will rhyme in your life. If this is the case, then you need a musician friend. Ah, but what kind of musician to bring?

Music is music, and good music like good food will satisfy the soul. Yes, you don't need a Christian chef to make good food and you don't need a Christian musician to make good music and remember, the music I am calling good, is the music that will bring your soul into a rhythm that will then release the rhyme.

Be assured that your soul knows the difference between binding rhythm and releasing rhythm and I tell you, your soul is longing for release, your soul is longing for rest, your soul is longing to be controlled and to hear the message from God which is carried in your spirit! So, let your prayer tonight be very simply this, "Lord, bring me a musician."

Listen: *"Then it happened, when the musician played, that the hand of the Lord came upon him. And he said, 'Thus says the Lord: "Make this valley full of ditches." For thus says the Lord: "You shall not see wind, nor shall you see rain; yet that valley shall be filled with water, so that you, your cattle, and your animals may drink." And this is a simple matter in the sight of the Lord; He will also deliver the Moabites into your hand. Also you shall attack every fortified city and every choice city, and shall cut down every good tree, and stop up every spring of water, and ruin every good piece of land with stones.' Now it happened in the morning, when the grain offering was offered, that suddenly water came by way of Edom, and the land was filled with water." 2 Kings 3:14-20 NKJV*

Pray: Lord, bring me music that will release Your message in me. Amen!

Night-Whisper | **WAIT**

The marriage of midnight madness and autumn mornings

It was American psychologist, Harry Levi Hollingworth, who wrote an introspective and analytical study of the psychology of drowsiness. In it, he apparently recalls a dream he has, where during the night, he saw the whole secret of the universe revealed to him and in such a state of excitement, moving from sleep to the state of drowsiness, lest he forget the secret, he managed to reach for a piece of paper at the side of his bed and scribble the revelation down. Having accomplished his fevered task, satisfied he then slipped from drowsiness back into the deepest of restful sleeps. Morning came and with it the remembrance of the written secret. He scurried for the folded paper which had been scribbled on in the middle of the night, opened it and read aloud the words of the revealed secret of the universe, here they are: *"A strong smell of turpentine pervades the whole."* It is Major General Sir John Kennedy who uses this "secret of the universe" to formulate some words of wisdom for us tonight. Here they are: "Bright ideas in the middle of the night are not always very bright in the morning!" I like that.

Revelation 2:28

and I will give him the morning star. NKJV

As I write this whisper, today is the first day of autumn, my most favourite of seasons. Though it is beautiful, sober and succulent, it always announces its first arrival with parididdled panache, always coating my morning toes with the pale blue of a semi-frosted crispness, which rises up through souls of my feet from the brown tiled kitchen floor, causing me to gaze outside at the already curling leaves of the trees, all staring back at me, bright eyed, semi solid and slightly shivering themselves with the same old cold surprise. Yes, autumn always begins with an epiphany of morning-startled coldness. I like that, for autumn is a most sensible season for it forces you to face your days with eyes wide open in cold and startled suprise.

Midnight madness is always tempered by morning light. For the cold light of day always brings with it an especial shining on plans and preparedness. When this happens, silly things will diminish and disappear in maniacal laughing, never to be seen again. Let them go. Never speak of them again. The solid things of the night however, shall remain. Those you must keep and talk of often for I tell you, that if you can then marry off this former seeming midnight madness to all the gorgeous autumn mornings, then their children, red-haired and vibrant, shall be well instructed ideas, well trained and well provided for, competent in every way. Yes they shall all succeed and prosper.

Venus is the morning star, the herald of the day appearing robed in light as the great darkness flees away. The planet, thus clothed in early light, becomes to us who wait for morning, a solid pledge of the faithfulness and goodness of God. In our opening text for tonight, it is evident that the Sun of Righteousness will give something of solid and shining beauty to those who hold fast to His teachings, to those who marry their midnight madness to All the mornings of His goodness. Be sure then to bring all your dreams to His autumn mornings and see if they will live. Yes, see if they will marry.

Listen: "My soul waits for the Lord more than those who watch for the morning — Yes, more than those who watch for the morning. O Israel, hope in the Lord; For with the Lord there is mercy,and with Him is abundant redemption. And He shall redeem Israel from all his iniquities." (Psalms 130:6-8 NKJV.)

Pray: Lord, I bring all my midnight thoughts to You, yes even to Your Word. Let the light melt the maniac and may I marry the remaining good to all Your greatness and all Your faithfulness. So may all my days be clothed in right and all my plans be made to prosper, in Jesus name I pray, amen.

| Vol | 01 | Q3 | NW00267 | September 23rd |

Night-Whisper | **GLORY**

The floodlight of the Father

Hebrews 1:3

"..who being the brightness of His glory and the express image of His person." NKJV.

Concerning the word "brightness" in our text for tonight, the Greek word "apaugasma" is only ever used here in the New Testament. It literally means an off flash, a solar flare, a glory hole into His holy furnace, a floodlight from the Father's heart shined on to hopeless humanity, all groping around in the dark, not even struggling to find the light switch. Concerning the glory of God then, Jesus is the brightness of that glory on two legs, a tangible and touchable torch of illuminating love. Jesus is God. God, the light of the world made manifest among us and moved into our neighbourhood.

In the darkness of this very night, should you be awoken by strange noises, probably the first thing you reach for is a light, some form of illumination to light your way and show you the danger as well as hopefully frighten away the predator! Jesus is such a light and you need him for the strange noises you hear in your spirit are the creakings of your sin and the distant clawing of demons who make ready at a moment's notice, to come and devour your soul. Yes, you really do need to reach for Jesus the light and let Him safely guide your path and frighten all your predators away. There is no other way to hush the distant clawing and close the mouths of predatory lions. So, get Jesus tonight, yes, ask for the floodlight of God to come and shine in the very centre of your dark beleaguered being.

Listen: "Then Jesus spoke to them again, saying, 'I am the light of the world. He who follows Me shall not walk in darkness, but have the light of life.'" John 8:12 NKJV.

Pray: Turn on Your light O God, turn on Your light and let all the darkness flee away. Turn on Your light O God, turn on Your light and make safe my bear trapped way. Turn on Your Light O God, turn on Your light and all fear and trepidation sever. Turn on Your Light O God, turn on Your light and drive the darkness back forever. In Jesus name I ask it, amen.

| Vol | 01 | Q3 | NW00268| September 24th |

Night-Whisper | **DROWN**

The drowning of two twins and the PO 8 Black Bart

I had been in Des Moine Iowa for the weekend performing some of my poetry. It had been my first time in the Mid West and in a place that is reported to have more pigs than people, I was pleased to find them all as pleasant as I expected them to be. Historically, Des Moines was as a prominent staging post for the Old Wells Fargo overland mail service and it was good to see this company was still prominent in the area, providing jobs to many people and giving its name to the 2005, 17,000 seat, Wells Fargo arena. Yes, the city of Des Moine wore its old-lady facelift very well indeed.

2 Samuel 13:26,27

"Then Absalom said, 'If not, please let my brother Amnon go with us.' And the king said to him, 'Why should he go with you?' But Absalom urged him; so he let Amnon and all the king's sons go with him."
NKJV?

Henry Wells and William Fargo spawned a number of companies, including American Express. However, it was the Wells Fargo overland mail company, owning the largest stagecoach empire in the world, that has fixed itself firm in all the legends and stories of the old wild West. Another spin off from The Wells-Fargo company, the Pony Express, together with the famous Six-horse Concord coach charging across the open plains of the old mid West, was in my youth, the stuff of every Cowboy and Indian-style robbery re-enacted on many a hot summer afternoon.

The Concord Stage Coach's treasure box was made of Ponderosa pine, oak and iron, and was usually kept underneath the driver's seat and body guarded by very unsavoury characters armed with sawn off shotguns. I say usually kept underneath the driver's seat, because should the coach not be carrying passengers, then the treasure box was bolted to the inside floor of the Coach. Now this last fact is important as I introduce to you Mr. Charles Bolt, or as he was commonly known then, the famous and daring stage coach robber-poet, Black Bart.

Farmer, gold prospector, wounded civil war soldier, Black Bart had tasted a life of adventure and would not go back to the simple farming life he had previously embraced. This man had more than an itch for adventure though, he had a grudge to go with it. Yes sir, we know from his letters to his wife that he had reported some kind of unpleasantness that had happened to him at the hands of Wells Fargo employees and he had vowed to get them back. A colourful little poem which he left at one of his always polite and courteous little robberies, reads as follows:

> *"I've laboured long and hard for bread,*
> *For honour and for riches,*
> *But on my corns too long you've tred*
> *You fine-haired sons of bitches."*

Charles Bolles or Black Bart, would sign his post-robbery pieces, PO8. Although he was reputed for his style, sophistication and eschewing of foul language, this little poem does reflect shall we say, not a little evidence of the terrible twins of resentment and revenge and I tell you now, that when these two twins get drunk at their many reunions, trouble is a brewing.

Coming full circle, Black Bart's last stage robbery took place at Funk Hill, the same place of his fist robbery! However, this time, the situation was completely different. Robbing the treasure box from a stage coach with no passengers meant that the treasure box was secured inside and

> *I do not believe in either abortion nor infanticide but resentment and revenge are two terrible twins that need drowning at birth!*

the loosening of the bolts took some time. He eventually made his escape, only to be wounded in the process by the hard man who had been riding shotgun. Fleeing, Black Bart dropped several items including a laundry marked handkerchief, which eventually led to him being traced, found and arrested. After serving four years in San Quentin, Black Bart emerged older and wiser. Wikipedia writes that, "Reporters swarmed around him when he was released. They asked if he was going to rob any more stagecoaches. 'No gentlemen,' he smilingly replied, 'I'm through with crime.' Another reporter asked if he would write more poetry. He laughed, 'Now didn't you hear me say that I am through with crime?' and promptly disappeared from the scene." He was never heard of again.

I do not believe in either abortion nor infanticide but resentment and revenge are two terrible twins that need drowning at birth! Drown them in the waters of confession, drown them in the waters of repentance, drown them in the waters of blessing those who hurt you and despitefully use you. If you don't, then as twins do, no matter what the distance in mileage, no matter what the difficulty in terrain, no matter how long the time, they will one day get together for a reunion and I tell you, when that happens, when revenge and resentment lift their drunken glasses high, then God help the person they are toasting!

In our text for this evening, Absalom and the twins are arranging a death party for all the sons of David and he especially wants Amnon to come and join the fun, for Amnon the slither, Amnon the cur, Amon the terrible, two years ago, raped Absalolom's sister Tamar. Since then, Absalom has said nothing, held his peace, bided his time. Now the drunken twins will have their way, and what a bad, red, way, it shall so surely be.

> *Do not be distracted by their kicking, neither be deterred by their self justifying screaming, their angry shouting and all their fussing, just hold them under these running waters until they kick no more.*

So, if you have resentment and revenge in your heart tonight, get up out of bed right now, go to the bathroom, run the water in the tub and then get down on your knees and take resentment in one hand and revenge in the other. Do not be distracted by their kicking, neither be deterred by their self justifying screaming, their angry shouting and all their fussing, just hold them under these running waters until they kick no more. If you do not do this, then it's death or prison friend, it's death or prison.

Listen: "Beloved, do not avenge yourselves, but rather give place to wrath; for it is written, 'Vengeance is Mine, I will repay,' says the Lord. Therefore 'If your enemy is hungry, feed him; If he is thirsty, give him a drink; For in so doing you will heap coals of fire on his head.' Do not be overcome by evil, but overcome evil with good." Romans 12:19-21 NKJV

Pray: Lord, take me to the waters and strengthen my hands for this work of drowning, in Jesus name I pray, amen!

Night-Whisper | **SHAPE**

Of big girls' blouses and warrior houses

Joab, Abishai and Asahel were of course the three sons of Zeruiah, one of the two half-sisters of David, and thus his three half-nephews. Heroes of David they were! Close of Kin and so close companions of King David they were as well but quite frankly, they were also a right pain in the rear to boot.

2 Samuel 2:18

"Now the three sons of Zeruiah were there: Joab and Abishai and Asahel."

Zeruiah was of course the older half sister of David, his mother most probably having been married before and on becoming a widow, then marrying David's father Jesse. You see, composite families are not new!

What is evident from the Biblical record is that Zeruiah's natural father, Nahash, is mentioned but once and that is in relation to him being the father of her sister Abigail. Zeruiah's husband's name is actually never mentioned in the Scriptures at all! And her three remarkable sons are always referred to as the son's of Zeruiah. I think it a right conjecture then, to surmise that Zeruiah was a strong, capable, tenacious, heroic and pushy individual! She had to be really, and oh may I remind you that she was also David's big sister and may I tell you, she was no big girl's blouse!

Interestingly I think, Zeruiah's name means wounded, or "squeezed of the Lord", and is related to being cracked under pressure. Not a cracking that produces madness mind you, but rather a distilled, squeezed out balsamed preciousness. A sweet smelling savour if you will. Now, we do not know just what this squeezing pressure might have been? A physical deformity maybe? Or maybe a prophetic name which was indicative of various life crisis? We don't know, but what we do know is that she was a very strong and influential women, especially as she raised three very competitive, hard, dedicated, and somewhat over-zealous warrior generals! Yes indeed, neither Zeruiah nor her sons could be classed as just big girls' blouses. Oh and did I mention that she was David's big sister?

There are two things I would like to say to say to you warrior women tonight.

First, that it is possible to take your cracked and broken lives to God and have Him squeeze out a very special inheritance for you, your family and your nation. Yes, it is possible for you to raise up generals!

Zeruiah was no big girl's blouse and neither were her sons. How about you girl? Are you manning up? How about your sons momma? Are they whiners or winners? Wise up girl! You have more influence than you can ever imagine.

Secondly, that you big sisters can have a great influence over your younger brothers, for I wonder if this particular big sister not only set a brave example for David the shepherd boy but on occasion, gave him a good old thump on his arm whilst telling him to, "Stop whining and man up?" I wonder? For I tell you, this Zeruiah was no big girl's blouse and neither were her sons. How about you girl? Are you manning up? How about your sons momma? Are they whiners or winners? Wise up girl! You have more influence than you can ever imagine. So, oh my goodness you mothers and big sisters all, in all your prayings, actions and leadings, do make sure that you are producing kings and generals and not pansies and drivelling dress makers.

Listen: "Joab the son of Zeruiah was over the army." 1 Chronicles 18:15 NKJV

Pray: Lord, rightly shape our mothers, that they may rightly shape their children and grant us shaping sisters to boot, in Jesus name I pray, amen!

Night-Whisper | **ROBUST**

The bare facts

I am not a pornographer. Though I could be. No, the abuse and the misuse of women in glossy magazines and internet titillation, is in my mind, an offence to all real men and is an abomination to God, for the marriage bed is holy and undefiled. Yes indeed, according to the Bible, sex is good and great and holy to boot! How wonderful! Imagine that. Not too much now...

Ezekiel 16:25

"You built yourself a high place at the top of every street and made your beauty abominable, and you spread your legs to every passer-by to multiply your harlotry."
NASU

So, taking a wonderfully holy thing like sex and dragging it through the dirt is a terrible offence to the gift of God and also a great stain on His beautiful creation. However, I have no problem with fine art and the odd bosom and bare behind. It is all a matter of context you see, a matter of what is being portrayed and said. Yes, the misuse of sex is a terrible thing, but the misunderstanding of naked portrayal is simply immature and silly, As a verbalist, in the same way I suppose, the naked words I use must also have some relevant artistic 'context' lest they too imply become pornographically offensive. Yes that sounds right doesn't it? However, God does not seem to follow these same cultural rules.

Take our text for tonight for example. It is raw and naked and contains no misunderstandings. It is real, it is straightforward and it is grossly offensive and, it is God that is speaking! Imagine a pastor or church member using that kind of language! They would be excommunicated! No, don't play the cultural context card here, for if anything, in that culture the impact of these words in our text have more offence and power than we can possibly imagine! God knew it and so God used it. God is very offensive. He doesn't care. He's not polite and He's not respectable.

You see the problem with naked words, words without any culturally respectable mores, is that the pictures they paint are shocking! Indeed, they sometimes paint so large a portrait that it is only the vast unbounded context of the mind that can house those word pictures painted upon it. We need to be careful don't we then, regarding just what kind of pictures we can paint with the words of our mouth? I mean last night's poetic quote from the 'Poet Bank Robber Black Bart,' was pretty offensive, I mean, fancy finding 'that' in a Christian devotional. It is a good job that it was only verbal art wasn't it? What's more important for me though, is that it is a good job I didn't go as far as Jesus did in giving astonishing cultural and religious verbal offense. Phew! Thank goodness I did not go as far as Jesus in being offensive in my language. You see God is often very offensive. He doesn't care. He's not polite. He's not respectable.

> *God is often very offensive. He doesn't care. He's not polite. He's not respectable*

Shall I be brave? Yes, I think I shall. Why not? Let me introduce you tonight then to some of the most offensive words ever spoken. Libellous they are! Outrageous they are! Astonishing even! Unfortunately though, the words are true and the passion in which they were spoken is rightly powerful, even spitting in its condemnation. So much so, that they got the speaker killed. Listen – Jesus speaking to religious hypocrites and says – "If God were your Father, you would love Me, for I proceeded forth and came from God; nor have I come of Myself, but He sent Me. Why do you not understand My speech? Because you are not able to listen to My word. You are of your father the devil, and the desires of your father you want to do. He was a murderer from the beginning, and does not stand in the truth, because there is no truth in him. When he speaks a lie, he speaks from his own resources, for he is a liar and the father of it." John 8:42-44 NKJV

Now friends, we have little felt import regarding the extreme offensiveness of being called, "A lying and murdering son of Satan!" When Jesus shouted and spat this verbal slap at the great and the gowned, all the listening mothers began holding their hands over the ears of their children. All the grandmothers were saying "Tush," and sucking their breath in deeply and shaking their heads in outrageous disbelief! All the Pharisees were reaching for rocks and all the disciples were wide eyed and open mouthed, staring at Jesus in disbelief! It's outrageous I know, but it's nothing compared to another place, where He's really going to go word wild on them and open up His big verbal guns and blast them with nomenclature like you've never heard before! Names that explode like hot shrapnel on the ringing ears of dumbfounded, pompously pious and polite big hypocrites, whose nice religious language has camouflaged a festering and a fallen reality. "Open graves!" He says, "White washed walls and nests of snakes," He says, and a whole lot more besides. Yes indeed, there is a many a religious and respectable Christian that should be thankful that not all the works and choice words of Jesus have been fully recorded for us.

> *I have to say to some of you tonight that it is time to grow up. It is time to get real, it is time to lay aside the large offense you attach to small words and become as Christ.*

Christianity is for real men. Men with swords, men itching for action, men willing to hazard their lives for the Gospel, men who can face lions and the strongest of charging bulls, grapple them by the horns, look them in the eyes and tell them the truth in full and not so glorious Technicolor, even if it costs them their lives. The words of Jesus are for men for they are spoken by the best of men.

Godly women, strong of life and sure of lip, throbbing in heart, weeping at His feet, serving with singing, tough and tender, ready to glean in the fields of Boaz, ready to labour long, love lots, hope much, and command the dignity they deserves in every market place that they may tread. The words fo Jesus are for real women who are sick of lies.

I have to say to some of you tonight that it is time to grow up. It is time to get real, it is time to lay aside the large offense you attach to small words and become as Christ. Christianity is not polite. Christianity is not respectable. Christianity is like its founder, like its Commander in Chief, it is righteous, robust and holy and that is the way you and your ears must become.

I spend my time encouraging folk to come to Christ! I spend my time encouraging folk to come to church, but I tell you tonight, that with some of you, I need to encourage you to put down your gold engraved red leather Bibles and go join the Masons or the Women's Institute or some other non-offensive little club. I say this because Christ and His cause is not for you. Frankly your polite and pressed suit approach to the beautiful and everlasting Gospel, is keeping people away from the Kingdom, yes it's keeping them away in their thousands. I invite you tonight to either get saved, get real, or get out for I wonder if you really know the real Jesus of the real Bible all red in word and raw.

Listen: "You stiff-necked and uncircumcised in heart and ears! You always resist the Holy Spirit; as your fathers did, so do you. Which of the prophets did your fathers not persecute? And they killed those who foretold the coming of the Just One, of whom you now have become the betrayers and murderers, who have received the law by the direction of angels and have not kept it." When they heard these things they were cut to the heart, and they gnashed at him with their teeth. But he, being full of the Holy Spirit, gazed into heaven and saw the glory of God, and Jesus standing at the right hand of God, and said, "Look! I see the heavens opened and the Son of Man standing at the right hand of God!" Then they cried out with a loud voice, stopped their ears, and ran at him with one accord; and they cast him out of the city and stoned him. And the witnesses laid down their clothes at the feet of a young man named Saul. And they stoned Stephen as he was calling on God and saying, "Lord Jesus, receive my spirit." Then he knelt down and cried out with a loud voice, "Lord, do not charge them with this sin." And when he had said this, he fell asleep. Acts 7:51-60 NKJV

Pray: Lord, forgive me for treating Your house, like a club for old ladies. Lord, let the words of my mouth, the meditations of my heart, the passion of my pulse and the presence of my true self, be acceptable in Your sight, Oh God my strength and my redeemer. Amen!

Night-Whisper | **BELIEVE**

Resurrection hopes

God is good but God is tough.

"Lord, don't mention me to the enemy. Lord do not say to him 'Hey, have you seen my servant Robert?' No Lord, please keep my name out of any conversation with him, lest I be tested like Job of old. As for Abraham, Lord just what were You thinking? Asking a man to kill his own son? Putting him through what can only be described as torture and for days and for what? Just so You could experientially know of his trust in You? I tell you Lord, if the social services ever get their hands on You, You're done! They shall lock You up and throw away the key, for abuse, yes, for abuse! There has to be a better way Lord of You conducting Your business, there has to be better way of You knowing and us, growing? Surely?"

Hebrews 11:17-19b

"By faith Abraham, when he was tested, offered up Isaac, and he who had received the promises offered up his only begotten son, of whom it was said, 'In Isaac your seed shall be called,' concluding that God was able to raise him up, even from the dead, from which he also received him in a figurative sense." NKJV

Abraham had to endure days of terrible torment, days of torment of heart and of mind. Jacob his grandson however, would undergo years of torment, thinking his Joseph was murdered, blaming himself every day for sending his lovely son on that last mission to Dothan. Joseph did no better, who whilst being sick with unfulfilled promises, spent years in prison for a crime he did not commit. I could go on and indeed, I will do so now and even with you. Yes, even with some of you reading this tonight.

For whatever reason, be it drugs, be it sexual sin, be it sickness of mind, be it raging anger, be it self-sealed pride, be it misunderstanding, be it distance, be it whatever! Many of you this very night wish you could exchange your circumstance for the comparatively simple test, which Abraham had to pass through! "Good grief," you say, "Abraham had that torture laid on his soul for days but mine, mine, I have had it laid upon my heart for weeks, for months, for years even and I don't know, I just do not know, how I can ever face the coming days, for each morning and each night, I lay my lost child, lost to drugs, lost to madness, lost to lifestyle, lost to self hurt, lost to dishonour, lost to anger, lost to God, lost to me! Oh God, every morning and every night I lay my lost child by faith upon on Your altar, hoping, pleading, praying, looking, longing, waiting, for a resurrection and I am still waiting Lord! I am still waiting!"

To all the Abrahams of this night, both male and female, I bless your broken hearts and pray with all my might, that your hopes would be resurrected upon this very earth you place your knees upon.

To all the Abrahams of this night, both male and female, I bless your broken hearts and pray with all my might, that your hopes would be resurrected upon this very earth you place your knees upon. May God grant you strength and continued belief for this oh most pressing miracle. If however, hope is dead, died even long ago, for maybe even your alter child died, when the circumstantial knife was not halted by an angel and when the sharp self-hating scythe, cut the limbs off life, then I am so sorry. I am so very sorry. Please yet believe, even let me believe for you, in a better resurrection still to come, for who knows if all your prayers were not answered and answered in *full*, answered even in the last moment of their time here on earth, answered in an elongated second, where all eternal business was transacted in its fullness and into which, all the abundant grace and goodness and the rescuing power of God, was poured forth in abundance. Who knows? Believe yet.

I hope my friend, that your daily and your nightly, altar-laid child, will rise to walk through your open door on this very morrow. But if not, even if that can never be, then I hope my friend, that your child awaits you, smiling, looking this time for you, to walk through that final door of your own eternal destination.

Tonight, millions of Abrahams lay their child on God's altar, believing in a resurrection by the good and able God. Join them in their prayers, join them in their weeping, join them in their hoping, join them in their believing, join them in their faith! For you are not alone and you are not forgotten.

Listen: "'Can a woman forget her nursing child, And not have compassion on the son of her womb? Surely they may forget, Yet I will not forget you. See, I have inscribed you on the palms of My hands; Your walls are continually before Me. Your sons shall make haste; Your destroyers and those who laid you waste Shall go away from you. Lift up your eyes, look around and see; All these gather together and come to you. As I live,' says the Lord, 'You shall surely clothe yourselves with them all as an ornament, And bind them on you as a bride does. For your waste and desolate places, And the land of your destruction, Will even now be too small for the inhabitants; And those who swallowed you up will be far away. The children you will have, After you have lost the others, Will say again in your ears, "The place is too small for me; Give me a place where I may dwell." Then you will say in your heart, "Who has begotten these for me, Since I have lost my children and am desolate, A captive, and wandering to and fro? And who has brought these up? There I was, left alone; But these, where were they?"' Thus says the Lord God: 'Behold, I will lift My hand in an oath to the nations, And set up My standard for the peoples; They shall bring your sons in their arms, And your daughters shall be carried on their shoulders; Kings shall be your foster fathers, And their queens your nursing mothers; They shall bow down to you with their faces to the earth, And lick up the dust of your feet. Then you will know that I am the Lord, For they shall not be ashamed who wait for Me.'" Isaiah 49:15-23 NKJV

Pray: Lord, lift up my head and my feeble, hanging hands, that I might hope in You once more. Amen.

Night-Whisper | **GREED**

The trail of tears

It was whilst first driving down Interstate 75 in Georgia in the late 90s, that I first noticed the white signs on brown backgrounds saying "Trail of Tears". Now the USA has a habit of naming its freeways after people of power, presence and prominence, but it was the first time I ever saw a highway called Trail of Tears, National Historic Trail. How interesting.

1 Timothy 6:10

"For the love of money is a root of all kinds of evil, for which some have strayed from the faith in their greediness, and pierced themselves through with many sorrows." NKJV

Another time on the same Highway when driving to the North Georgia Mountains and to Ellijay, Georgia's apple Capital, I was tired and couldn't wait to kick back, relax a little and smell the Roses, indeed knowing that a white rose is Georgia's state flower, it made the prospect of relaxation all the more attractive. How interesting.

I was off to a men's retreat on the Coosawattee River. The very names of Ellijay and Coosawattee when said out-loud indicate the roots of a very different language. Indeed, these places were once part of the vast and enchanting, ancestral home of the Tsilagi People, or the Principled People, or as we know them, the Cherokee nation.

After a good night's sleep, the following day I took my laptop and drove to the Crimson Moon Café in the small town of Dahlonega, a beautiful tourist trap, selling trinkets and flavoured coffee! Dahlonega's quaintness and beauty however, hide the fact that this was a major boomtown in the Georgia Gold rush, the first in U.S. history actually, and indeed, even became a branch mint for the United States Mint. The name Dahlonega is Cherokee as well and means, yellow money.

The examination of history is a complicated affair. However I believe it is safe to say that ultimately, it was the discovery of gold in these same

North Georgia mountains that led to the forced removal of over 16,000 Cherokee Indians, to diseased holding forts and then to a journey of over 1,000 miles on foot, to their new and very different lands in Oklahoma.

This forced march resulted in the death of between 4,000 and 6,000 Cherokee. It is reported that the mothers of the Cherokee were grieving and perpetually crying on the journey, because they were unable to help their children survive.

This Georgia state flower, this wild Cherokee Rose, grows along the route of the Trail of Tears into eastern Oklahoma even today.

The Cherokee elders prayed for a sign that would lift the mother's spirits and so give them strength to continue. The next day, a beautiful rose began to grow where each of the mother's tears had fallen. The rose is white for their tears; a gold centre representing the gold taken from Cherokee lands, and the seven leaves on each stem represent the seven Cherokee clans. This Georgia state flower, this wild Cherokee Rose, grows along the route of the Trail of Tears into eastern Oklahoma even today.

Make no mistake about it; Chief Dragging Canoe was correct when he said that it was the "continual advancing banners of a greedy host" that consumed the ancient nations in the USA. Spiritually speaking, greed always leads to a trail of tears. So then, may I ask you what might be greedy for tonight? How might that end in tears for other people, even for you? Think about that. If greed destroys nations, how will you fair in succumbing to that self same lust?

Many Cherokees had become Christians by the time of the trail of tears and missionaries who travelled with them, report that they were great singers. On this trail of tears, the Cherokee Christians sang one particular song, which since then has become the unofficial national anthem of the Cherokee Nation. That song is "Amazing Grace". Translating it back from the Cherokee it reads:

God's son
Paid for us,
Then to heaven He went,
After paying for us.

But He said,
When He rose,
"I'll come again,"

He said when He spoke.

All the earth will end
When He comes.
All will see Him
All over the earth.

All the good people living
He will come after.
Heaven always,
In peace they will live

The first book to be translated into Cherokee was a hymn book. Along your trail of tears, the answer to destruction of the pursuit of great greed is always amazing grace. Did you get that?

Listen: "Let your conduct be without covetousness; be content with such things as you have. For He Himself has said, 'I will never leave you nor forsake you.' So we may boldly say: 'The Lord is my helper; I will not fear. What can man do to me?'" Hebrews 13:5-6 NKJV

Pray: Lord I set my eyes on You. Deliver me from greed, especially the covetous greed of another persons, goods, land, property and relationships. By Your amazing grace, help me O Lord to be content with what I have. In Jesus name I pray, amen.

Night-Whisper | **SATISFY**

No more to the dance

A friend of mine quoted a champion athlete who had reached the top of his game, the pinnacle of his career, the desire of his dreams, saying that when questioned regarding his success, he replied, "Well frankly it's a little disappointing, I really expected more." In the church, many people would like to say the same about their experience of Christianity and I have observed many people are leaving the church because of this same reason. They expected more! The fact is that many people entering the world of church rarely become solid in Christ, no, so very soon, many come to the conclusion that they have been sold a pup and they leave.

Psalm 65:4

"Blessed is the man You choose, And cause to approach You, That he may dwell in Your courts. We shall be satisfied with the goodness of Your house, Of Your holy temple."
NKJV

This disappointment in Christianity, in Christ, is very noticeable even in long term members of our churches and usually comes out sideways in these people. In other words, this disappointment in Christ eventually makes itself manifest in depression, manifest in sickness and manifest most usually, in sin. They are disappointed because they expected more!

The answer this disappointment, the answer to this dis-ease in Zion, has to be an active relationship between desire and satisfaction. A person in Christ must desire Christ and then must find satisfaction, in Christ, which will in turn kindle desire, which when burning in Jesus will lead to satisfaction, which will fuel desire, which will burn in satisfaction, which will fuel desire, which will burn in satisfaction, which will, well, you get my point. We need to begin this upward spiral of satisfaction in Jesus and we need to begin it right now!

Like it or not, this means feelings. Like it or not, feelings are important. The absolute facts of the Gospel are what we hang our hats on, are what we hang our all upon, but these absolute facts will not fuel us with energy to continue and win the race. No, only the very felt presence and the manifest footsteps of God walking along with us, will keep us warm through the lonely valleys, in the darkened dale of this old world. We need to feel our Christ, we need to feel our Christianity. Our experience of Jesus must become a felt reality.

> *"He who affirms that Christianity makes men miserable, is himself an utter stranger to it."*

Spurgeon begins his opening volley of Daily devotions today with this stunning statement: *"He who affirms that Christianity makes men miserable, is himself an utter stranger to it."* If that is the case, then let us acknowledge but one thing tonight dear friends, and then let us make sure of but one more.

First then, let us acknowledge that the vast amount of what we see in the present days of the church are indicative that most people do not truly experience Christ. Secondly, let us make sure that we do truly experience Christ.

There is a need here folks for some active pursuance of God. There is a need here for stout hearts in winning this fair prize of the felt presence of God. Maybe tonight you need to throw some rocks at the windows of the Father and demand that He get up and give you some bread. Maybe tonight you need to get out of bed and run around the city looking for your lover, weeping in desperation until you find Him. You may brush with the religious police as they find you out of your pew so late this very night, they may even give you a right royal beating, but He shall hear about it! A report shall be made in heaven concerning the mad pursuing love which has come upon you, and who knows, tonight, when you hear the turning of your door knob, your lover may slip in and slide between your waiting sheets. He who has ears to hear, let him hear.

Listen: "My beloved put his hand By the latch of the door, And my heart yearned for him. I arose to open for my beloved, And my hands dripped with myrrh, My fingers with liquid myrrh, On the handles of the lock." NKJV

Pray: No more to the dance O Lord but bring me to Your house and to Your banqueting table dear Jesus. Let me be familiar with the language of love and ask You then to fed me on Carmel and Bashan; Oh come and satisfy my soul in the mountains of Ephraim and Gilead. Amen. (Jer 50:19)

| Vol | 01 | Q3 | NW00274 | September 30th |

Night-Whisper | **DIG**

The Honking Questioning of Blind Birds

Tonight, the geese arrived.

In North America, the transition of the seasons from summer to winter is heralded in cacophonic announcement, by the arrival of those curl tipped winged and honking hoards, who, as chatty winners at an old ladies' bingo club, slide elegantly down the invisible banisters of the air and take their place in seats of water, cold and silver in the setting sun. The Canada geese have come to town, carrying their annual message in all their barking bills.

Job 28:7

"There is a path which no fowl knoweth, and which the vulture's eye hath not seen" KJV

It is said, that the skies of the promised land were often darkened by the rising smoke of millions of burnt sacrificial offerings. Of course, all the offal from this daily carnage would have been thrown away, making Israel a continual 24-hour all you can eat buffet, for the sharp clawed raptors that scratched the air for blood. The other birds, the vegan varieties of fowl, the democratic doves of peaceful destinies, even to this day, eschew, rebuff and hold in great contempt, all the red flagged hawks of the republics of running blood. These two birds do not mix. These two birds do not talk to one another, make no deals, have no real fellowship, but from two distinct aerial perspectives, these birds quite simply get on with their jobs, seeing in detail, even from the heights of the whirling skies above, all their destinies and dishes, the raptors always beholding by bright and zoomed in focus, their prey at prayer, either scurrying across the earth, or swimming in the waters, maybe even lying and waiting to be plucked like grass, from the smoothed out rocks, gowned with glowing green, hid beneath the dancing surface of many a giggling brook. These birds always see their meals from afar.

You see, most birds whether those with monocular or binocular vision, have eyes that are flatter than human eyes and it is this flatness, that allows birds of both perspective, even the hawk and the dove, to have a much larger area in focus, whilst we more rounded and human individuals, focus on a much, much smaller area. In other words, birds see far better than we do! However, our text for tonight says, even to these far and better sited fowl, *"Precious pathways, beneath the furnace earth, full of rubied treasures, lay hidden from even their more full and far focused sight."*

Some of us will hunt upon the surface of our souls, some of us will scavenge and feed upon the offal of other men's sacrifice, some of us will play a life of bingo, occasionally dipping our heads beneath the surface of the shimmering silvers, to graze on green and pluck the unseen harvest from the winter coated rocks, which lay shivering in the dark. However, some us will stop the grasping and the grazing, the occasional dipping into the deep and go and dig for ourselves treasure from beneath the surface of the earth. Yes, some of us will dig for victory even though we cannot see it from above. Yes, some of us will become treasure hunters.

> *Tonight the geese arrived, carrying a message in their honking bills, "Time is passing," they said. "Another year has gone," they said. "Show us the treasures that only you can find."*

Tonight the geese arrived, carrying a message in their honking bills, *"Time is passing,"* they said. *"Another year has gone,"* they said. **"Show us the treasures that only you can find,"** they said, *"Show us the burning eyes of sapphire that we can never see, show us the long streaked silver and the shining of the yellowed sun gold, show us,"* they said, *"show us all the treasures of darkness which you have plucked from far beneath all the air circled earth, this long year passed."*

So my friends as autumn begins to take its grip and winter follows hard on its red and orange coat tails, just what hidden pathways have you pursued this year. What treasures have you plucked out from the recesses of your mind, from the caves of your soul and the depths of your spirit? What treasures have you found from all the mining in the very heart of your being? What treasure trove have you found hidden beneath your earth? What have you gotten from your mines and distilled from the smelters hot refining fire?

Listen: "Surely there is a mine for silver, And a place where gold is refined. Iron is taken from the earth, And copper is smelted from ore. Man puts an end to darkness, And searches every recess For ore in the darkness and the shadow of death. He breaks open a shaft away from people; In places forgotten by feet They hang far away from men; They swing to and fro. As for the earth, from it comes bread, But underneath it is turned up as by fire; Its stones are the source of sapphires, And it contains gold dust. That path no bird knows, Nor has the falcon's eye seen it." Job 28:1-7 NKJV

Pray: Lord, lead me to the mines, lead me to work, lead me to hidden pathways, lead me to all the secret treasures, hidden beneath my earth. In Jesus name I pray, amen.

DID YOU REMEMBER?

DON'T FORGET TO ORDER YOUR NEXT QUARTER OF NIGHT WHISPERS.

Check us out more at WWW.NightWhispers.com

Buy at WWW.TheologyShop.com

THE MISSION STATEMENT OF THE 66 BOOKS MINISTRY

WWW.66Books.tv | Our Mission is:

1. "To proclaim Jesus, the Savior of the whole world, from the whole Bible, because He is wonderful!"

2. Indeed, we are constrained by the love of God, to communicate the rawness of the Bible to real people, in real ways, and our driving and major project of '66Cities' shall take us to the 66 most influential cities of the 250 nations of the world in the next 25 years. That's 16,500 cities!

3. We are aiming to build relationships with grass roots, real people, that is, ordinary people, who, in their own countries and cities, want to do extraordinary things for Jesus and the Kingdom of God, to bring a Biblical Gospel message that is relevant to now, in a world that has come to believe that Jesus is irrelevant to their lives.

If you would like to partner with us in this great task. Then we want to hear from you! Contact me today on vr@66books.tv

MORE ABOUT 'THE 66 BOOKS MINISTRY'

WWW.66Cities.com | By the year 2047, by the grace of God and according to His will and favor, The 66 Books Ministry shall be preaching consecutively from each of the 66 Books of the Holy Bible, the Gospel of the Lord Jesus Christ in 16,500 of the most influential cities of the world on an annual and ongoing basis!

We do not underestimate the quality teams of trained people that this will take, together with the need for vast amount of materials and finances which will also have to be raised. However, as most futurists indicate that the growing global population will be gathered mostly in major world cities in the coming years, there is a necessity laid upon the church to present and proclaim the God of the whole Bible, through the primacy of preaching in these cities. We are convinced that this is a paramount and pressing concern.

"For since, in the wisdom of God, the world through wisdom did not know God, it pleased God through the foolishness of the message preached to save those who believe" 1 Corinthians 1:21NKJV

"Preach the Word! Be ready in season and out of season. Convince, rebuke, exhort, with all longsuffering and teaching." 2 Timothy 4:2NKJV

The church is looking for a revival. The 66 Books Ministry, however, is trying to start a revolution of a return to the preached Word, from the whole of the Bible as a precursor to any and all coming revival.

For "whoever calls on the name of the Lord shall be saved." How then shall they call on Him in whom they have not believed? And how shall they believe in Him of whom they have not heard? And how shall they hear without a preacher? And how shall they preach unless they are sent? As it is written: "How beautiful are the feet of those who preach the gospel of peace, Who bring glad tidings of good things!" Romans 10:13-15 NKJV

We are unashamedly looking for and seeking to foster a massive, huge, releasing, transformative, and exceptionally disruptive reversal and revolutionary change, both within the church and then in the world. We are not just another mission trying to do the same as every other mission. We are intent on revolution!

To this revolutionary end, we have no fear of seeming failure and will cultivate that audacious atmosphere within our ministry. We want to attract grass roots people who are people of faith risk takers, for we believe it is people of such life hazarding attitudes that are used by God to make breakthroughs in the world for the Kingdom of God. Hanging back for fear of seeming failure, hanging back and waiting for the trained professionals, both wastes the time of the church time and kills the spirit of victory.

In that spirit then, we therefore are believing that this task can be accomplished by such people within the time frame we have given ourselves.

Fully assured then, that we are in full obedience with the great commission of our great God and Savior Jesus Christ, we do, with great confidence in Him, turn ourselves happily to this so great a task in the hope that, like a happy hound straining at the leash to be let loose, we believe that many other people will smile along with us and be part of this brand new grass roots 21st Century Global City Mission.

If you want to know more and want to be part of what we are doing then go to www.The66BooksMinistry.com or call us in the USA on **855 662 6657**, or email V.R. directly on vr@66Books.TV

AUTHOR BIO | PURPLE ROBERT

It won't take too much investigation for you to find out that Purple Robert is in fact, Victor Robert Farrell (Born 1960 and alive until now and still kicking) was born in Chesterfield England to Scottish parents with Irish grandparents, which is an obvious recipe both for writing and emotional disaster if ever there was one!

He grew up a culturally excluded Roman Catholic (his parents were divorced,) which is one of the reasons why he hates religion with a passion, and that's an interesting enough fact by itself, because he is also an ordained protestant minister to boot.

Purple Robert. became a Christian whilst serving on board a Polaris Submarine at the end of the cold war. He has gone on to do many things, including being a broadcaster, App developer, performance poet, and the long-time author of 'Night Whispers,' which is read in over 100 counties and is also translated into Spanish (see www.Night Whispers.com)

Currently, Purple Robert is also President of The 66 Books Ministry: a grass roots global city mission endeavor. I suppose it is this concoction of background and experience which means Purple Robert's communication is always raw and emotive. After all, and as he says, *"If Christianity can be relevant on a Monday morning, several hundred feet underneath an unknown ocean, in a pornographic sewer pipe carrying enough nuclear weapons to destroy a continent whilst hiding from the Russians, then it can be relevant anywhere and everywhere!"*

Purple Robert sees himself as a servant of the 'Word of the Lord' to tasked communicate the God of the whole Bible. His proclamation of the same is done in very raw terms to very real people, is both his burden and his passion.

| **May 26th** | Reading 147 of 366 |

- **MORNING** → | HISTORICAL BOOKS |
- BOOK 11 of 66 → | 1 KINGS 16,17 |
  - Signpost Words → | "AN ANSWER" |
  - Highlight Verses → | 1 Kings 16:31-34 |

And it came to pass, as though it had been a trivial thing for him to walk in the sins of Jeroboam the son of Nebat, that he took as wife Jezebel the daughter of Ethbaal, king of the Sidonians; and he went and served Baal and worshiped him. Then he set up an altar for Baal in the temple of Baal, which he had built in Samaria. And Ahab made a wooden image. Ahab did more to provoke the Lord God of Israel to anger than all the kings of Israel who were before him. In his days Hiel of Bethel built Jericho. He laid its foundation with Abiram his firstborn, and with his youngest son Segub he set up its gates, according to the word of the Lord, which He had spoken through Joshua the son of Nun. NKJV

  - Some Observations → |

This is nothing but an extended killing time, and it is God who is slaughtering His wayward nation. Decade after decade the decadent mobster kings steer the people more and more out of the way of the Lord. Dogs lick up the blood from slaughtered corpses, birds peck the watery eyeballs out of the maggot eaten heads. Death and destruction stalk the land, yet still the people rise up to pray to an idle and engage in sexual sin. The mercy of God is seen on two legs and heard from one mouth, even the prophets of the Lord. Now, dropped from heaven, out of nowhere, in answer to the madness of Ahab the loon, a prophet like no other arrives on the scene. Elijah the Tishbite!

  - A Call To Action → |

Fine pulpits and finer churches, are rarely the abode of the prophet.

- **EVENING** → | PAULINE EPISTLES |
- BOOK 46 of 66 → | 1 CORINTHIANS 15 |
  - Signpost Words → | "ASSURANCE OF SALVATION" |
  - Highlight Verses → | 1 Corinthians 15:1-11 |

Moreover, brethren, I declare to you the gospel which I preached to you, which also you received and in which you stand, by which also you are saved, if you hold fast that word which I preached to you — unless you believed in vain. For I delivered to you first of all that which I also received: that Christ died for our sins according to the Scriptures, and that He was buried, and that He rose again the third day according to the Scriptures, and that He was seen by Cephas, then by the twelve. After that He was seen by over five hundred brethren at once, of whom the greater part remain to the present, but some have fallen asleep. After that He was seen by James, then by all the apostles. Then last of all He was seen by me also, as by one born out of due time. For I am the least of the apostles, who am not worthy to be called an apostle, because I persecuted the church of God. But by the grace of God I am what I am, and His grace toward me was not in vain; but I labored more abundantly than they all, yet not I, but the grace of God which was with me .... NKJV

  - Some Observations → |

The two 'wee' words we Evangelicals dislike to discourse upon are 'if' and 'unless.' I believe that once we are saved we are always saved, 'IF' we continue on receiving, believing and standing. I believe that once we are saved we are always saved, 'UNLESS' we prove ourselves to be unfaithful and reprobate in forsaking the Christ of the Scriptures. Paul did not believe he was saved by our works, yet by grace he worked his little heine off!

  - A Call To Action → |

Continuance in the work of grace is the key to your own assurance.

JOIN THE FELLOWSHIP OF THE BOOK

WWW.TheFellowShipofTheBook.com

The Fellowship of The Book is a Daily Bible Reading Fellowship. It is a morning and evening devotional of four books available each quarter of the year. It includes

Signpost Words
Highlight Verses
Some Observations
Call To Action

Consecutively, Chronologically and in many other ways, Read The Bible Thru in 1 just one year, with both Morning and Evening reading to keep your mind focused on the Lord of the Word and the Word of The Lord. Buy this and several other ways to 'Read the Bible Thru in a Year Books' at www.whisperingword.com

ANOTHER BOOK BY THE AUTHOR, VR

Habakkuk A Prophecy For Our Time

As the Church in the West is found to be mostly dead and covered with Laodicean lukewarm vomit, as The Lord, slips the dead things silently over the side of the storm tossed ship into the dark oblivion of the waves of secular humanism and rising Islam, what remains will need to be fortified with steel to live in a quickly changing anti-Christian world of persecution. There is no better prophecy more equipped to speak to such a remnant who shall be so very besieged. Welcome to Habakkuk, 35 of 66, a prophecy for our time.

Buy at www.whisperingword.com

ANOTHER BOOK BY THE AUTHOR, VR

The 66-Minute Bible

I am told that there are 788,258 words in the King James Bible and of these 14,565 are unique. That's a lot of words! I have been reading the Bible for nearly forty years on an almost daily basis. It still remains to me the most exciting book on the planet, however, it never gets any easier. Bible reading is a spiritual discipline and for me the emphasis is on discipline. I created this resource to aid you in your Bible reading, it gives your brain a sixty second overview of the Bible, a loose enclosure to herd the narrative of the book into something that can be seen as a whole. It was never created to be a substitute, but an aid. Just saying...... Friends, welcome to the most exciting book on the planet! V.R.

Buy at www.whisperingword.com

AN INTRODUCTION TO 'PURPLE ROBERT'

Some Dangerously Different Devotionals!

Now, before I go any further, this guy comes with warning shots! The opening parts of his currently seven volumes pf poetic works says quite clearly, *"If you are easily offended by low level expletives...**Go no further. Do not read this book!** If you are prudish in any way ...**Go no further. Do not read this book!** If you do not want to be challenged...**Go no further. Do not read this book!** If you want to be stroked into unchanging sleep and into the stupor of remaining as you are...**Go no further. Do not read this book!** If you hide under the respectable covers of a comfortable religion...**Go no further. Do not read this book!** If you are frail in faith and dishonest about life under this sun...**Go no further**. If you have no real integrity regarding the state of your own heart,* **then do not read this book!** *If however, you are grown up, honest and have a basic human integrity, ENJOY!"* So, there you go, you have been warned!

Purple Robert is a Performance Poet and a Metaphysical Biblical Realist. If you want to hear some of his work and get hold of the 66 Poems each of the Seven volumes contain, then go to www.PurpleRobert.com and purchase them today.

Also Buy at Buy at www.WhisperingWord.com

Night Whispers
'Blood Work'
Volume 01–Q3

July-August-September

Copyright © Rev. Victor Robert Farrell

2019

All Rights Reserved

No part of this book may be reproduced in any form, by photocopying or by any electronic or mechanical means, including information storage or retrieval systems, without permission in writing from both the copyright owner and the publisher of this book.

ISBN Number 978-1-910686-04-1

First published in this format
June 2015 by WhisperingWord

All current contact and sales information can be found at

www.NightWhispers.com

Printed in The United Kingdom

for

WhisperingWord Ltd.

www.ingramcontent.com/pod-product-compliance
Lightning Source LLC
Chambersburg PA
CBHW031614160426
43196CB00006B/129